HARDPRESS.NET
HOME OF HARD-TO-FIND BOOKS

# Tafilet
by Walter Harris

Address:
HardPress
8345 NW 66TH ST #2561
MIAMI FL 33166-2626
USA
Email: info@hardpress.net

# Tafilet

Walter Harris

90

EX LIBRIS

GIT

# TAFILET

BERBER VILLAGE IN THE VALLEY OF THE GHADAT.

[*Frontispiece.*

# ·TAFILET

THE NARRATIVE OF A JOURNEY OF EXPLORATION IN THE
ATLAS MOUNTAINS AND THE OASES OF THE
NORTH-WEST SAHARA

BY

## WALTER B. HARRIS, F.R.G.S.

AUTHOR OF

'A JOURNEY THROUGH THE YEMEN,' 'THE LAND OF AN AFRICAN SULTAN
TRAVELS IN MOROCCO,' 'DANOVITCH, AND OTHER
STORIES,' ETC., ETC.

*ILLUSTRATED BY MAURICE ROMBERG*
*FROM SKETCHES AND PHOTOGRAPHS BY THE AUTHOR*

WILLIAM BLACKWOOD AND SONS
EDINBURGH AND LONDON
MDCCCXCV

TO

CLEMENTS R. MARKHAM, Esq.,

C.B., F.R.S., F.S.A.,

PRESIDENT OF THE ROYAL GEOGRAPHICAL SOCIETY,

𝔗𝔥𝔦𝔰 𝔅𝔬𝔬𝔨

IS DEDICATED BY

THE AUTHOR.

# PREFACE.

VERY few words of preface are necessary for this book.

To three friends I owe hearty thanks for assistance toward the successful accomplishment of my journey—namely, to Alexander Peckover, Esq., D.C.L., F.L.S., F.R.G.S., &c.; James Mason, Esq.; and R. G. Haliburton, Esq.

To the Proprietors of the 'Illustrated London News' I am gratefully indebted for the use of the drawings made from my original sketches and photographs, which have been most generously placed at the disposal of my publishers and myself.

WALTER B. HARRIS.

*November* 1895.

# CONTENTS.

# ILLUSTRATIONS.

## FULL-PAGE ILLUSTRATIONS.

## ILLUSTRATIONS IN THE TEXT.

## MAPS.

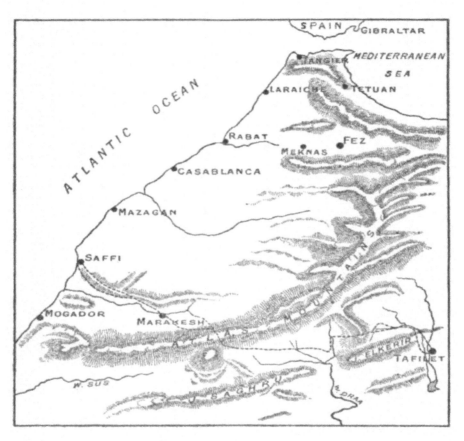

SKETCH MAP OF MOROCCO,

Showing Mr W. B. Harris's Routes to and from Tafilet.

*Author's route*..................................................

# TAFILET.

——

## CHAPTER I.

### PREPARATIONS AND START.

It had long been my intention to make a journey
of exploration into, and if possible beyond, the Atlas
Mountains ; and though on several occasions my plans
had been already formulated, I had been obliged,
almost at the last moment, to abandon the idea.

However, the close of the year 1893 offered an
opportunity which could not be neglected ; but before
entering upon the description of my journey, a few
words must be said as to what not a little helped
it toward success.

Mulai el Hassen, the Sultan of Morocco, had been
meditating for some years an expedition into the
southern regions of his dominions, toward that in-

definite frontier which divided his country from the wastes of the Sahara desert. Until, however, the spring of the year 1893 he had been so occupied with summer expeditions, organised to crush petty rebellions and intertribal strife, that he had found no favourable opportunity of making any protracted absence from the seat of his Government; for so miserable are the means of communication in Morocco, that, once across the Atlas Mountains, he was practically as distant from his capital — and still more from the residence of the European Ministers accredited to his Court, who reside at Tangier—as Kamskatka is from London.

However, during the summer of 1892 the tribes had been so punished for their many rebellious offences, and so heavily taxed in consequence, that his Majesty felt but little anxiety in carrying out his projected visit to his trans-Atlas dominions.

But there were other questions almost as serious to be considered — first, his relations with foreign Powers; and, secondly, the reception that might await him in those far-off corners of his realm.

With regard to the former, while avoiding all political questions, one or two words must be said. First, it must be understood that Mulai el Hassen, the late Sultan, was not only an autocratic ruler, but his own Minister of Foreign Affairs; and a great difficulty therefore arose as to who, in the case of sudden foreign complications, should be directed to fill his place. No one knew the temperament of his Ministers and Viziers better than the Sultan, and probably no one could trust them less; for although their patriotism might be all that was desired, it was very possible that this same over-zeal might lead them into difficulties. For this reason the relations of his country with the European Governments were temporarily put into the hands of a council, in which the acting Minister of Foreign Affairs, Sid Fadhul Gharnit, held but only an equal voice with the rest; while the powers vested in Sid el Haj Mohammed Torres, the Vizier-resident at Tangier, were more fully specified and amplified, for alone of all the members of the Sultan's Government this man could be said to possess the confidence both of the European Ministers and his master.

Having announced the manner in which all questions of foreign affairs were to be regulated during his absence, there was to be considered the second serious difficulty of the enterprise—the reception he would receive. For the purpose of ensuring success in this respect, long before his Majesty started from Fez for the south, influential members of his family, already acquainted with the tribes in question and their attitude toward the Sultan, were sent out to bully and bribe. Of the two, the latter did the most toward ensuring his Majesty's safe passage through the Berber tribes, and by March 1893 everything was prepared for a start to be made.

It is usual for the rulers of Morocco to change their residence from year to year, spending the winters in one of the larger cities, either Fez, Meknas, or Marakesh, and during the summer and autumn to make the long marches from the north to the south of the empire, or *vice versa*. The enormous retinue accompanying the Sultan, the quantity of baggage to be transported, to say nothing of the insufficiency of all commissariat arrangements and the entire absence of roads, renders these royal progresses matters often of several months' duration.

None can have known better than the Sultan the difficulties—even dangers—of the journey before him ; for, although he possessed no personal knowledge of the country to be traversed, he was well informed as to the climatic changes that would have to be endured, as to difficulty in finding food for his troops, and still greater difficulty for his horses and mules, and as to the physical aspect of the country, which presented, along the proposed routes, not only the heat and cold of the desert, but the passage of mountain-passes, one alone of which reaches an altitude of over 8000 feet above the sea-level,—and this amongst subjects who, by birth a different and a semi-conquered nation, would provide nothing or little for his welfare, and whose reception, if hearty enough in words, would lack any real enthusiasm.

There can be no doubt that influence was used to prevent Mulai el Hassen starting out upon this journey, the expenses of which, even to a European Government, would be enormous, while the dangers were scarcely less; but so persistent was his Majesty in carrying out his idea, that he showed little favour to those who tendered him advice, and let it be clearly understood that the matter rested with him alone.

In April a start was made from Fez, the direction being due south, and a halt of a few days was called at Sufru, a small town some sixteen miles away from the capital. Here the European officers attached to the Sultan's suite were informed that it had been decided that they were not to accompany his Majesty, and they forthwith returned to Fez. The sole exception made was in the case of the French doctor, M. Linares, who was commanded to remain with the army, and to make the journey with the Sultan.

After weary months of hard travel and equally hard delays, Mulai el Hassen reached his goal, Tafilet, the home of his ancestors, in the first week of November.

There is no need here to recount the march from Fez to that oasis; suffice it to say that, in spite of the physical difficulties of the country, the scarcity of provisions and fodder, and the half-hearted reception of the Berber tribes, it was successfully accomplished.

It may be thought that I have already digressed too far from the purpose of my book in making these introductory remarks; but as it was owing to the Sultan's presence in Tafilet that I was able to undertake my journey at all, and happily bring it to a successful end, I have felt constrained to briefly state the reasons that had taken Mulai el Hassen to the far-away oasis in the desert from which his dynasty originally sprung.

As to the motives of the Sultan, it is difficult to state anything with certainty. No doubt religious zeal to pray at the reverenced tomb of his ancestor, Mulai Ali Shereef, had much to do with the desire to undertake so long and trying a journey, for it could have been from no hope that by so doing any considerable sums of money could be collected or extorted, as was generally believed to be the case, for none could have been better aware than he of the poverty of the country and its inhabitants. Probably it was solely the religious point, touched with some anxious curiosity to see the home of his ancestors, that led him to empty the treasury upon an expedition from which no real, and but little moral, benefit could accrue.

I had meanwhile been carefully watching such glimpses of information as from time to time reached England as to the whereabouts of the Sultan and his army, and scanty and contradictory as they were, I was able by the beginning of September 1893 to gather that his Majesty's journey, in spite of a general belief to the contrary, would be successful, and that Tafilet would be reached.

I therefore left England in the middle of September, and collecting the few necessaries for my journey at Tangier, reached Saffi, some 400 miles down the Atlantic coast of Morocco, in the second week of October.

The journey from Tangier to Saffi was one that presented but little of interest. The coast-steamer in which I travelled visited the various ports, — Laraiche, Rabat, Casablanca (Dar el baida), and Mazagan, all of which I knew well. The weather was rough, and we had some difficulty in communicating at more than one of the ports, lying for some twenty hours off Rabat before the lighters were able to issue from the mouth of the river—the Bu Regreg—that separates that town from Sallee, the home of the old rovers, whose depredations upon English sailing-ships were at one time so well known and so much dreaded.

However, on the fifth day after leaving, Saffi was reached, and fortunately the sea was calm enough to allow of our landing in one of the strangely built and decorated surf-boats in use at that port.

*Landing in Saffi.*

What a shouting and yelling there was of the boatmen, as my Riffi servant Mohammed, of whom more anon, and I, perched on the top of our little pile of baggage, were tossed to and fro by the curling seas that one after another broke along the beach! In silence the steersman watched his opportunity, and with a smooth gliding motion we were borne between rugged rocks, and our boat lay high and dry upon the beach.

Saffi has been too often described to need more than the merest mention here. It is a strange, flat-roofed, white town, reaching from the sea-beach high up the semicircle of hills by which it is enclosed, the summit capped by the windowless walls and peaked towers of the great castle, once a palace of the Sultans, now little more than a deserted ruin.

Within the town the streets are narrow and dirty. In rainy seasons the mud is almost knee-deep, and a torrent flows through the main street. The native inhabitants are poor, and accordingly but little signs of luxury or trade are to be found, with the exceptions of the large stores of the few European merchants who reside there. The town is walled, in parts of Moorish workmanship, in others the remains of the old Portuguese occupation; for Saffi, like most of the other towns of the Atlantic coast of Morocco, once formed a small colony of the "King of the Algarves."

The few days I spent at Saffi passed pleasantly enough, for I was entertained by Mr Hunot, her Majesty's Vice-Consul, whose knowledge of Arabic

and Morocco, gained from a residence of some forty
years in the country, is exceptional; and though I
chafed at the delays that always meet one in dealing
with Moors, he did much to render my time as agree-
able as could be to a man who was intent upon
nothing but in making a start.

Small as my preparations were, they caused me
several days' more delay than I liked; but before the
week was out I found myself on the eve of departure,
with a couple of mules, an old man who was to be
my guide, philosopher, and friend, his son and his
nephew, a black slave-girl belonging to his establish-
ment, a stray Sahara pilgrim, and my Riffi servant.

Adopting the dress of the country on my departure,
and mounting a pack-mule on the top of the luggage,
we set out one morning, not at sunrise as I had hoped,
for the old man forgot everything that he could forget, and remembered an enormous quantity of things
he should have left behind, and it was near mid-day
before we passed out under the old gateway of the
town and climbed the steep hill, in the valley below
which the only gardens that Saffi can boast are
situated.

The heat was intense and water scarce, and both
we and our poor animals suffered the entire road to
Marakesh, or, as it is more commonly called, Morocco
City, a distance of about a hundred miles.   There

had been no rain for some five months, and even the *metafir*, as the natives call their underground cisterns, were nearly dry, and many quite so.

The road from Saffi to Marakesh presents no aspect of peculiar interest. The tribes of Abda and Beled Ahmar are passed through, the latter boasting the dreary circular salt lake of Zima, near which is a cluster of white buildings, a *mdarsa* or sort of college, where the late Sultan and many of his sons received their education. The inhabitants are all Arabs, but their villages are few and far between, or lie off the road. The country, at this time of year a dreary stony waste, is in the spring one great field of waving corn ; and the horses of Beled Ahmar are famous. Owing to the heat, we did not arrive at Morocco City until the fourth day, and did not actually enter until the morning of the fifth, preferring to spend the night just outside the walls.

There is one scene, however, that presents itself as one nears the city that cannot be passed over without mention, though I myself, amongst others, have described it before. Yet so strikingly grand is it, and so unique, that it demands reference in any work that deals with this portion of Morocco. I refer to the first view of the wide valley of the Tensift, with its wonderful background of the range of the Atlas Mountains.

We had been climbing the steep slopes of Jibeelet, the name given to the range of hills that form the north boundary of the wide valley of the Tensift, for some little time before the plain beneath came into view. The ascent had been a hot and tiring one,

*A Well at Sunset.*

and we and our mules were thirsty indeed. Nor were there any means of obtaining water, for during some hours we only passed one small village belonging to a few shepherds of the Arab tribe of Ulad Dlim, and their water-jars were empty. The well was a couple of miles away, and not till sunset were they going to fill the jars again. Dirty and poverty - stricken their little collection of thatched hovels and grimy tents were, but picturesque all the same, with a group of women in dark-blue cotton in the foreground, wearing necklaces of large amber beads and coral, and with long plaits of untidy hair, while dogs and naked children stood by and watched our little caravan pass. Up we toiled until, passing through a narrow gorge, the scene opened out before us in indescribable beauty. At our feet lay the valley of the Tensift, far below us, stretching away some thirty miles or so to where the great range of the Atlas rose majestically from the plain. Green was the valley, green with crops and groves of date-palms, while here, there, and everywhere sparkled and glittered the river Tensift and the many canals that carry water from its stream to irrigate the surrounding country. A haze hung over the valley, that sufficed, without in any way hiding its beauties, to soften the effect of the fierce sunlight; so that beyond the river the plain appeared to shimmer in semi-unreality until there arose from the level ground the great barrier of mountain beyond, its summit white with snow, its base blue with distance.

Inexpressibly grand it was, yet not with the grandeur that rugged cliffs and precipices can give, for beyond everything appealed to one the richness

of the scene.    After the hot weary march across
waterless plains, the vegetation was surpassingly welcome ; and the dark forest of palm-trees, stretching
for miles along the valley, was as cheering to our
eyes as are the lights of his village to the storm-
tossed mariner.    There are few views in the world
that can equal the first sight one obtains of the
Tensift valley and the Atlas Mountains,—the strange
mingling of tropical vegetation, of fields green with
crops, and of peaks 13,000 and 14,000 feet high, one
and all capped with snow, forming a unique scene.
There, too, was the city, its minarets, like little
needles, peeping above the level of the feathery
heads of the palms, but still far away.

The glimpse of shade and water gave energy to
our weary bodies, and we pushed on as fast as was possible for the tired mules, who, nevertheless, needed but
little urging, for to them, too, the scene must have
appealed as much as, if not more than, to ourselves.

At a stream we drank ; then entering the palm-
groves, threaded our way, here through a forest of
tall straight stems, there through fields of green
maize, until within a mile or two of the city we
camped for the night at a small *nzala*, or resting-
place for caravans.

As often in these pages this word *nzala* will be
found, it may be as well to explain its purport here.

Owing to the lawlessness of the tribes, small villages
have been planted by the native Government along
all the tracks which in Morocco answer the purposes
of roads. Usually the inhabitants of these wayside
caravanserais are natives of some other tribe, brought
there and given a small grant of land. The villages
consist merely of thatch huts and the brown *ghiem*
or tents of the Arabs; but there is always a large
*zareba*, or open space enclosed with a high and thick
thorn hedge, in which travellers and their pack-
animals spend the night. The village community
furnishes a guard at the only entrance to this *zareba*,
and in case of robbery the inhabitants are held responsible by the Government. In return for this
responsibility they collect a small tax from any who
make use of their protection. The system is a good
one, and theft is very uncommon, it being greatly
to the villagers' benefit to carefully guard the traveller's property and exact the small fee, rather than by
stealing call down upon themselves the wrath of the
native Government and the rapacity of the local
officials.

So at the last *nzala* on the road from Saffi to
Marakesh we spent the night, pitching our one
little tent in the *zareba*, and hiring an elderly
female, who possessed only one eye, to cook us
some supper in her hut of thatch; and, considering

that her fire consisted only of bunches of thistles, which had to be replaced almost as soon as they were lit, she performed her task with skill and success.

*Berber Tribesmen.*

The next morning, at the tail of our little caravan, I entered Marakesh on foot, grimy and travel-stained, and reached my destination, the house of

Sid Abu Bekr el Ghanjaui, without attracting any attention as a Christian in disguise.

Here comfort, even luxury, awaited me, and pleasant indeed were the eight days I spent in the city before continuing my journey—this time into unknown regions.

Sid Abu Bekr el Ghanjaui is almost the best-known man in Morocco, and probably the most disliked, a fact in which he takes particular pride. Protected by the British Government, to all intents and purposes a British subject, he has by these means been able to amass a large fortune without the native Government having annexed it and imprisoned the possessor. Whether this fortune has been altogether collected by creditable means, according to European ideas of business, I am unable to say, nor is it a matter of any importance. Suffice it that his fortune has made him many enemies, whose jealousy at seeing him easily and safely amassing wealth, while they have been under the constant dread of confiscation by officials, and continual taxation, has reached such a pitch that they have not hesitated to spread all kinds of scandalous reports about his goings on. These reports reached the ears, amongst others, of British philanthropists in England; and while Sid Abu Bekr was engaged in building fresh houses and buying new gardens in his native city, the House of Commons was being harangued as to the perfidies of

B

the so-called "Government Agent" in Morocco City. It did not stop there ; newspapers, even foreign European Governments, took the question up, and his name became of common mention in official despatches. As long, however, as his personal liberty was not affected, he merely laughed at these hazardous statements, until one day it was brought to his ears that things looked serious, and that the only English newspaper in Morocco was calling him a slave-dealer, a brothel-keeper, and, if I remember right, a murderer.

Then Abu Bekr girt up his loins to fight, and for some ten days his action for libel occupied the time of the High Court of Gibraltar. I was present on the occasion, and shall never forget the scene when, seated in the witness-box, Sid Abu Bekr, robed in silks and fine linens, answered calmly and expressionlessly the extremely unpleasant questions put to him by the defendant—unpleasant in that they referred to that, to the Moor, most private of questions, his wives and his daughters. Every atrocity, every crime, was stated to have been committed by him ; but with no result more than the fact that Sid Abu Bekr won his action with costs, and 500 dollars damages, and an injunction that the libel should not be repeated.

Thereupon, his character legally cleared, he returned

once more to Marakesh, where, surrounded by his
little daughters, to whom he is devotedly attached,
he lives in luxury and wealth.

In the house of this man my days were spent, just
as I lived another three weeks with him on my return
journey, and I received from him then, just as I have
always done, every mark of kindness and hospitality.
Even the interior of his house was open to me,
and many a pleasant hour I passed playing with his
little daughters, whose dresses of silks and brocades
sparkled with jewels.

By this time I had found opportunity to take stock
of my travelling companions, who, as they played a
by no means unimportant part in the success of my
journey, deserve some notice.

The chief of our party, by position, age, and, he
himself would probably add, acquirements, was the
elderly Shereef. In person he was dark, of a sort of
coffee-colour, with a grey beard and moustache; a
short figure inclined to stoutness, and a bad habit of
trying to sing. Himself a native of the Sahara, it
was on him that I principally relied for success in
my undertaking, my personality and disguise being
concealed under the bushel of his reputation and
accomplishments. Principal amongst the latter was
his knowledge of medicine, a hereditary knowledge it
must be understood, part of the *baraka*, or blessing,

of his august family, for he was a descendant of the
Prophet Mohammed.   I unfortunately had no opportunity of seeing the result of his skill, for when in
his company I was never in one place sufficiently
long to obtain any information as to the potency of
the draughts he administered out of one of the three
empty soda-water-bottles he had with him.   It was
entirely my own fault, though, that I did not see
him perform the operation he was most skilled in—
namely, cataract—for before leaving Tangier I had
received a letter from him asking me to bring a large
bottle of chloroform and a knife suitable for the
purpose.   This I steadily refused to do, and I think
that the old man felt the slight I had unintentionally
offered him, and fancied that I doubted his skill.   At
least he was always holding forth upon the subject,
and continually repeating the story that when in
Algeria he had been offered a fabulous salary—the
sum varied each time the tale was told—to remain in
charge of the military hospital at Algiers, an honour
which he had declined.   He never tired of narrating
the facts and details of his most successful operation.
There is a sect in Morocco called "Hamacha," who
are followers of a certain saint by name Sidi Ali
ben Hamduch, who lies buried near Meknas.   These
devotees amuse their audience—and themselves too,
let us hope—by throwing into the air heavy cannon-

balls, which they allow to fall upon their shaven crowns. On the occasion in question a Hamdushi had unfortunately evidently been wanting in religious power, for the cannon-ball crushed his skull. My old Shereef friend had been called to the rescue, and according to his account, which, let us hope, for the sake of science as well as his own reputation, is a true one, he removed the broken patch of skull, replacing it with the rind of a green pumpkin, and closing the skin over it. In a month's time the patient was not only convalescent but was once more hard at work practising his religio-acrobatic feats, with not only a remodelled and renovated skull, but even a new crop of hair! Such, then, was the skill of the leader of our caravan.

But there was another member who aspired to play the chief part in our little camp—the black slave-girl. Of all the mischievous impertinent hussies that ever saw the light of day she was the worst. Alternately shrieking with laughter at her practical jokes, and howling with rage because she couldn't get what she wanted for supper, she was equally annoying in either capacity. At the same time, one could not help laughing at her strange antics. Why she had come at all was at first a mystery to me, until it leaked out that she had insisted upon doing so, and had pulled the old man's beard until, with tears in his eyes, he had promised to take her—anyhow, come she did. Her mother was a slave of the Shereef's wife—the wife who lived at Saffi, for there were a couple more at Dads, where he had formerly resided, and where his home really was—who had been bought with her little daughter, our fellow-traveller, some ten years before. The girl was fearfully ugly, as black as jet, with all the typical features of the negro. However, one readily forgave her this, and all her sins as well, for many a laugh her antics caused us when hunger and cold made a laugh worth double its ordinary value. When she was riding she wanted to walk; as soon as she commenced to walk she wanted some one to mount her again on the mule, from which, if she did not purposely alight, she would invariably tumble off. Such was the lady of our party, and she accompanied us as far as Dads, leaving there with the old Shereef some four days before I arrived at Tafilet. She stood the cold and fatigue of the journey well, and ought to be made a Fellow of the Royal Geographical Society, for she had a wonderfully retentive memory of the road and all the places we had stayed at, though as often as not she managed to forget the sternly delivered command that she was not to eat our complete store of dates while our backs were turned. Enough of Embarka, for such was her name.

The next individual in our caravan was of a very different kind and class,—a long, tall, delicate, thin man of some four-and-twenty years of age, with one of the most beautiful voices in speaking I ever heard. He was himself a Shereef, a nephew of the old doctor's; and a man of absolute fearlessness in danger, and equal gentleness and sweetness of manner in time of peace. He never complained of cold or hunger, though we suffered much from both, but bore all the hardships of the journey, and they were many indeed, not only with every fortitude, but also without ever losing an opportunity to attempt to add to my comfort. As we trudged along the weary desert roads he would for hours together, with a voice that would be the fortune of a Member of Parliament, and gestures that an actor might spend years and never acquire, relate to me strange stories of the past, page after page of Moorish history and tradition, in Arabic as pure and as poetical as any that can exist.

The very opposite was the old Shereef's son, a boy of some twelve or thirteen years of age. Heavy in body and mind, he had neither the intellect to be amusing nor the inclination to be useful, and served no other purpose of advantage than to be the object of the black girl's practical jokes instead of any other of us.

There was, too, in our party the returning pilgrim,

a devotee of the sect of Mulai Ali el Derkaui, as was apparent from his green turban and the string of large wooden beads he wore suspended round his neck. A strange quiet man he was, always ready to help us load our animals or pitch our one little tent, but seldom speaking; never missing the hour of prayer, and often himself bearing part of the load of his little donkey, on which he was carrying to his native village a few bars of rough iron to be forged into ploughshares. We saw but little of him : he was always a hundred yards ahead or behind, counting his beads as he came along ; and often when we missed him altogether we could see away back along the road his figure, or its shadow, for his colour and that of his clothes corresponded too truly with the yellow sand, as he rose and fell in prayer. I was much struck by his quiet, patient, uncomplaining way. He didn't belong to us, but travelling in the same direction, he joined our little caravan, and we made the journey together. I of all our party had some conversation with him, for kind as were they all to the solitary stranger, he was timid and retired. However, we often talked together as I trudged beside him, and he seemed to be a man of no little power of reasoning and thought. Often in discussing theological questions, and he would talk of nothing else, it became apparent that a battle was raging in

his heart, a battle of common-sense against prejudice
and fanaticism. He had travelled to Mecca and back,
and his eyes had been opened, and he seemed to
realise the narrow-mindedness of the school in which
he had been brought up. He spoke openly to me,
for to the day he left us at Dads to turn aside to his
home, he never knew I was a Christian and a European, and often we prayed together by the roadside.

There remains but one more man to mention, my
servant Mohammed er-Rifi, who followed me faith-
fully throughout the long journey, and returned with
me to Tangier to commence again the humdrum
existence of waiting at table and sweeping floors. An
excellent youth he is, all good nature and smiles,
strong and trustworthy, but preferring the luxuries
and warmth of my kitchen to sharing the hardships
of a desert tramp of several hundred miles. However, he never complained until the end of the journey, and then, arrived once more in Marakesh, he
cursed the desert, and all that in it is, with all the
curses he could muster—a very tolerable lot, on the
whole. However, I cannot speak too highly of his
fidelity and of the patience with which he bore what
must have been to him a most terrible journey—nor
forget to say that at times he hints that he and I
should set out afresh for pastures new.

I have entered somewhat at length into the charac-

ters and description of my men, but some word of
praise is only due to them ; for had I not been surrounded by a faithful and uncomplaining band, my
success in reaching Tafilet would never have come
about.

The usual delays occurred in Marakesh before we
got started once more, this time again the fault of
the old Shereef, who wanted to buy presents to take
to his relations at Dads,—the existence of whom, although he had two wives and quite a number of children there, he had apparently forgotten for several
years,—and could not decide what to purchase.

So having found quarters for my men and my
mules, I determined to enjoy the last few days of
rest and plenty that I was destined to know for
several months.

*From Saffi to Morocco City : a weekly Market.*

# CHAPTER II.

I HAD already several times visited Marakesh, or Morocco City, and had therefore no difficulty in finding my way all over the town, through the streets of which, ruinous as they are, it is always a pleasure to pass; for all kinds and species of human beings congregate in this southern capital of the empire, from the fair mountaineer to the swarthy negro from Timbuctu and the Sudan, from the rich merchant of Fez to the lithe shy Berber of the snow-clad peaks of Mount Atlas.

But before I speak of the inhabitants and the strange sights to be seen within the city, some general description of the place must be given.

Marakesh shares with Fez and Meknas, both lying far to the north, the title of a capital, and it often forms the residence of the Sultans of Morocco for considerable periods at a time, the royal palace here being one of the largest in the country. The city lies in a wide plain, formed by the valley of the Wad Tensift, some fifteen miles to the north of the foot-hills of the great Atlas range, at an altitude of some 1600 feet above the level of the sea, from which it is distant about a hundred miles. A wall from 20 to 30 feet in height surrounds the city, which covers a very large extent of ground, though no inconsiderable portion of the enclosed extent is composed of gardens. This wall is defended at intervals of 120 yards by towers, some of which are formed of stone, but most of native concrete or *tabia*, and without lime being employed. Seven gates give entrance and exit to and from the town, but none presents any remarkably handsome features, being more attractive from their yellow colouring and general picturesqueness than from any architectural beauties. On almost all sides the city is surrounded by luxuriant groves of date - palms, stretching for some miles to the north, but more scanty on the south. These are irrigated and the water - supply brought from the Wad Tensift, which flows to the north of the city, and in which there is, summer and winter, a considerable volume of water.

Approaching Morocco from almost every direction except the south, the place lies hid behind the forest of palms until one is close upon it, and even then little is to be seen but the dull yellow walls with

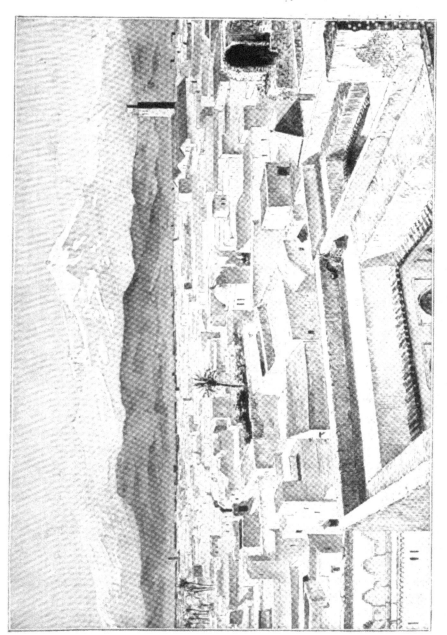

A GENERAL VIEW OF MOROCCO CITY.

their square towers, above which rise the many minarets of the form common to Morocco.  These do not
in the least resemble those of the East, being of far
more solid construction and form, and are almost
universally square, though now and again octagonal
or sexagonal.  Often decorated in gorgeous green
tiles, they add, wherever they are met with, a glimpse
of colour and form to a city that is otherwise but
gloomy,—its buildings and soil, its inhabitants and
their clothing, seeming to be all more or less tones
of one colour, a greyish yellow.  Such is Marakesh as
seen from without the walls.

As soon as one has entered its gates the state of
dilapidation in which the city now is becomes apparent.  Surrounded by ruinous houses and mosques are
large open spaces of ground, as often as not filled
with the refuse of the city.  From these the streets
give entrance into the more habitable quarters, where
some pretensions to comfort, though few to cleanliness, are to be found.

The streets are wider, as a rule, than in Fez, though
many are narrow enough ; but the size of the houses
bears no proportion to those of the northern capital,
being for the most part of one storey in height, except in the thoroughfares and quiet back-streets in
which the richer portion of the population live.  The
smaller one-storeyed buildings all more or less adopt

the same form of construction, being built round an open court. *Tabia*—concrete, or rather consolidated soil—is the material in use, with here and there mud bricks. Only two stone buildings, I believe, exist in the whole city,—the handsome gate leading into the " Kasba " near the Government mosque, and the still more handsome minaret of the " Kutubía."

Some little signs of prosperity, however, are apparent in the bazaars, which are large and well supplied. The new " Kaiseríeh "—parallel arcades arched overhead and lit by open skylights—are of by no means contemptible size or construction, and in good repair. They present of an afternoon, when the goods are for sale by auction in the arcades and by retail in the many box-like shops that line them, a picturesque and lively scene. All manner of goods can be purchased here—from the newest design in Manchester cottons to old silver daggers and brass candelabra. As in nearly all oriental cities, the different trades possess their separate bazaars, one whole street being given up to the *attarin*, or sellers of sugar, spices, glass, and china, &c., who answer much to our grocers ; another to the brass and copper workers ; a third to the saddlers ; and the longest of all perhaps to the shoe-workers, for Marakesh is celebrated for its leather. The merchants and inhabitants generally of the city are very different in type

and character to those of Fez. Whereas the latter
are fair, and generally most fanatical, the native of
Marakesh is a good fellow, smiling and cheery, with
far more of the traits of the negro than of the
Moor of the north. In colour, too, he is much darker
than the Fezzi, and many show more or less remote
signs of negro blood, owing, no doubt, to their
proximity to the darker tribes, and the fact that the
slave-trade of entire Morocco filters through this
city.

The residential part of the town is divided into
several districts, separated from each other by open
spaces, or by streets of shops. Just as in Europe,
there are the fashionable and unfashionable quarters,
the " Medina " or city being perhaps the most sought
after. So largely does fashion hold sway over the
people, that the rents of houses of equal size only a
few hundred yards away from one another vary often
fifty per cent, a palace in the district of " Bab Dukala "
not bringing anything like so large a sum as a minute
house in the " Medina." It was in the latter that I
resided during my stay, in the house of Sid Abu Bekr
el Ghanjaui, who owns very considerable property all
over the city, and particularly in this neighbourhood.
The houses here are high, and, like most Moorish
residences, have but few windows looking towards
the street, one and all possessing central courts on

to which the rooms open.　But even in respect of
windows Morocco City is different to Fez, for whereas

*A Street in Marakesh.*

in the latter from the streets one sees but few, and
those generally closely barred, in Marakesh they are

in considerably larger numbers, though, as I stated above, by no means general.

After the "Medina"—the trading quarter—the "Kasba" is the most important. This district, the residence of the Government, and which contains the palace, is separated from the remainder of the town by walls, much resembling those that encircle the city, but higher and in better repair. Nor do the houses reach to this wall, for between the city proper and the "Kasba" are large open spaces and many gardens, adding a most picturesque effect to this quarter. These gardens for the most part are walled, and as a rule only the tree-tops, amongst them the handsome cypress and date-palm, are visible, while the minarets beyond cap the scene.

One enters the "Kasba" through the handsome stone gate of which I have already made mention, and of which tradition says the stones were brought from Spain, and after passing a smaller and less important gateway, one emerges opposite the large "Jumma el Makhzen," or Government mosque, with its handsome minaret of stone and tiles, and its huge modern courtyard, opening on to the street by large gates. With the exception of the tower, now fast falling into decay, it presents no particular features of architectural beauty, though its courts and green tiles and turreted walls are by

c

no means despicable.　A long straight road with one-storeyed houses on both sides, for the most part quarters of soldiers and *employés* in the Government service, leads on to another series of walls, those of the Sultan's palace.

As in all the Moorish cities, the great courtyards of the palace are public thoroughfares, though they can be closed any moment by the strong gates which are found in every direction, and one of the principal entrances and exits of the city is through the royal squares that lie between the palace and the great park, or " Agdal," of the Sultan.　These squares, three in number, are surrounded by high walls of modern construction and in good repair, and open into one another by handsome gateways, decorated in colour-tiles and painting,—the latter an art peculiar almost to this portion of Morocco, and though met with here and there elsewhere, it is known throughout the country as a Marakesh fashion.　For the most part it consists of red and black designs upon a ground of yellow ochre, and has by no means a bad effect, especially when employed under the overhanging roofs of green tiles in the palaces and mosques.

Although it covers a very considerable amount of ground, the palace at Marakesh, as seen from the outside, does not present any very particular features of beauty, though the pointed roofs of brilliant green and highly glazed tiles, capped with globes of gold, are picturesque enough. The interior it is impossible to see, and the one or two courtyards which I had visited on a previous occasion were in bad repair, noticeable only for their size and absence of decoration. Probably, however, in the portion of the palace put aside for the private use of the Sultan and his many women, there exists a great deal that

*Inner Court of Sultan's Palace in Marakesh.*

is beautiful in the way of architecture and decoration, though the constant love of the Sultans for pulling down and rebuilding has no doubt destroyed much of the older work, which in all probability was the best. It must by no means, however, be denied that even the modern architecture of the Moors, as exemplified in the finer houses of Fez, is excellent. It is the custom of writers on Morocco to detract in every way from the present state of the country and its inhabitants, especially as regards architecture; but this is no doubt owing to the fact that they have no opportunity during their stay in the towns of entering the houses of the official and richer classes, for the Moors are very shy of strangers, and it requires a long acquaintance with the language and the people before they will admit one, as a rule, into the interior of their abodes, and then generally not unless the native costume is adopted, for fear of falling into bad repute if " Christians " are seen to enter. I have myself not only had many opportunities of seeing the finest houses of Fez, but have resided in them for several periods of no little time, and can vouch that some of the dwellings of the richer men are little short of the Alhambra in beauty. The one great drawback to their modern architecture is the entire absence of marble pillars, in place of which much heavier work is erected, usually richly decorated in tiles. Beautiful as they often are, the airiness and lightness so apparent in the Alhambra, for instance, is entirely wanting. The mosaics of finely cut tiles to-day being worked in Fez surpass in design and skilful application any I have seen in Spain. However, I have wandered rather far from Morocco City, for there but little if any great beauty is to be seen, the inhabitants being, as a rule, much poorer than those of the northern capital, while the materials used in the construction of their houses are not nearly so good or so lasting.

On the opposite side of the three squares to the palace are the walls of the "Agdal," the great enclosed park of the Sultan. On a previous visit to Marakesh I had been allowed to wander at will in these gardens for hours at a time, and though, according to our ideas, they have fallen into a state of ruin, they are still very beautiful. Water runs in every direction; and at one spot is a huge tank, or reservoir, reached by a handsome flight of steps, and of such dimensions that a steam-launch plies upon its waters. As for the gardens, they are a forest of olive and palm and orange trees, half smothered in many places in dense creepers, while the soil is covered with a thick undergrowth of shrubs and flowers, that shelter not only the partridge and the hare, but even foxes and jackals. The Sultan, in spite of the dilapidated state of his gardens, draws no small revenue from the sale of its fruits, which are put up to auction annually, and sold when still on the trees, the purchasers having to pluck and send them to the market, as well as to guard them against theft.

There are several fine mosques in the Marakesh, one surpassing all the others in its magnificent minaret, which may be said to be almost the sole existing example in the whole country of the remarkable

architectural capability which the Moors undoubtedly
possessed at one period of their existence.    This

*The Kutubía in Marakesh.*

mosque and minaret are known as the "Kutubía,"
or "Mosque of the Library," from its having contained at one period a vast collection of manuscripts.

The tower, built of squared stone, is 280 feet in height, and is surmounted by a smaller minaret, which again is capped with a dome. On the summit of this dome are three gold globes, one above the other and decreasing in size. On the summit of the lower tower is a parapet of Moorish design. The whole building is of a dull red colour, and the niches of the windows and the centres of its faces are carved in a very pure style of Arabic design. Originally tilework filled most of these niches, but a great quantity of this has fallen away, though a broad band of green and black encircles the whole immediately below the parapet. Just as in the two sister towers,—the Ghiralda of Seville and the Hassan tower at Rabat, the latter uncompleted,—a sloping incline takes the place of steps within, on account of this forming an easier ascent for the beasts of burden that carried the stones during its construction. The architect of all three of these towers is said to have been a certain Fabir, who worked in the employ of the Sultan El Mansur, in whose reign the Kutubía was completed. The mosque beneath, though covering an enormous extent of ground, is in by no means just proportion to the great minaret, being built of brick, and white-washed, while the roof is tiled. Below the flooring is said to exist a great cistern excavated by the Sultan El Mansur. The pillars

supporting the roof of this mosque are all of marble,
and the courts are paved in the same stone and
coloured tiles.

From whatever point Marakesh is looked at, the
great tower of the Kutubía is the first object to
catch the eye, and it forms an excellent landmark
in steering one's way over the bewildering plain that
surrounds the city on all sides. I was told when
crossing the Glawi Pass, on the fourth day after
leaving Marakesh for Tafilet, that from a point near
the road this great work, the sole reminder of the
genius of the old-day Moors, was visible.

Although the largest mosque, and possessing the
handsomest minaret, the Kutubía seems much deserted as a place of worship, possibly from its being
somewhat removed from the more inhabited portions
of the city. Two shrines have annexed all the
veneration of the townspeople and the surrounding
tribes,—those of Sid bel Abbas, the patron saint of
the city, and Mulai Abdul Aziz. A pretty story is
told about the first, which, though common amongst
the Moors, I have never seen quoted. Sid bel Abbas
arrived outside the walls of the town, a beggar in
rags; but although his poverty was apparent, he had
a great reputation for sanctity. Before entering he
sent to the Shereefs living within to ask their permission to be allowed to reside in the city, a course

that much perturbed the said saints; for up to that moment they possessed the monopoly of the business —in Morocco a most lucrative one—of demanding and receiving alms on account of their descent from the Prophet. Wishing, however, to avoid an abrupt refusal, they resorted to delay, during which Sid bel Abbas took up his residence on the summit of a rocky barren hill—Jibel Glissa—which rises amongst the palm-groves to the west of the walls, and on which a little mosque to-day commemorates the event. At length, seeing that some answer must be sent, the Shereefs filled a bowl to the brim with water and sent it out to him. The bowl represented the city and the water themselves, and the bowl was full, which said pretty plainly, "Business already overstocked—much rather you wouldn't come." However, they gave him an opportunity of getting over their device, for the message they sent was couched in more poetical language. "If you can add," they said, "to a bowl of water already full, enter." Thereupon the saint plucked a rose and held it in the sun until its stalk thirsted for moisture, when he gently laid it in the bowl. The water displaced was drunk up by the thirsty flower. In this manner he sent the bowl back—but with no answer. When, however, the Shereefs saw that he had succeeded, and also paid such a pretty compliment to himself as to

liken them to the water and himself to the rose, they
withdrew all opposition, and the saint entered the city,
and, judging from the reverence paid to his bones,
must have entirely monopolised the business.

The "Zauia" of Sid bel Abbas forms a sort of
almshouses, and food and money are distributed there
to the poor. An entire quarter of the city—the extreme north-west — belongs to the *zauia*, and it
owns enormous tracts of palm-groves and agricultural land in the surrounding plain. These posses-
sions have been offerings from the faithful, or bequests
at death, and in some cases purchases made with the
constant flow of money that pours into the coffers of
the mosque.

Another almost equally holy spot is the shrine of
Mulai Abdul Aziz, which lies either in or just on
the borders of the "Medina" quarter. A very handsome building covers the tomb, like that of the rival
saint, gorgeously decorated, and full of lamps and
candlesticks of precious metals. But of all the trea-
sures stored in these sanctuaries, clocks are the most
numerous. When this invention began to penetrate
into Morocco—that is to say, in comparatively late
years—they were naturally looked upon as the most
valuable and wonderful things, and a fashion promptly
set in to bestow them upon the ashes of the dead
saints. Every one who could afford it gave a clock,

THE SÔK JUMMA-EL-FANAR, THE PRINCIPAL PLACE IN MOROCCO CITY.

and often in talking of local saints I have heard
Moors say, "Ah! he was a saint indeed, God's mercy
upon him; and there are four clocks in his tomb!"
It is said that the burial-place of Mulai Idris at Fez
presents a bewildering scene of clocks, great and
small, half going, and all wrong. I myself have had
opportunities of visiting one or two tombs in Morocco,
and have listened, bewildered, to the ticking of fifty
or sixty of these much-reverenced presents. Most
seem to be tall "grandfather" clocks, made in England, and dating from about the end of the last
century. Some are remarkably fine, with silver dials,
showing the quarters of the moon, &c. Even to-day
the natives adore the great, loud, ticking horrors
manufactured for the native market in Algeria—
monstrosities of gaudy decoration and painted wood
—and no good house is considered complete without
one or more. I have dined in houses at Fez where
there have been six or seven in one room.

None of the other mosques of Marakesh calls for
much remark, though those of Ibn Yusuf, El Mansur,
and El Muiz are large, the former possessing a very
handsome, though more modern, minaret, rich in green
tiles. As is customary all through Morocco, no Christians are allowed to enter the sanctuaries, and even
whole districts, *zauias*, are sacred. One or two
streets near the tomb of Mulai Abdul Aziz are crossed

with chains, marking the boundary of town and saintly property, and within these limits even the assassin is safe from arrest, for they answer the purpose of marking the boundary of the refuge. The result is that all the *zauias* are full of refugees of all classes, from political prisoners to the pilferer of the stalls in the markets.

Two large markets are held weekly, one outside the Bab (gate) el Khamis—as its name implies, on Thursdays—and the other within the city walls in the square of Jumma el fanar. Both collect large crowds of the country-people, as well as the natives of the town, and the trade is considerable in native produce. The more picturesque of the two is without doubt that of the "Khamis," for the great open space that serves as the market-place is surrounded on two sides by the palm-groves, and on the other two by the long straight line of the city walls. A few cypress-trees and a white-domed saint's tomb add not a little to form a fit background to the strange grouping of figures and animals that are crowded together in the market. Here herds of oxen, cows, and calves are for sale, tended by the long-robed Arabs from the plains; there camels, goats, and sheep. Mules occupy a spot to themselves, and one at a time is mounted by the auctioneer to show its paces; while a professional rider gallops to and fro, shouting as he goes,

upon the various horses, for which he yells for bids.
All classes and kinds of people congregate in the
market—from rich Shereefs, accompanied by slaves,
and riding great fat mules with crimson saddles, to
the ragged hungry
soldier; from the timid
Berber of the Atlas
peaks, in his black
cloak, to the *gamin*
of the streets; from
the respectable grain-
merchant to the most
disreputable of Jew
money-lenders. Here,

*A Jewish Banker of Marakesh.*

too, the shoesmith has his tents, and women sell
baskets and embroideries, pots and pans of earthen-
ware, and wooden dishes, embroidered *kuftans* and
woollen girdles. All the city seems to adjourn of a
Thursday morning to the great level space outside the
Bab el Khamis to buy and sell or look on.

The Jews, as in nearly all Moorish cities, possess a
quarter to themselves—the "Mellah," or salted place.
In Marakesh it lies quite close to the "Kasba," and
almost adjoins the Sultan's palace. If anything this
division of the town is dirtier than any other, while
the ever-present smell of *mahia*—the strong spirit
made in the place—adds a nauseating aroma to the

many already emitted by the offal and filth thrown
out into the street. There are many well-to-do Jews
in Marakesh, and one or two possess nice houses,
scrupulously clean within, but with manure-heaps,
several feet in height, at the door-step—the refuse
of the place, which they merely throw there and
leave to rot.

Drunkenness seems very common in the streets
of the *mellah*, and it is this fact that gave rise
to the recent complaints as to the persecution of
the Jews. As far as the Sultan is concerned, they
can get as drunk as they like in their own quarter,
for they are under a Sheikh of their own; but he
naturally objected to them selling *mahia* to the
soldiery, for whose crimes he was responsible. However, in spite of the fact that the Jews are, or ought
to be, almost all Moorish subjects, the Sultan has not
been able to prevent this nuisance, for the cry of
persecution at once arises. I was asked on the last
two occasions that I visited Marakesh to make inquiries as to the state of the Jews there, and had
opportunities of speaking with, and consulting, the
leading and most respectable of the Israelites. They
one and all made light of the complaint of general
persecution, but mentioned that individual cases did
exist where Jews had been hardly treated on insufficient evidence. However, such is far more often

the case with Moors. I have met with much kindness on my travels from the Jews of the interior, and also at times with no little show of fanatical hatred; and I think that the most respectable of their tribe in all the towns acknowledged that the cry of persecution was more an attempt to become exempt from taxation than for justice for wrongs done. There can be no doubt, however, that in former times the Jews were cruelly used; but the late Sultan, Mulai el Hassen, was a broad-minded man, and never refused to listen to their petitions. No one mourned his death more sincerely than the peace-abiding members of that tribe, whose wrongs he was ever ready to redress, though only naturally he put opposition in the way of those who, taking advantage of European protection or his own leniency, practised nefarious usury with his subjects.

The population of Marakesh to-day does not probably number more than some 40,000 souls, though it is said that within a hundred years of its founding by Yusuf in 1062 A.D. it contained some 700,000 inhabitants. There is no doubt, though this figure is probably an exaggeration, that it was at one time a city of great importance and learning, for even Europe sent its sons to be educated at the great colleges that existed there at that time.

I have written but little as to Marakesh. It is

a city that has so often been described by other
travellers, that it has been my purpose here merely
to sketch its peculiarities and to give a general

*A Street Scene in Marakesh.*

impression of the place. Briefly, it presents a maze
of yellow streets, leading, here, between the crumbling walls of tottering houses; there, through narrow
dimly lit bazaars with their tiny boxlike shops; and

here, again, amongst the high white walls of the residences of the richer class. Then out into great open dusty spaces, surrounded by half-ruined mosques with tiled minarets, or gardens above the walls of which appear the tops of palms, olive, and orange trees, and the straight stems of glowing cypresses. Then perhaps one turns a corner and comes face to face with a drinking - fountain of exquisite tilework and carved wood, to stumble, as one gazes at it, into a manure-heap or a hole in the road, broken in the roof of some aqueduct. And beyond the wonderful range of white snow-peaks, rising some 12,000 feet above the level of the city, the silent majesty of the great Atlas Mountains.

# CHAPTER III.

### THE ASCENT OF THE ATLAS MOUNTAINS.

ON the afternoon of November 1 a start was eventually made for our journey of exploration. My party consisted of the same men as had accompanied me from Saffi, with the addition of a dull and lazy negro, whom I had taken into my employ on the recommendation of a native of Tafilet to whom I had confided my plan. He turned out to be worse than useless, complained the entire route of the hardships of the journey, and insisted upon riding the whole distance, while I had to go most of the way on foot, gaining his point by constant veiled threats of exposing my identity. I had to humour him as long as we were upon the road, for fear of his making known the fact that I was a European in disguise ; but on my return to Marakesh he paid the price of his impertinence and perfidy in a manner more in use in Morocco than in England—for on my making a statement to

his master of his conduct, which was amply corrob-
orated by all my men, he received, without my knowledge, though I do not think I should have objected,
the flogging he deserved. His presence was a constant
cause of anxiety and danger during the whole journey ;
and his coarse impertinent manner, his threats, his
treatment of my other men and myself, so exasperated me, that on one or two occasions I felt that
I could have ordered him to be flogged myself, and
enjoyed the sight of it. While every one else was
making light of the cold and our hunger, he would be
cursing at me for having brought him, and stealing,
if he could get it by no other means, the share of food
belonging to the rest of the men. The least remon-
strance brought a threat that he would inform the
natives of my disguise, and thereby ensure my death.
On one occasion it was only by an effort that I succeeded in restraining my men from murdering him,
which was their intention during some night. Fear
of discovery there was none, and their moral code certainly would allow of the taking the life of a man
whose presence caused danger to every other soul in
camp, and who used this power to obtain everything
procurable that he set his heart on, caring little
whether the rest of us fell by the wayside from
fatigue so long as he could ride, or died of starvation so long as he could obtain his fill of food. I

have no pity even now when I think of the salutary
hiding he got when he returned to Marakesh, for a
worse villain never, I believe, existed.

We split up our little party and left Morocco City
by different gates, so that in case any information
had reached the ears of the native officials there
would be less chance of their being able to arrest our
progress ; but nothing occurred, and an hour after
bidding adieu to my host, Sid Abu Bekr, our united
caravan of men, three mules, and a couple of donkeys,
had entered the palm-groves and was threading its
way toward the open plain.

Before us lay the Atlas, blue and white in the sunshine, and seeming to bar all farther progress in that
direction, of so equal an altitude are the snow-peaks.
The scene was a charming one—the constant peep of
the glistening snow seen through groves of palms.
But the forest, which to the west and north of Marakesh extends to a great distance, does not to the east
protrude far into the plain ; and in an hour or so we
had left the last palm-tree behind and entered the
open level country, which stretched away to where
the unbroken line of mountains rises from the plain.

At a small *nzala*, the merest collection of thatch
huts with the usual *zareba* of thorn hedge, we spent
the night, crowding into the little tent, before which
our animals were hobbled ; and soon our tin kettle was

boiling, while the black slave-girl unpacked the tiny glass tumblers that take the place of tea-cups, and the old Shereef made a brew of the favourite beverage of Morocco, green tea with piles of sugar and mint.

Every one was in the best of humours. At length all delays were over, and we were started upon our adventurous journey, in the success of which all, with the exception of the negro, felt a common interest; and as we squatted round the tent we talked and laughed together, as cheery a little band of men as could be found anywhere.

Before dawn on November 2 a start was made. Impatient as I was to reach country where I should be safe from the interference of the Moorish Government, it was decided that our pace must be very slow, for a long and weary road lay before our pack-animals, and their strength must be husbanded for the climb over the mountains. So it was that we pushed on quietly, seldom travelling over three miles an hour at this part of the road, although the soil was good and the country level.

Our course took us in an east-by-south direction across the plain of Misfiwa, which forms one of the large *bashaliks*, or governorships, of Southern Morocco. There were many signs of cultivation on both sides of the road; but the dry summer had turned the soil to a light yellow hue, which rendered it no easy matter to see how much was agricultural land and how much merely used for grazing. That crops are largely raised in this part is a well-known fact, yet judging from the appearance of the soil at this season of the year it looks poor enough. The villages are few and far between, and although mostly inhabited by the Berbers, the original inhabitants of Morocco before the Arab invasion, their dwellings had not as yet begun to show the neater and superior style of building we were so soon to notice. However, as we proceeded and forded the Wad Urika, placing a longer distance between us and the city, the improvement in the habitations became visible, and instead of the thatch *nuail*, or huts, of the villages that we had been passing, we found houses built of *tabia* with flat roofs, which, though possessing no particular appearance of comfort or size, were greatly superior to the others.

Two rivers were passed before we left the plain to enter one of the valleys of the Atlas Mountains, at Imin Zat. These were, namely, the Wad Urika, which I have already mentioned, and the Wad el Melha, or salt river, which owes its name to its brackish waters. Both rise in the Atlas Mountains,—the Urika in the valley above Akhliz, which I had visited some five years previously ; and the Wad el Melha farther to the·east, issuing from the hills by a narrow valley a few miles to the east of that of the Urika. Although such of the last winter's snow as disappears in summer had already melted, and the fresh fall had not as yet taken place, there was a considerable body of water in both streams, a sure sign that while we had been parching in the sun-dried plains heavy rains had fallen amongst the mountains. The water of both is largely used for purposes of irrigation, although that of the Wad el Melha is salt, and a considerable amount of labour and time has been expended in banking up the small canals which carry the precious liquid to the fields far removed from the actual course. After flowing some ten miles into the plain from the Atlas foot-hills, these two rivers unite in the province of " Uidan "—" the rivers "—and finally empty themselves into the Wad Tensift some six or seven miles to the north-east of Morocco City, near the *zauia* and tomb of Sidi Abdullah ben Sessi.

The plain at this point presents the appearance of an almost dead level, though, in fact, it ascends to the east, until the termination of the Tensift valley is reached, some thirty-five miles higher up, where a concourse of smaller streams flowing from the north-east and south unite to form the main river, which supplies with water the entire country round Marakesh, and the city itself, finally to reach the sea between Mogador and Saffi on the Atlantic coast.

The district of Misfiwa, through which we were passing, is bounded by three powerful *bashaliks:* on the north Rahamna, the hills of which, a continuation of the range of Jibeelet, which we had crossed between Saffi and the capital, are clearly visible ; on the east Zemran, with its capital and seat of government at Sidi Rehal ; on the south Urika, including the country of Beled Ersdigi, famous for its mulberry-trees and silkworms.    All of these districts are governed by powerful Bashas, who may be reckoned amongst the richest and most important of Southern Morocco.

Nearly all the population of Misfiwa, although Berbers, speak Arabic in addition to their own language, Shelha,—a fact that is due, no doubt, to their constant communication with the city of Morocco, which forms their market and source of supply. Yet, in spite of the fact that Arabic is spoken amongst them almost as freely as Shelha, they are true to their traditions in their intense dislike to the Arabs.    Aware previously of this trait in the character of the Berbers, I had carefully chosen the men who accompanied me, of whom one and all were by extraction Berbers, and who all spoke Shelha with the exception of my Riffi servant, whose native tongue, " Riffia," is so much allied to it that he could gather the gist of every conversation and make himself tolerably well understood in turn. This fact, that the language of the natives was equally the language of our party, helped us not a little in obtaining the welcome everywhere extended to us by the Berber people.

A word or two must be said as to the system of cultivation and raising crops extant in this portion of Morocco. The ground is ploughed with the primitive native implement as soon as the first rains of autumn fall, and the grain, especially the barley, sown early. By May the harvest is in full swing, and the reaping and gathering of the crops takes place. The ear is merely severed from the stalk close to the top, so that long straw is left standing. The ears are carried in nets upon the backs of mules, mares, and donkeys to the *nuadder*, where the threshing takes place. A clear hard space of ground, puddled with clay if necessary, is left bare, and upon this the grain, still in the ear, is thrown, and over the whole are driven round in circles the mares, horses, mules, and often donkeys of the farmer, until the grain is thoroughly separated. Pitchforks of wood are then made use of, and by raising the straw and grain into the air the chaff is carried off by the wind, the seed alone remaining. This is then stored in subterranean granaries—*metammer*—sunk in the soil, the outlet to which is a small hole

at the top closed with stones and clay.  The whole
is lined with a coating of stiff clay, which prevents
the ingress of water.  Grain remains in a good state
of preservation for long periods when housed in this
manner.    On to the reaped fields the cattle and
sheep are now turned out to graze, finding means
of subsistence through the dry summer by cropping
the standing straw, and at the same time manuring
the soil for the next season's crops.

It was still comparatively early morning when we
reached the termination of the level ground at a spot
where the Wad Misfiwa leaves the Atlas foot-hills.
The Berber name for this spot is Imin Zat, the mouth
of the Zat, the latter being the local title of the river.
The word *imin*, " a mouth," is of very common occurrence in geographical names amongst the Berbers,
and corresponds exactly to the Arabic *fûm*, both in
meaning and the term implied.    It does not, as our
word " mouth " geographically does, imply the estu-
ary of a river, but any gorge or outlet by which a
river or a track enters a different district or a different
kind of country.    In the following pages the word
will be found more than once in its latter meaning.

We found the ford of the Wad Misfiwa at Imin Zat
by no means an easy one.    The river was not very
deep, it is true, but so fast was its current and so
stone-strewn its bed that the footing was insecure,

and we were fortunate in crossing without any mishap, more than a wetting to two or three of our men, and a partial soaking of the pack of a donkey, which fortunately contained nothing that could be damaged. Not so, however, a party of mountain Jews who crossed at the same time, one of whom was washed completely off his legs, and both he and his donkey carried some little way down the stream before they were able to regain their footing. The water was very cold, and the sudden immersion, no doubt a rare occurrence, which the Jew obtained caused him to become a pitiful object, and he shed liberal tears of annoyance at getting wet.

Nothing prettier than the entrance to the valley of Imin Zat can be imagined. The hills slope gently down to the river's edge, clothed in groves of olives, under which the stream flows crystal clear, leaping and dancing over the rocks and stones, and adding to the charm of the scene its sweet music. For a background rose the snow-capped peaks of the Atlas, standing out clear and defined against a sky of azure blue. The village of Imin Zat stands on the west bank of the river some little way up the hillside, and a delightful site it possesses, clinging to the slope and rising tier above tier, its deep yellow houses contrasting well with the dull green of the olive-trees and the cobalt of the mountains and sky.

As from this point of our journey to its very conclusion the buildings—whether the great *ksor*, or walled fortresses, of Tafilet or the humble cottage of the Berber of the northern slopes of the Atlas—are all constructed of the same material, *tabia*, it may render more clear the constant use of the word in the descriptions of scenery and villages if I describe here the manner in which *tabia* is used, and of what it consists. Roughly it may be said to be cement without lime—in other words, the soil, of sand, gravel, and pebbles, beaten into a consolidated mass. The manner in which it is employed is the following. The foundations of a building are sunk and the ditch filled in ; then from the level of the ground to the height of usually some 2 to 3 feet stakes are driven into the earth at each side of the ditch, and on the inside planks are arranged parallel with the soil. Quantities of loose gravel and pebbles are now brought, and the space intervening between the planks is filled up with the material, which, by means of being constantly beaten down with heavy blocks of wood at the end of poles—*mrakas*, the Moors call them—becomes a solid mass. Upon its drying the planks are removed and replaced above the first stratum of wall, the gravel being treated in the same manner. In this way a solid and tolerably durable material is obtained, subject to but one destroying action, that of water. On the northern slopes of the Atlas, where the rains are heavy, the walls of the houses are protected almost always by overhanging roofs, constructed on beams which project 2 feet or more over the wall. Across the beams and at right angles to them is laid a flooring of dried canes, which again is covered with brushwood. Beaten into the brushwood is a flat roof of adhesive clay, which is held firmly in its place by the twigs which intersect it in every direction. On the southern side of the Atlas range, however, the rainfall is exceptionally small, and there is no necessity for the overlapping roofs, the material being of sufficient durability and strength to withstand the rare showers that fall there.

It is a curious fact that as one proceeds south from Marakesh, while the dwellings of the natives improve, their welfare decreases ; for as soon as the fertile plains are left behind one leaves the farmer class altogether and enters amongst a population dependent for its livelihood upon the scanty stock of olives and vegetables they can raise in their small gardens, and more generally upon the firewood and charcoal that they carry, often two or three days' journey, to the capital. Many of the richest farmers of the most fertile districts of Morocco have no roof to cover them but their brown goat-hair tents or thatch huts, while almost the poorest peasant amongst the Berbers possesses a cottage of *tabia*, which nearly always presents an appearance of cleanliness and order.   While the rich Arab of the plains is content to spend his days seated on the manure-heap in front of his hovel, the hardy and poor Berber of the mountains builds himself a little verandah on the roof of his house, where he can pass his time shaded from the sun or rain in peace and quiet.

It is almost as soon as one enters amongst the Berber people that one begins to find out how infinitely superior they are in morals and character to the Arab.   Their every word and look speak of greater honesty and truth than one finds in a month amongst the Arabs.   But of the Berber character I shall have more to say anon.

As soon as we had passed over the ford of the Wad Misfiwa, our road took a turn to the south, following the course of the river, a little way up the side of the hills on its east bank.   Gradually ascending as we proceeded, we camped early at a miserable *nzala* on the summit of a steep incline, from which a fine view was obtainable both up and down the river—up, to the snow-peaks of the Atlas; down, to the plains we had now left behind and the hills of Rahamna far away beyond.   Very different was the thatched *nzala* from the neat and trim villages that dotted the valley below, surrounded by their carefully terraced gardens of olives and vines, walnuts and almonds; but the people where we camped were evidently very poor, and eked a miserable pittance out of the small fees they collected from passers-by—for the road over the Atlas is one not often travelled, even by natives.

The change in the costume of the natives made it clear that we had left the people of the plains and entered into the country of mountaineers, for the length of their garments was much curtailed about the legs, and instead of the draggling and mud-stained skirts of the Arab there appeared the sinewy limbs of the children of the mountains. But peculiar to the Atlas we noticed here for the first time in general use the *khanif* or *haidus*, the strange black-hooded cloak with its eye-shaped pattern in yellow or red in the centre of the back, the object of which no tradition seems to make mention, and no history to hint at. All that we know for certain of this strange garment is, that while it is not found throughout Algeria, it crops up again in the mountains near Tripoli. Putting aside all speculation as to the origin of the design, it must be added that the material of which these cloaks are made is an excellent one, the closely woven black goat-hair being impenetrable to cold and rain, and therefore excel-

lently suited to the mountaineers of the bleak heights
of the Atlas range.

A few words must be said as to the general difference of costume between the Berbers and the Arabs.
While the former wear the *jelab*, a hooded garment
closed down the front, it is never found amongst the

*Berbers.*

Berbers, whose one desire as to clothing seems to be
absolute freedom of limb.   The *haik*, or toga-like garment of the Arabs, is used amongst the better-class
Berbers, but merely as a luxury.   Their typical costume
consists of the *chamira*, or long loose shirt reaching
from the neck to below the knees, and the *haidus*

above, the open hooded cloak called by the Arabs
*s'lham.* This in the case of the mountaineers takes
the form of the black goat's-hair article, and in that
of the Berbers of the plains of a thick but finely
woven garment of white wool. The one distinguishing mark in the costume of the two races, however,
is the following : while the Arab loves to gird his
waist with a sash or leather belt, the Berbers have
the greatest objection to anything of the sort, and
seldom, if ever, wear either. Some exception to
these customs can always be found in the case of
Berbers who have left their native lands to work
in the Moorish cities, and here they can often be
found in dress absolutely resembling in every detail
that of the poorer class of townspeople ; but this is
owing far more to necessity than option, for the local
Berber materials cannot be found, except rarely, in
the Moorish towns.

In appearance, too, besides the difference of feature
of which I shall have opportunity to refer anon, there
is considerable variance of fashion and custom. While
the Arabs leave unshaven their beards and only trim
their moustaches, the Berbers of the Atlas and the
country beyond shave the entire face with the exception of a small pointed beard on the chin, which is
connected with the ears by a fine closely cropped line
of hair. This shaving of the head is general through-

E

out both people, the only class who fail to do so being
devotees, the sects of " Ulad bu Sba," who leave the
entire skull covered with hair; the followers of Sid
ben Aissa, or " Aissaua," who leave crown alone unshaven; and the Riffis and mountaineers of the north,
who wear the *gitaya* and *kron* respectively, the former
a long lock on the centre of the back of the head, the
latter grown on one side above the ear.   It would be
interesting to discover the origin of these various but
unvaried customs of locks of hair, for the common
explanation that they are to be pulled up to heaven
by is not only absurd but altogether an insult to the
high system of theology possessed by many who wear
them.   So systematically are these customs preserved
that there can be little doubt, especially in the case
of the Berbers, that they date from a period long
anterior to the introduction of Islam.

Leaving the valley of the Wad Misfiwa on the
morning of November 3, we turned directly to the
east and crossed the spur of the Atlas that lies
between the valley of the former river and the Wad
Ghadat.   This slope of the lower Atlas takes the
form of a plateau, with an average altitude above
the level of the sea of some 3000 feet, and is known
as Tugana, a district under the jurisdiction of the
Kaid of Misfiwa.

But very few villages or habitations were to be

seen, and the greater part of the soil seemed capable of but little cultivation, being here torn into deep water-courses, there covered with brushwood. One stream alone is crossed, the Wad Masin, a small clear river of no size, but which, from the appearance of its banks, floods in the rainy season. Near the ford were a few gardens, and dense bushes of oleanders lined its course. A very short distance beyond, one of the customary weekly *sôks* or markets is held; but not being market-day, the place was deserted and left to a mangy dog or two, and a few ravens which sought for food amongst the offal and dirt. There are no buildings at the market, for the native shop-keepers bring their little tents—*gaiaton*—in which they expose their wares for sale, packing up the same in the afternoon and pushing on, probably to be in time to visit another *sôk* elsewhere the following day. The usual custom is for the consecutive *sôks* along the main roads to be held on following days, so as to allow all the travelling vendors of goods to visit one after the other in succession. I have some-times travelled for a week and found each day some market by the roadside in full swing, by having hit off the right day at the first *sôk* and followed them up in succession, though it is far more common to miss the entire number, and never see a full market-place at all upon a long journey. These *sôks* are always known by the name of the day on which they are held, with the name of the place added as a distinctive mark. Thus one finds "Had el Gharbiya," "Sunday of the Gharbiya," and "Arbaa of Sid Aissa," "the Wednesday of Sid Aissa," so called from its proximity to the tomb of that saint. Near this *sôk* of Tugana is a small semi-deserted village of stone-built huts, a dreary poverty-stricken-looking place. From this spot we had a choice of roads to the summit of the Atlas—namely, either to pursue the one we eventually followed, *viâ* the Wad Ghadat and Zarkten, or to turn to the south, and skirting the side of the steep mountains on our right, strike as straight a line across country as the nature of the land would allow. The latter, a mere track, often passing along the face of precipices and at all parts difficult, leads *viâ* Gadaruz and Tizi Aït Imiger to Zarkten, where the two unite. However, we chose the longer but more practicable, and even that was bad enough. What the other must have been like it is impossible even to guess; but the fact that it is only pursued by the native mountaineers and sturdy mountain mules would probably have meant that for us it would have been impassable.

Ten miles after leaving the *nzala* in the valley of the Wad Misfiwa, we descended by an execrable path to the level of the Wad Ghadat, close to

*Fording the Wad Ghadat.*

where a ruined or incompleted bridge raises its broken arches from the stony river-bed. The ford was bad enough, even though the river was not high, and it was only by piling the loads bit by bit on to the top of the pack-saddle of the highest mule that we succeeded in getting our baggage across at all, for the stream was strong and wide and swift.

No history or tradition seems to contain any record of the bridge, which, if ever completed, must have been a fine work with its five high arches; but it is easily apparent that it is of Moorish workmanship, and was no doubt erected by one of the early Sultans of the present dynasty, probably in the seventeenth century, for previous to that period the communication between Morocco and Tafilet was almost *nil*, the two countries forming as a rule separate kingdoms, though now and then falling under the jurisdiction of one Sultan, as in the case of three successive rulers of the Beni Merín dynasty. After the seizure of the thrones of Morocco and Fez by the Filelis, who still govern Morocco, it would be only more than probable that one of their first acts would be to keep communication open with the desert, whence their armies were drawn; and even to-day the river Ghadat at the time of the melting snows prevents all farther progress up or down the road over which we were travelling, which would not be the case were the bridge in repair, though the snows in the heights above would as often as not effectually bar all farther progress beyond.

The distance from the bridge over the Ghadat to Zarkten, the principal village and residence of the deputy governor of the district, cannot be more than about ten miles as the crow flies; but the river was too full to allow us to follow its bed, the shortest route, and we were obliged to climb by a precipitous path high up the mountain-side on the east bank of the river. Keeping parallel with the Wad Ghadat, except that we had necessarily to follow the escarpment of the range, we toiled on over a stony and rock-strewn track for some four hours. Tiring as the rough walking was—and it required, too, all our energies to prevent our mules and donkeys slipping on the smooth rock—the scenery amply repaid us for the disadvantages we had to suffer.

Perhaps the valley of the Ghadat was not so wild as some of the Atlas scenery we were yet to see; but it certainly possessed one feature that all the others lacked — namely, vegetation; for here on the cool north slopes of the range rain falls in plentiful supplies in winter and spring.

Away above us the mountains towered—here clothed to their summits with pine, arbutus, gum cistus, and evergreen oak; there rearing precipice upon precipice of bare forbidding rock to where the eternal snows formed a line of white against the sky. Below us, for our road ascended high up the mountain-side, lay the valley, clothed in verdure, through the centre of which, now in a wide stone-strewn bed, now dashing between high walls of rock, flowed the river, the roar of which was the only sound that broke the silence. Here and there we looked down on to the flat roofs of the Berber villages, where a small patch of land would be reclaimed, and walnut and other trees planted, through the branches of which peeps of narrow terraces, green with vegetables, appeared. Strange beautiful shapes the mountains take, at places rolling in sweeping curves, at others broken into rock projections and precipices, but everywhere presenting some point of grandeur and beauty.

At length towards sunset Zarkten came into sight, ahead and far below us, and we hurried on, hoping to reach the Sheikh's house before dark, and thus obtain provisions for the night and our next day's journey; but when, in fast falling twilight, we reached the rocky bed of the river, we found all hope of fording it to be impossible, and reluctantly retraced our steps to a few stone hovels we had passed a quarter of a mile back, near which we found space to pitch our tent. The cold was extreme, and it was only by untiring efforts that we were able to persuade the inhabitants to sell us a fowl, which, of its kind the very poorest, was no meal for eight people. Bread

*A View from above Zarklen.*

and the native *kuskus* were neither to be obtained, and a few dried figs was all that our stock consisted of.

At daylight we descended once more by a precipitous path, and, after a weary hour and a half of labour, succeeded in getting our animals and our baggage across the river. So tired were the poor mules and donkeys with their struggle of perhaps 100 yards against the swift current, that we were obliged to call an hour's rest on the farther bank, where we lay down under the shade of the grove of trees that surround the residence of the Sheikh.

A picturesque castle it is that the deputy governor of the district has built himself at Zarkten, though probably he gave more thought to its defence than to its appearance in designing it. The main body of the castle, for such it is, is a large square block, with a high tower at each corner, the latter gradually tapering as they ascend. The whole is built of *tabia* of dull yellow colour, but the summits of the towers are decorated with a coating of whitewash. Surrounding the whole building is a wall, parts of which form outhouses and rooms for retainers and guests. Standing in its groves of trees underneath a peaked mountain wooded with pines, it presents not only an effect of great picturesqueness, but also appears to possess the undoubted advantage in such a lawless country of being impregnable.

We had passed but few caravans or travellers on the road hither—merely a mountaineer or two singing cheerily as he came along driving his little mule before him, probably laden with the dates of Tafilet, which change hands many times before they reach Marakesh. A few of the mountain Jews, too, we met now and again—long gaunt figures, many carrying arms, and one and all a finer type of man than their co-religionists of the plains; for they have a hard existence these Israelites of the Atlas, and though not persecuted, find it difficult enough to scrape a living from their trades, for, as a rule, they are gunsmiths, workers in silver, or dealers in hides. As soon as our animals were rested, we lifted our scanty baggage once more on to their backs, and set out afresh upon our journey.

At Zarkten the valley splits into two parts, one continuing the general direction—north and south—that we had been following, while the other turns away to the west. It is from the latter that the Wad Ghadat flows, rising in the snows of Jibel Tidili, or Glawi, while the other is drained by the Wad Tetula, so called from a small settlement of Berbers, higher up its course, but locally known as the Asif Adrar n'Iri, "the stream of Mount Iri." Just above the Sheikh's house, and within 100 yards of it, the two rivers unite.

Turning a little to the west, we ascended an incline amongst gardens and fields and pine-trees, above the

*The Sheikh's House at Zarkten.*

river Ghadat, until we reached the main portion of the village of Zarkten, a mile farther on. The place is poor enough, a few stone and *tabia* houses of mean appearance lying on a dreary level of bare soil at the foot of the great mountains beyond, and we did not turn aside to examine it more closely, for the view we obtained of the place from the distance of a few hundred yards was depressing enough. There is a considerable settlement of Jews at Zarkten, from whom we had hoped to obtain provisions; but it being Saturday, they would not sell, and the man we sent to the *mellah*, or Jews' quarter, returned empty-handed.

Our road turned once more to the south, and we commenced a steep ascent by a sandy track up the side of a well-wooded mountain, at the summit of which I found that we had reached an altitude of 5600 feet above the sea-level, and nearly 2000 feet above the Sheikh's house at Zarkten, the elevation of which I made out to be 3710 feet above the sea.

An adventure, which happily ended only in laughter, happened to us at this part of the road. The track, never of any width, was here extremely narrow, and our impatient donkey, desirous of being the first to cross the Atlas, tried to push his way past the mules. There being no room, however, to perform this manoeuvre, he nearly put an end to his existence by falling over the precipice. Happily he alighted some 40 feet down, legs up, in the branch of a pine-tree. The difficulty was how to rescue him from this perilous position, for the poor little fellow carried on his back all my personal belongings — small though their quantity was. We were obliged, accordingly, to unpack the mules, and by tying together the ropes which held the tent, &c., in its place on their backs, I managed to descend, and, cutting the pack-saddle loose, had the happiness of seeing my luggage rescued. Then letting the rope down again, I made it fast to the four legs of the donkey, which I bound together to prevent its struggling, and the others hauled him up, I eventually reaching the track by being pulled up in much the same manner. The donkey was none the worse, and as soon as he had recovered his equilibrium, and found, to his satisfaction, that he was unhurt, issued a prolonged series of cries, and kicked violently at everything his heels could reach.

Every step we took the scenery increased in grandeur, and from one spot we could obtain views of the three valleys. To the west lay that of the upper stream of the Ghadat, through which the river twisted and turned, a thin thread of silver 2000 feet below us. The lower slopes of the valley were mostly wooded, but towering far above them on the west and south rose the central peaks of the Atlas range, Jibel Glawi, or Tidili, a dome of pure white snow dominating the whole, which presented a panorama of exquisite beauty. To the north we could see the gorge of Zarkten, and far down the valley formed by the united streams of the Ghadat and the Tetula; even the plains beyond and the distant hills of Rahamna were visible in the clear atmosphere. Less pleasing, but offering features quite distinct, was the scene directly to the south of us, where the smaller river, the Tetula, dashed between walls of rock that seemed in places almost to meet over its stream. Here were no signs of vegetation, except in the immediate foreground, and all was bare limestone and snow above and shales below, a dreary but impressive scene.

We were leaving all vegetation behind us, and already I missed the *azif*—palmeto—so common all over Morocco, and in its place there appeared the *arar*—calitris—and juniper and pines, while scattered about rose the twisted trunks of evergreen oaks.

Proceeding for a time along a level track over a mountain the name of which is Telettin Nugelid, and at an average elevation of about 5000 feet, we descended once more and forded the Tetula, or Asif Adrar n'Iri, near the pretty village of Agurgar, the name of which—walnuts—is due to the existence of a fine clump of these trees. Here the district of Aït Robaa, which extends along the west bank of the Tetula as far as this point, was left behind, and we entered the small and bleak tribe-land of Aït Akherait. Agurgar, from its sheltered position, is pleasant enough, and the village seemed clean and well built. A few of the natives, wild mountaineers, met us and brought us a welcome meal of boiled turnips. The bed of the Tetula is very narrow at this spot, the river rushing between enormous boulders, which bear every appearance of having been heaped up in their present positions by the action of glaciers, which have long since ceased to exist in the Atlas,—for throughout the whole range, as far as it has been at present explored, and that, it must be confessed, is very little of it, no extant glacier has been discovered.

Ascending again, this time on the right (east) side of the river, we quickly left all vegetation behind, except for an occasional wind-bent stump of an evergreen oak, and entered a wild dismal country, the soil of which consisted for the most part of black and grey shales, and above peaks of limestone, and they again capped with snow. Not a sign of life, either animal or vegetable, was to be seen; yet every now and then the cliffs gave back the echo of some strange Berber song which told us that although no human being was to be seen, even these dreary wastes of rock were inhabited.

At a tumble-down hovel of loose stones, where the natives had scratched an acre of soil, poor enough but sufficient to grow a few turnips, we spent the night of November 4, finding protection from the cold in a dirty stable—for, with the exception of the cultivated patch, there was not an inch of soil into which one could drive a tent-peg. However, the dozen or so inhabitants of this dismal abode asked the old Shereef and myself into a grimy room, windowless and without a chimney, and filled with dense smoke, where we were able to sit for an hour or two in warm discomfort over the fire of half-burned charcoal, the fumes of which were stifling. Poverty seemed in possession of the little place, for not a blanket did they appear to possess; but they were cheery good people, and spoke a little Arabic, so that conversation was possible. In winter, when the entire district is under snow, they drive their one or two cows into the house and hibernate,—only the men, and they very seldom, ever leaving the house at all during the two or three months of bitter cold.

They told me the name of the place was Afuden Nugelid, and I found the elevation to be 5800 feet above the sea-level.

F

A few miles above this spot is a little oasis, the
tiny district of Tetula, sheltered from the bleak
winds by a semicircle of mountains, amongst which
the few acres of gardens and trees nestle.    The
village is a large one, compared with most that we
had passed, and the natives seemed better to do than
our friends of the night before.   It is from this spot
that the last steep ascent to the pass over the Atlas
commences, and after an hour and a half's scramble
up slippery paths and amongst enormous boulders,
we found ourselves by ten o'clock A.M. on November
5 on the summit of the Tizi n'Glawi, or Glawi Pass,
at an elevation of 8150 feet above the sea-level,
where, weary with the steep ascent, we threw ourselves down to rest in the warm sunlight, sheltered
from biting wind by a huge rock.

# CHAPTER IV.

## THE ATLAS MOUNTAINS AND THE BERBERS.

ALTHOUGH the Atlas range is said to extend from the Atlantic Ocean to the Gulf of Syrtis, it is my intention to deal here with only such a portion of it as is found in Morocco, and of that but briefly, for in my journey to Tafilet I crossed the range at the same spot on my going and return, and was therefore unable to gather much of its nature beyond the portion I absolutely came in contact with. On two previous occasions, however, I had visited this portion of the Atlas, and on both followed it from due south of Marakesh to near the Atlantic—to the point, in fact, where the mountains decrease in altitude and spread out, forming the watershed between the rivers Sus on the south and the Tensift on the north.

Although geographers claim for the many ranges that occur between Morocco and Tripoli the name of Atlas, it must not be thought that a continuous line of peaks extends from one point to the other; for, speaking of the Moroccan portion, it ends more or less abruptly where the plains of Beni Mgil occur, to the western side of the Wad Muluya, the river which runs into the Mediterranean near the frontier of Algeria and Morocco. In fact, it is not far to the east of Fez that the peaks decrease in altitude, falling away to the long plains which succeed. From this point, however, south and westward they extend in unbroken line to near the ocean, taking a general direction of south-west and then west. The entire portion from Fez, from which the snow-peaks in-habited by the Beni Mgild and Aït Yussi are visible, to but a little way beyond Demnat, some fifty odd miles to the due east of Marakesh, is unexplored, the nature of the succession of Berber tribes inhabiting its slopes rendering it inaccessible to the traveller. From Demnat to the Atlantic the tribes are less wild, and live in greater fear of punishment from the Government in the case of molestation of Europeans, with the result that not only the explorer but even the most casual globe-trotter can travel in safety, and enjoy the grand scenery which presents itself. Yet how few Europeans ever go!

I have already described the appearance of the Atlas Mountains from the north, and farther on in the narrative of my journey more than one allusion

*The Atlas Mountains from the South.*

will be found to the barren scene they present from the south. It may be here added, however, as a general remark on this portion of the range, that while the northern slopes contain fine wooded valleys, their lower parts rich in olive and fruit trees, the south stretches away, a dreary waste of stone and shales, presenting no feature of beauty beyond its gloomy grandeur. The reason is not far to find, for the desert wind in summer blows in terrific gusts, drying up what soil does exist, while little or no rain ever falls. This very scorching wind it is that renders so fertile the northern valleys and the plain beyond, in which Marakesh lies, for, following the slope of the mountains to the altitude of their highest peaks—and the range must hereabout average nearly 11,000 feet above the sea—the wind is transformed by the change of temperature into cloud, and falls in heavy showers. The difference as one ascends the luxuriant northern slopes, where fine vegetation is found to the altitude of some 5000 to 7000 feet, to the scene that meets the eye when the summit is crossed, is a most extraordinary one, and from the Tizi n'Glawi, the pass over which I crossed, one could obtain the two views at the same time—north, down the deep valley of the Ghadat, with its woods and forests; south, over range beyond range of bare limestone and shale mountains.

The main range at this part forms in reality but one of four parallel chains. To the north of Marakesh the hills are known as Jibeelet, and extend from near the Atlantic beyond the eastern end of the tribe-land of Rahamna, terminating a few miles beyond Kalá. South of this some twenty miles, and parallel with it, is the principal range, beyond which, at an average distance of some twenty-five miles, is Jibel Saghru, or the Anti-Atlas. However, although the first two mentioned run directly east and west, Jibel Saghru forms a large district of broken chains of mountains, the valleys of which lead in every direction, for it empties such streams as flow in rainy seasons east into the Wad Gheris, west to the Draa, north to the Dads, and south to the desert. Yet in spite of this the system takes an easterly and westerly direction, the same being more apparent after the spot where the Wad Draa divides the range into two portions. The natives call only the eastern portion Saghru, not connecting it with the hills to the west of the Draa, which form eventually the southern side of the Wad Sus. There is yet another line of hills still farther to the south, Jibel Bani, which rise near the Draa south of the *zauia* of Tamgrut and continue to the west. It has always been a question as to where they terminate; but I was pointed out at Tafilet, from above the hill at Dar el baida, the end

of a chain of mountains to the south, which sink
gradually to the valley of the now united course of
the Wad Gheris and Wad Ziz. Beyond there appeared to be nothing but desert sand, and this, I was
informed, was the western extremity of Jibel Bani.

It is difficult to hazard an opinion as to where the
highest peak of the Moroccan Atlas will be found to
exist, for at present but very few observations of the
high altitudes have been taken, though both Sir
Joseph Hooker and Mr Joseph Thomson reached to
about 12,000 feet. In the native opinion Jibel
Ayashi, in which most of the large rivers of Morocco
rise, surpasses the other peaks in altitude; but, as far
as I know, no European has ever seen it, much less
been there. Some geographers are of the opinion
that the highest point will be found amongst the mountains almost due south of Morocco City. So equal
are the summits in this direction that it will take
many ascents before any definite result can be arrived
at, though, with the exception of the obstruction
of the native officials, no great difficulties ought to
arise, as the snow in summer and early autumn
almost altogether disappears, and no glaciers are
found throughout the whole range; nor do the
mountain-tops rise in precipitous peaks, but, as a
rule, are flat and undulating.

But little game is to be found in this portion of

the Atlas. The Barbary wild sheep (*muflon*), it is true, exists, but is by no means easy to obtain, as every native carries a gun, and should chance give him the opportunity, fires at them whenever he may catch a glimpse. The Berbers, too, are sportsmen ; and the Kaid of Glawa, and other governors, are in the habit of organising large hunts, that have done much to kill off this fine beast and drive the remainder into the most inaccessible parts. The lion is unknown, and the leopard very rare, though farther to the north, in the forests of Beni Mgild, both are said to be common, and I have often seen the skins for sale, and captured lions in the Sultan's palace at Fez. Hyenas seem to be found throughout the entire range, and foxes and jackals abound. Bird-life seems most noticeable for its absence, and I have never seen, though I have spent several months at different times in and near the Atlas, either a vulture or an eagle. Smaller hawks and one or two varieties of kites are common. Amongst game-birds I have seen only the red-legged Barbary partridge and the pintail sand-grouse, and the latter only in the foot-hills. A guinea-fowl is said to exist, and I have seen in the possession of the Shereefs of Wazan specimens brought from Zimmour, to the west of Rabat on the Atlantic coast. It is a small variety, dark in colour, with a blue head and dark crest, and not half the size of the fine plump bird of which I have shot so many in Somaliland and around Harrar. A pretty grey-striped rock-squirrel is common in the mountains, and much prized by the Berbers for his meat, which is said to possess medicinal properties.

The commoner vegetation of the Atlas, which differs according to altitude, are pine, *arar* or calitris, evergreen oak, cork, white poplar, wild olive, arbutus, laurustinus, lentiscus, palmeto, oleanders in the river-beds, and juniper, while at places the gum cistus is found in large quantities.

The principal rivers of Morocco all rise in the Atlas Mountains, with the exception of the Wergha, the large tributary of the Sebu, which has its source in the hills to the south of the Riff country. The Draa, Sus, the Gheris, and the Ziz are the principal rivers to the south of the range; while to the north the Tensift, Um er Ribía, Bu Regreg, and Sebu are all fed by the Atlas snows; and on the west the Muluya, which empties itself into the Mediterranean.

Brief as these notes on the Atlas are, they will suffice for the objects of this book. Those who desire to know more of their geology and botany will find two works upon the subject, the results of the explorations of Sir Joseph Hooker and Mr Joseph Thomson.

With regard to the inhabitants of the Atlas, they

*Approaching Marakesh from the North.*

are Berbers, and the following notes upon that race in general, together with the constant mention of their customs and habits which crop up in the succeeding chapters of my narrative, will, I trust, not only bring before the reader a tolerably clear picture of these people, but add possibly to the scanty information that exists as to this trans-Atlas branch of the Hamitic people.

It would be out of place in a book which professes to be no more than a narrative of exploration to enter at length into the subject of the Berber race, and interesting though such would be, the slight description of the people here appended must suffice. Nor have I even collected into this chapter all the notes I was able personally to make upon my travels, but have preferred in many cases, such as in the descriptions of their dwellings, costumes, &c., to make mention of these details when I come across them, rather than drag them out of the context and place them all in one chapter. This I have thought best to do for more than one reason, but mainly because remarks *àpropos* of the Berbers of Dads are not equally applicable to those of Aït Atta for instance, though these two tribes are neighbours. So rather than cause confusion by mentioning peculiarities noticed in only one spot in a chapter which deals with the race as a whole, I have spread my notes over the entire journey, and included them at the points at which I find them jotted down in my original diary—that is to say, at such portions of my journey as I first noticed them.

Nor can mention at any length be made even of the race as a whole, for though the country through which I passed was almost entirely inhabited by this strange people, their territory is vastly more extensive, and they may be said to inhabit districts along the entire northern portion of Africa, from Egypt to the Atlantic Ocean. Therefore it will be seen how impossible a task it would be to enter at any length into the peculiarities of a race which at different points presents such vastly different characteristics, both in the physical aspect of the country they inhabit and in their manners and customs. For this reason it is the safest course to mention only what can refer to that portion of the Berber tribes amongst which I found myself, with but a few general remarks that apply equally to the entire race.

As to the derivation of the name considerable doubt exists, nor was I able to trace any tradition amongst the people as to its origin. Barth asserts that it sprang from the name of their traditional ancestor Ber, but it seems more probable, at least a safer surmise, to connect it with the Greek and Roman term Barbari, for, I believe, without exception the name is not applied by the Berbers to themselves, though in this respect the Arabs use it. The general name by which they call themselves in Morocco is " Shloh," a word meaning " noble," and thus the same as the more classical term " Amazigh," which, though well known all through tribes inhabiting the districts south of the Atlas, I heard only once or twice used. Amazigh is certainly the older name of the two, and was known to both the Greeks and the Romans, and seems to-day, though rarely used in Southern Morocco, to be the classical title of the race.

Although to-day found all through North Africa, from beyond Tripoli to the Atlantic Ocean, the Berbers seem to be entirely cut off from one another, and to have no great intertribal feeling of patriotism, or to be connected by any ties. Yet there can be no doubt that, divided as the tribes are, they have a common origin, being the Hamitic and original inhabitants of North Africa.

Yet even in so small a space of country as that through which I travelled one finds the Berber tribes not only split up into minute clans and factions, but so strangely differing from one another that they might almost be the descendants of different races. Nothing more unlike could be imagined than four typical Berbers, for instance, of four portions of

Morocco—the Riff, and the natives of Aït Yussi, Dads, and the Sus—and yet there can be no doubt that they are of the same family, and the language, though split up into dialects, is practically the same. Yet in appearance the type is absolutely different in these above-mentioned portions of Morocco, and no feature in common, even to the dressing or shaving of the head, or costume, is to be found amongst them, though one and all are proud of their aboriginal origin.

But one tradition did I hear amongst the Berbers as to their antiquity, and this tradition seems to be general amongst their tribes, for we came across it on several occasions on our journey. It is difficult to perceive how it could have sprung up, as it seems to hint at an entirely different origin to that which history, and even other traditions of their own, has set down to them. It runs as follows. A certain maiden of the original Berber people, at the time when the race lived in a far-away country swept by strong east winds, once, in passing a strange king, had the misfortune to expose more of her person than was decent, owing to her attire having been raised by the gale. On the king laughing at the girl's misfortune, the tribe in very shame departed by night, and wandered to the country that they now inhabit. So the story runs, and I leave it to those more versed than myself in sifting traditions and folk-lore to find the signification and value of the tale, which, it may again be said, is not only common throughout the Berbers of the trans-Atlas Sahara, but is known and repeated amongst the Riffis, and between these two districts hundreds of miles of country exist, while no communication takes place one with the other.

No doubt the fact that the Berbers have been many times conquered has done not a little to account for their difference of type, for the Phœnicians, Romans, Vandals, and Arabs have each in turn invaded their country.  But from whatever reason it may be, the fact remains that a more divided and subdivided race could not be found, and marriage, or even cordiality, between the tribes is unknown ; while they exist, in Morocco at least, in a state of perpetual warfare with any one they can get to fight with them.  Not only are their hostilities levelled against the Arabs, for whom their hatred is most deep, but whose religion they have adopted with extraordinary fervour, but also against every other tribe, and failing these, village against village, and even household against household.  Mention will be found more than once in the ensuing pages of cases of this, in which it was the custom for neighbours to fire at one another from their windows and roofs whenever the opportunity presented itself. Yet in spite of this the stranger passes in safety through them, for with him they bear no quarrel.

A few words must be said as to the manner in which native travellers proceed in safety through districts in which bloodshed and murder are of every-day occurrence. The system under which immunity from murder and robbery is accorded to the stranger is known by two names, *mzareg* or *zitat*. *Mzareg* originally means a spear, and the term was thus applied from the fact that in old days a spear was given by one of the tribe to the traveller, which, being recognised as the property of one of their number, accorded him safety in his journey. However, spears have long ago disappeared from these districts, though the name *mzareg* still remains. Nowadays the common custom is for a member of the tribe, in consideration of a small fee, to conduct the traveller in person, both being sacred from attack while passing through the land over which the tribe in question holds jurisdiction. As soon as the limits are reached, a new *mzareg* or *zitat* has to be obtained. Sometimes, especially in the case of the Jews living and trading in the Sahara, some mark or token is given, such as a turban or handkerchief, which is considered sufficient; but in cases of caravans and total strangers a man invariably is employed, who answers the double purpose of guide and protector. From Dads to Tafilet I was accompanied on my journey by a *zitat*, without whom I could never have reached my destination, as amongst the many Berber tribes we passed through his presence afforded me immunity from inquisition and annoyance. Here again I was fortunate, for I was not obliged to change my *zitat*, the fact being that members of the tribe of Dads can travel in safety amongst nearly all the other Berber tribes, by a reciprocal arrangement by which the caravans of the others are allowed to pass through their district without fear of plunder. Dads has gained this unique privilege from its situation, blocking as it does the entire road from east and west.

With regard to the Jews living amongst the Berbers a similar practice exists to the ·*mzareg*, only in their case it is known as *debeha*, or sacrifice. This name has been applied from the fact that the system first arose from Jews seeking the protection of the Berbers by sacrificing an ox or a sheep to them : nowadays the native Jews no longer need to perform this, the patronage of the Berbers being hereditary, the vassalage descending in both families from father to son. Any injury suffered by the Jew is revenged by the protecting Berber as though it had been committed to a member of his own family. In this manner the

Israelites are able to live in tolerable security from murder and theft; in fact, they are the only people who do, as the Berber is never happy unless he has some one to kill, or is running a risk of being shot himself from behind some stone. As may be expected, the Berbers do not allow their influence to be used for nothing; but so poor are the Jews, and also the entire country in which this state of things exists, that it is little or nothing that the "lord" can screw out of his vassal.

In the same way the tribe of Aït Atta, one of the most powerful of the Berber tribes of the Sahara, recently added a large district to the south of Mesgita, on the Wad Draa, to their already extensive territory. However, the inhabitants—Haratin—could not be enrolled as are the Jews, as they are Moslems; and though exactly the same principle is carried on, the term implied is *neïba* — agents or representatives. They, as in the other case, are protected by their conquerors from attack from elsewhere, in return for which they pay an annual tribute.

With regard to the language of the Berbers. Generally speaking, it is known in Southern Morocco as Shelha, but as a matter of fact it consists of many different dialects. Although along most of the road we travelled over the dialect was much the same, I was told that in the heights of the Atlas, as again in

the districts of the Draa, it was very different, and
that it was no easy matter for natives of each place
to render themselves comprehended by each other.
The Berber language as spoken in Morocco may be
divided into four distinct dialects, which are again
much subdivided : (i.) Shelha proper, as spoken
generally throughout the Atlas, from the tribes
of Ghiata, Aït Yussi, and Beni Mgild, to the south-
east of Fez, as far along the Atlas as about due
south of Marakesh ; (ii.) Riffía, spoken by the Riffis
inhabiting the mountains of the north coast, from
the south - west of Tetuan to the French frontier
of the province of Oran ; (iii.) Susía, spoken from
along the Atlas and the Sus valley to the south,
from where Shelha proper terminates, about due
south of Marakesh, to the Atlantic coast ; and (iv.)
Drauía, the common tongue all along the valley of
the Wad Draa from Mesgita, where the junction of
the Dads and Idermi form that river to where it
flows into the Atlantic.   So various are these dialects
that, although my Riffi servant could catch the gist
of the remarks of the Shloh amongst whom we
travelled, and was with difficulty understood in return, he found it impossible to comprehend the
Haratin of the Draa, who speak Drauía, though the
Shloh of Dads and the intermediate *oases* can do so.

I was able only to learn of one feast celebrated
amongst the Berbers which had not been adopted

from the Arab calendar, so completely have they
embraced the religion of the latter. This feast appears to be a kind of harvest-home, and is known as
the *Ayur Nûgârûmûn*, the meaning of which not
even the Berbers seem to know. Curiously enough,
it is held in the Shahr el Fukra, which points out
that it is annual only according to Arab ideas—that
is to say, counted by lunar months — whereas one
would have expected, if it were a survival of great
antiquity, that it would have been at a fixed period
in the solar year. The programme of the feast is
simple. Guns are fired during the day, and great
dishes of food are brought into the streets and there
partaken of, the poor being asked to join. One other
custom only differing from the Arabs was I able to
hear of—namely, that the bride remains three days
in her husband's house before the marriage is
consummated.

That some civilisation had reached the Berbers
long before the Arab invasion is certain, but, as far
as we know, the Romans never crossed the Atlas.
Yet, curiously enough, all foreigners are known to-
day amongst them as *Rumin* (sing. *Rumi*), though
this may be owing not a little to the fact that it was
not until the Arab invasion that the Berbers were
driven to the remote districts they now inhabit, but
were spread all over the country; for it was principally through the prowess of these men, whose desire

for booty the Arabs stirred up, that Spain was invaded and conquered. Therefore it must be certain that the Berbers of Morocco knew the Romans as well as the Romans knew them, and that they carried away with them into the Atlas and the districts beyond the traditions of the forefathers who had been in actual contact with the Roman colonists. Yet there is no doubt that remains of even pre-Roman date exist in the Atlas and the Sahara, and I think it is risking but little to suppose that they were erected by Phœnician colonists. That the Phœnicians were strong in Morocco at one time is shown by the ruins of the great colony of Lixus, on the river Kûs, near El Araish, and I can see no reason why they should not have pushed much farther afield. And to them, I think, may be put down the workings of former mines in the Atlas and Anti-Atlas, and the building of the stone remains which are found in more than one spot—and invariably without mortar—in those ranges. One may go even further, and ask the question, whence the Berbers obtained their existing architecture; for the great *ksor*, with their many towers, have no resemblance to any Arab architecture that I have ever seen, either in Arabia or Africa, while they do most strangely resemble the elevations given in such works as those of Messieurs Perrot and Chipiez of Phœnician castles.

The change on passing from Arab Morocco into Berber trans-Atlas Morocco is in no way more marked than in the architecture. One leaves behind one the mud huts and tents to enter an immense district, every habitable portion of which is thick with great castles, often over 50 feet in height, and with richly decorated towers, unlike anything else I have seen elsewhere in the world, either with my own eyes or in the works of other travellers; and I see no reason why one should not at least surmise that the style of building in vogue to-day amongst the Berbers of trans-Atlas Morocco is not a remnant of their conquest by the Phœnicians. Another instance, slight though it may be, may help to form a link in the chain, that at Dads I saw children modelling in clay little figures of men on horseback, the very image of the Phœnician figures, which no Arab or Moor either could or would do. Excellently modelled they were too. I asked a native, and he laughingly replied, " We all did that when we were small." Yet in all my travels in Morocco, and in the inquiries I subsequently made, I have never seen or heard of modelling of human figures or animals amongst the Moors. An idea of the artistic talent of the Arab youth, in comparison to that of these young Berbers, can be gathered from the drawings they have learned to make in Tangier on the walls of the houses, &c. ; and this only from seeing artists at work. However, they confine themselves to ships, which are just recognisable and nothing more, whereas my Dads friends' models of men and their steeds were excellent in every feature, even the bits and reins and stirrups being represented. In short, it is my belief that when the regions I passed through come to be diligently explored and excavated, remains will be found of a large former civilisation which will be proved to have been Phœnician. In the case of the one ruin I was able to take any notes about at all, it corresponds almost exactly, so far as the general idea, to some of the plans of buildings given in books upon Phœnicia and its colonies ; but unfortunately, travelling in disguise as I was, it was impossible for me to take measurements, or anything, in fact, more than the most scanty notes of this curious ruin.

As to the general character of the Berbers, their manner of living and their looks, I have retained my remarks upon these subjects in the places in which they were originally jotted down, for reasons already given in this chapter, that there is such great divergence of appearance and costume in the different parts of the question. It is for that reason that I have given at this spot only such notes as can be safely applied to the tribes in general amongst which I travelled during my journey.

# CHAPTER V.

## THE DESCENT FROM THE ATLAS.

HAVING digressed for a chapter from the account of my journey, I take up again the narrative from where it was broken off—when on the morning of November 5 we had reached the summit of the Tizi n'Glawi, and were resting after our exertions.

The Glawi Pass scarcely deserves such a name, for there is in reality no pass at all. One ascends to the very summit of the mountains to descend as suddenly on the south side, the narrow strip of footing at the top being only a few yards wide. It is true that the surrounding mountains on either hand rise to a very considerable elevation above that at which we found ourselves—8150 feet ; but the road merely crosses a connecting line of quartzite, overlying the shales, which runs from Jibel Glawi on the west to Adrar n'Iri on the east, the flat-topped snow-capped mountain that gives its name to the stream up the valley of which we had been ascending. The views in either direction were fine, but totally different; for while to the north our eyes wandered over the valley of the Tetula, and lower down the Ghadat, with the steep mountains densely wooded on their lower slopes, before us to the south lay range after range of broken limestone mountains, bare and bleak, and without a single sign of vegetation. But one exception there was, the circular valley of Teluet lying 2000 feet below us; but at this dry period of the year, for as yet only the very slightest rain had fallen, it looked as bare and dried up as did the hills that surrounded us.

The descent could be seen twisting in and out the escarpment of the mountains, amongst boulders of rock from which here and there unsightly wind-bent trunks of evergreen oaks appeared.

A few villages dotted the little plain below, whose flat roofs upturned to our gaze had a strange appearance as we peered down on them from so far above. For the most part they were perched upon rocky eminences, raised slightly above the level of the small valley. It is here that the great castle of the Kaid of Glawa is situated, but from our vantage-point it was indistinguishable, being hidden in the slight descent that leads from the valley to the course of the Wad Marghen. This *kasba* of the Kaid of

Glawa, Sid el Madani, was the last point at which, should I be discovered, my return would be insisted upon, for beyond this the Moorish Government holds little or no real jurisdiction, so it was not unnaturally that we gave the place as wide a berth as possible. On my return journey, when disguise was no longer necessary, I spent a night at the *kasba*, and when the time comes shall describe this mountain fortress, which even in Europe would be considered a building of great size and strength.

Descending the 2000 feet that led to the valley of Teluet, we met at the bottom almost the first large caravan we had as yet come across. They were bound upon the same road as ourselves, though their destination was Dads, while I hoped to push on as far as Tafilet. The men forming the caravan were one and all Berbers, and natives of Dads, added to which they were friends of the old Shereef whom I was accompanying. Therefore I had nothing to fear from them, and the little Arabic they spoke was so mixed up with Shelha that there was no possibility of their detecting my foreign accent. Some twelve men there were in all, with as many mules and donkeys. The cheerfulness of this augmentation of our little caravan was damped by the news they gave us, for from them we learned that the road *via* Warzazat was blocked, owing to the tribes being in

*A Pass on the Road.*

revolt, and that they had been obliged to turn back only some six hours from where we met them. It had been my particular desire to proceed *via* this route, as there are rumours of ruins in the valley of the Warzazat; but I at once perceived that we must follow the inevitable and pursue the road *via* Askura, which possessed this attraction to the explorer, that it had never before been traversed or described by any traveller. It was good luck that brought us in contact with the Dads' caravan, for in these wild lawless regions there is safety in numbers, and I noticed that the old Shereef especially cheered up at the sight of the dozen antiquated flint-lock guns the men bore.

We at once decided to join company and pursue the road together, and for the five following days the Dads tribesmen and their little mules formed part of our caravan. Good sturdy fellows they were, always laughing and running races, in which the brisk cold often tempted me to join them. At this they were much amused, for my slender—not to say thin—form and limbs, as yet but slightly tanned with the sun, led them to suppose that I could ill stand the hardships of the road. That I was a European in disguise never once crossed their simple trusting minds, and amongst this wild band I obtained a reputation of very considerable sanctity, on account of the fact that I said my prayers in orthodox style with the old Shereef, and that I wore suspended round my neck, over my torn and ragged *jelaba*, a string of wooden beads, the insignia of the sect of the Derkaua, or followers of Sidi Ali el Derkaui, who may be almost said to be the patron saint of the Sahara.

With one of these caravan men, Hammu by name, I made great friends, and one of my pleasantest recollections of Dads was the feast he gave me in his house, to which half the village was invited, and which lasted from somewhere about mid-day to somewhere about midnight. He was a simple gentle fellow this Hammu, but as good as could be ; and many a time when we lay huddled together of a night for the sake of warmth he would cover me up with his thick *haidus* of black goats'-hair as I slept, and swear in the morning that he had not done so—that it was merely owing to the fact that he had kicked it off in my direction that accounted for his having slept in only a light cotton *chamira* while I was warm and comfortable. Poor Hammu ! he never learned, so far as I know, that I was a European in disguise,—not that I believe he would mind much, for the friendship that sprang up between us would break through all such barriers as this. He eventually finished, on the day I departed for Tafilet, by embracing me and asking me to return with him to Dads, and share his home, with his sister as my wife. He even promised her a dowry of a few yards of blue cotton, a pair of bracelets, and a cow. My Riffi man nearly exploded with his attempts to conceal his laughter, but I took the compliment as in the manner meant, and clasped his good strong hand with a grip of real friendship, for I could not but recognise that the wild tribesman, with his handsome face and fine bearing, meant every word he spoke.

But I digress from the narrative of my travel. It being out of the question that we should pursue the route *vid* Warzazat, there was no option about the matter, and we turned to the east across the plain of Teluet, fording the Wad Marghen, or Wad el Melha, some two or three miles above the Kaid of Glawa's *kasba*. The stream is not a very large one, but clear, fresh, cold water flows from the snows of the western slopes of Jibel Unila throughout the entire year. Although slightly brackish the water is drinkable to cattle, but the inhabitants rely for their supply upon the many streams and springs that form its tributaries. The river flows along the Teluet valley from east to west, and at the south-west corner of the plain passes out through a gorge to flow into the Idermi, which, eventually joining the Wad Dads, forms the Wad Draa, the largest and most important

river of trans-Atlas Morocco.   The second name of the
river, Wad el Melha, or salt river, is the local title
of every stream the waters of which are brackish.

Ascending by the dry bed of a torrent on the south
side of the river, we skirted the eastern end of Jibel
Teluet, which forms the southern boundary of the
valley, and descended some four miles farther on to
the larger stream of the Wad Unila.   The ascent and
descent we had crossed forms a small watershed for
the tributaries of the two rivers, though apparently
these mountain torrents only flow in the wet season.
At one spot, rather more than half-way, we passed
extensive salt-mines, where quite a number of natives
were engaged in working rock-salt.   The scene was
a wild one, the half-nude men with their rough picks
hewing away and singing the while, as others piled
the salt in native panniers on to the backs of their
sturdy little mules.   The power of these mountain-
mules in overcoming difficulties in the roads is extraordinary, and at one spot we saw a couple literally
descending a precipice, followed by a man who only
kept his footing by the aid of a sort of alpenstock.
The manner in which both man and beasts succeeded
in descending seemed to us, as we stood and watched,
incredible, yet we were told that he made the journey
every day to this spot in the face of the precipice, to
collect rock-salt from a small deposit that existed there.

At one place where an unusually large supply of the
precious mineral existed, a roughly constructed fort
had been built, for the mines had been the cause of
war for generations amongst the tribesmen living
near, their value being, for the arid bleak district,
extraordinary. No doubt to more or less reserving
to himself the monopoly, as is the case, is owing to a
great extent the wealth to-day in the possession of
Sid Madani, the Kaid of Glawa. The soil at this
part consists principally of shales, strewn with boulders of limestone, no doubt portions of the peaks
above, which time, water, and glacier have carried to
their present position.

The Wad Unila, where our path struck its course,
flows nearly due north and south, issuing from a
gorge 100 or 200 yards above, and descending for
half a mile through a narrow valley before reaching
the district of Tiurassín, in which we spent the night
of November 5.

This settlement of Berbers of the Imerghan tribe is
a large place, lying on the banks of the river where
the valley is sufficiently wide to form a small triangular plain, which is again bisected by a torrent, at
this period waterless, which flows from the east. The
*ksor* are many and large, and present a remarkable appearance, each a castle, or sometimes several castles,
with high towers at the corners, the summits of which

H

are roughly decorated in sun-dried bricks and white-wash. The great size and solidity of the buildings struck one as extraordinary, after the hovels the Arabs erect as habitations, and a rough measurement of one of the towers gave an altitude of at least 70 feet, no mean height when it is taken into consideration that they are built without any of the appliances we know in Europe, and altogether without mortar or lime. The plain I alluded to as formed by the valley may be perhaps half a mile across, and consists of gardens of walnut and almond trees, with a few other varieties of fruits.

The Wad Unila, the river of the place, rises to the north-east at the summit of Jibel Unila, from which the stream takes its name. This mountain forms one of the finest of the Atlas peaks, and is said never to lose its cap of snow. The summit, the natives told me, consists of a circular lake of great depth, from which the river takes its rise. So important to the land through which it flows are the waters of the Unila, for the natives are entirely dependent upon its supply for irrigating purposes, that this lake, which is said never to vary its level, has become a place of pilgrimage and veneration, and in the spring of each year sheep are sacrificed to its patron saint. Before uniting with the Wad Marghen (Wad el Melha) at Aït Zaineb, four districts are watered—

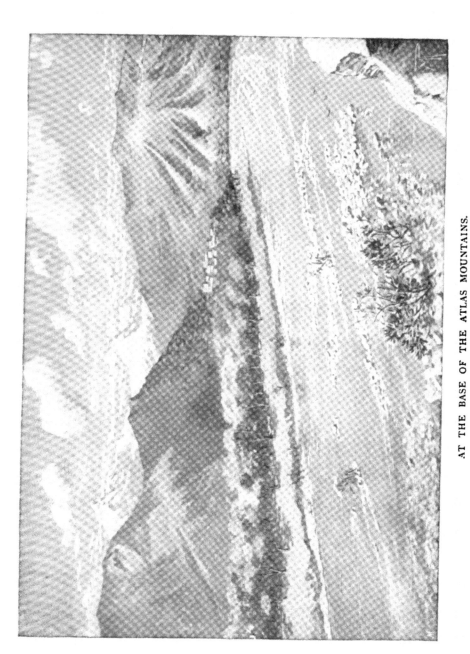

AT THE BASE OF THE ATLAS MOUNTAINS.

namely, taking them from the river's source, (1) Unila, (2) Assaka, (3) Tisgi, and (4) Aït Zaineb ; but the valley thoughout is a narrow one, shut in by high mountains, and only at its widest parts, such as Tiurassín, is it inhabited. But very little wheat is grown, maize and turnips taking its place as the articles of subsistence amongst the natives. The walnuts and almonds, however, flourish to such an extent that a large quantity are yearly exported to Morocco City, being taken by the road we had followed across the Glawi Pass.

The only traveller who had preceded me at Tiurassín was De Foucauld, the French explorer, but from this point our ways separated—he having continued his journey south along the river's course, while I turned off to the east, *en route* for Askura and Dads. He followed the river as far as its junction with the Idermi, which, joining the larger stream of the Dads at Kheneg el Tauria, form together the Wad Draa.

A few of the inhabitants of Tiurassín belong to the tribe of Unila, which geographically occupies the slopes of the mountain of the same name ; but the larger proportion is formed of members of the powerful tribe of Imerghan, which is found split up into many divisions scattered all over this portion of trans-Atlas Morocco. The constant state of warfare existing amongst the Berber people has no doubt caused this disintegration of the larger tribes, by the changing, acquisition, and losing of territory. The people of Dads were the sole exception, and their position, offensive and defensive, has prevented their being so divided, a fact that adds not a little to their strength and importance.

We spent the night of November 5 at the large *ksar* of Aït Yahia u Ali, pitching our one little tent in a walled-in yard, which answers the purpose of a caravanserai for passers-by. A great number of natives crowded about, offering to sell us barley for our animals, and chickens and eggs for ourselves; and though the last we found to be unprocurable, in spite of all their protestations to the contrary, our mules and donkeys fared better than usual. It was not long before one of the reasons of these visits was discovered, for the opportunity was not lost to the pilfering Berbers of stealing a fine powder-horn belonging to one of my men, and formed of the horn of a Barbary wild sheep (*muflon*), set in brass and silver,—a tempting bait to these mountaineers, who set great store upon such highly decorative articles of warfare. The cold was extreme, and it was as much as we could do by crowding together in the tent to keep warm. Although many natives visited us and paid their respects to the old Shereef,

not one for a moment eyed me with suspicion, and
Arabic seemed scarcely spoken at all amongst them.
I found the elevation of our camp to be 5480 feet
above the sea-level. The small caravan with which
we had fallen in on the plain of Teluet camped with
us, and we were not sorry to have increased our
numbers, for the inhabitants of Tiurassín seem to be
a hungry lot of devils on the look out for loot.

Our companions were loudly regretting the fact
that they had been obliged to abandon the route
*viâ* Warzazat, as that road is considered much the
safer, the Arab tribe of Askura, whose district we
were to pass, being much dreaded on account of their
lawless depredations. Nor do they deserve much
else but discredit, for this very little caravan was
pillaged under our own eyes by the robbing Arab
tribe, whose reputation is the worst of all the peoples
of this portion of the country. No love is lost at any
time between the Berbers and Arabs, and this curious
settlement of the latter, in the very midst of the
strongholds of the former, does much to keep the
hatred alive.

The next morning by sunrise, and in bitter cold,
we were threading our way up the dry torrent-bed
that I mentioned as bisecting the little plain formed
by the junction of the rivers at Tiurassín. As we
proceeded the steepness of the climb increased, and

it was not for some five or six miles that we found
ourselves at the summit of the spur of the Atlas that
our road crossed.    Reaching quite suddenly a level
piece of country some half a mile in extent, a magnificent view met our eyes as we turned and looked
back.   Stretching away before us, a panorama of a
hundred miles of snow-capped peaks met our view,
and glorious they were in the early sunshine, one
and all glowing pink and gold.    Beneath we could
see far down into the shadows of the gorge that we
ascended, steep clay and shale slopes crowned with
pines and evergreen oaks.    Certainly the Atlas range
presents as fine a view from the south as from the
other side, but the great plain of the Tensift was
missing to add to the effect of their great altitude.
In return, however, for this, there is a foreground
of far wilder appearance, broken crags of limestone
rock rising range above range until the snow capped
the whole.    The peaks, too, do not bear from this
vantage-ground the same look of equal altitude that
forms so prominent a feature from the north, but each
rises singly and is easily recognisable could any definite system of naming be discovered.    Such, however,
is not the case, and often a mountain known here by
one title is a few miles farther on spoken of by an
entirely different one, the nomenclature being purely
local.    So it is with the rivers all over Morocco, with

but one or two exceptions, and these only the largest, for the smaller streams often take their names from the villages they pass through or near, and I know one river in Northern Morocco, the length of which cannot be more than some twelve to fifteen miles from its source to its mouth, which boasts no less than six separate names. I could identify, how-ever, every peak to which some more or less recognised title seems to pertain. On the extreme west, and to the south somewhat of the others, was Jibel Sirua, a snow-clad peak, which lies slightly away from the main chain, forming the base of the valley of Wad Sus, between the districts of Tifinut and Ras el Wad. It is the principal elevation of the chain that divides the basins of the rivers Sus and Draà. Then, taking them from the west, Jibal Miltsin, Tidili, Glawi, Taurirt or Adrar n'Iri, Adrar n'Deren, and lastly Unila, of all the most beautiful in form, adding almost a proof to what the account of the deep circular lake had forced one to believe, that it forms the cone of an extinct volcano. Even from here, and far more so from the north, one could not but be struck by the equality of altitude presented by the view of the range, a fact proved by the altitude of the Glawi Pass, the lowest at this part of the chain, and yet 8150 feet above the sea. Supposing, then, that the average height of the peaks

reaches 12,000 feet, it will be seen that only at one
spot is the altitude below 8500, and probably in few
others reaches much below 9000, and where the exception is found, probably only in cases of tortuous
gorges entirely hidden in a panorama such as presented itself from where we stood ourselves at an
altitude of 6800 feet above the sea-level. Jibel
Sirua, it is true, is connected with the main chain
by a low ridge of peaks, and Unila stands more
alone than any of the rest; but neither of these
can reach the altitude of Miltsin and Tidili, which
can be roughly estimated at some 13,000 feet.

Although but very little snow was reported to
have fallen as yet this winter, all the peaks were
well covered, and judging from the altitude at
which we were, and the fact that the *arar*—calitris
—and evergreen oak abounded, I should estimate the
snow-line at this particular period at 10,000 feet.
However, as a general rule, no true estimate can be
formed as regards the snow on the Atlas, for so much
depends upon the severity of the winter or the heat
of the summer; and to the best of my belief, based
upon statements made to me on the spot, snow
altogether disappears from the Atlas in very dry
seasons, with the exception of sheltered spots and
crevices. Probably the least snow is found about
the end of October, after a previous dry winter and

a hot summer. In May and June, before it has had time to melt, I have seen a far greater expanse of snow-capped peaks than I did on my return from Tafilet in December. Generally speaking, the deepest snow is found in March and the least in October.

Descending from this elevation of 6800 feet by the bed of a now dry torrent, we continued our journey in an east by south direction, passing through one or two narrow gorges between rocks that were remarkably fine. It is no difficult matter to see that in winter and wet weather this road must be impassable, for the sole track is in the bed of the stream, and there were signs on the rocks of the water having risen to some six feet above the level of its stony course.

Here one began to notice the first clear signs of the fact that while the valleys of the northern slopes of the Atlas run almost due north and south, those of the side on which we were take an east and west direction, parallel, in fact, to the backbone of the chain ; the intermediate hills forming a small range along the foot of the southern side, such as is found, only at a greater distance away, on the north. I refer to the hills of Jibeelet and Rahamna.

The system of the Atlas at this part of its chain may be said to consist of five distinct ranges, all running east and west and nearly parallel. To the extreme north are those I have just mentioned, Jibeelet and the hills of Rahamna; then the main chain of the Atlas itself; then the hills at its feet on the south, to which no distinct name seems to pertain, and which are so close to the range as to form part of itself; then again the Anti-Atlas, or, as it is more properly called, Jibel Saghru; and farther south still, the unexplored line of Jibel Bani, which leaves the Wad Draa near where it turns to the north, and not far from the *zauia* of the Shereefs of Tamgrut—Ulad Sid ben Nasr—and extends as far as the southern limits of the oasis of Tafilet, near the hills known as Jibel Belgrul.

Following the course of a valley, our road proceeding nearly due east, we passed the ruins of a *ksar*, or more properly a fortress, known as the Teherumt of Majdáta, the latter being the name of this inhospitable and nearly uninhabited district. The fort is in bad repair, half of it tumbling down, but in what remains a few poor Berbers have taken up their residence, and managed to till an acre or two of the soil in the immediate neighbourhood and plant it with turnips. Although a tolerable amount of vegetation is visible, we saw no herds or flocks, though it was stated that in spring a few goats are grazed hereabouts. Almost immediately after passing the Teherumt—" fort "—two small rivers are forded, the easternmost of which is known as the Wad Igurian, while I was unable to find the name of the other, only an insignificant stream. Both appear to unite after reaching the plain, from which only a low range of hills now separated us. The valley we were following, though scarcely deserving of being called a valley, for its watercourse was dry, descended to the western of these two rivers, only a few hundred yards of hill dividing the two streams, and after passing the Igurian one commences to ascend again by the course of a dry torrent, the hills on the south taking the form of high perpendicular cliffs of remarkably fine appearance. But little vegetation was to be found here, a few oleanders along the bed of the stream being almost all there was. Again passing a small watershed, we descended toward the river of Agurzga, parallel to the two we had passed, both of which crossed the road, which proceeded between the parallel ranges of mountains on the north and hills on the south, at right angles. I could hear of but few inhabitants in these districts, though our men said that a small tribe of Aït Minzeru lived higher up in the mountains, near the eastern slopes of Jibel Unila.

Where the road runs under the high cliffs the name of "Kaiserfeh" has been given to the spot, the same implying the narrow streets of the bazaars of a town.

At Agurzga, on the banks of the river of the same name, we spent the night of November 6.

Of all the picturesque and romantic spots we passed on the entire journey, I think Agurzga deserves to be

*Agurzga.*

considered the first, for not only is its situation, shut in with high precipices of bare stone, fine in the extreme, but the hand of man has done much to add to the scene by perching strange great castles, rich in decorated towers, on every pinnacle of rock that

juts up in the narrow valley, and by terracing a sufficient quantity of land to allow of a strip of gardens
along the edge of the river. The stream enters
this portion of the valley by a narrow gorge, between
precipices some thousands of feet high, and taking a
semicircular bend, still between high walls of rock,
opens out into a stony bed, one bank rising sheer in
broken boulders to some height, while on the other
side are the gardens of walnut, almond, and fig trees,
terraced one above the other. Rising again high
above these gardens are rocky eminences on which
the great castles are perched, in one case the summit
being crowned by a huge block of building, in others
by tier above tier of strange yellow *ksor* and white
square towers, the summits of the latter richly decorated in brickwork and turreted. Just as the Wad
Agurzga enters the district to which it has given its
name, so does it leave it again, flowing out to the
level country through a gorge in the range of hills
along the northern slopes of which we had been
travelling. Through this narrow gorge, guarded by
a ruined fort, we could catch a glimpse of the wide
plain beyond, across which the rivers flow before
entering themselves into the Idermi or the Dads,
as the case may be. This plain, of which I shall
have more to say anon, forms the centre of the Draa
basin, and extends from the foot-hills of the southern

slopes of the great Atlas range as far as the northern extremity of Jibel Saghru, the so-called Anti-Atlas, to the south. The river of Agurzga, flowing from the snow-level, is always well supplied with excellent water, which whirls and eddies along in crystal clearness over its stony bed, here in deep blue pools, and there in tiny rippling rapids. In winter-time it is liable to sudden floods, and often entirely unfordable.

We pitched our tiny tent at an elevation of 4850 feet above the sea-level, just opposite a large *ksar*, near a few solitary trees, and sent to the village for supplies, which we found difficult to obtain. However, without my knowledge, my men made out a tale that I was a poor Shereef on my way to make a pilgrimage to the tomb of Mulai Ali Shereef at Tafilet, and accordingly we obtained what money alone had failed to do, an excellent supper of boiled turnips and almonds and walnuts—not very nourishing, it is true, but hot and satisfying to those who had tasted nothing all day, as had been our case. The poverty existing in this spot is extreme, for the small quantity of land under cultivation is only sufficient to sustain the life of the inhabitants without allowing them to sell food, and all along the road we found the greatest difficulty in purchasing provisions. The money we offered was to them a large sum, but its acceptance in return for what little they had of grain, eggs, fowls, or turnips would have eventually placed them in the position in which we found ourselves—namely, in possession of money but unable to purchase food with it. It is extraordinary upon occasions like this how one realises the worthlessness of money in places where there is nothing to be procured with it ; and our little hoard of silver, small as it was, seemed but to mock our hunger.

However, my supposed sanctity did more for us than coin could do, and we supped after all. It was not until the following day that I learned the ruse by which my men had been obliged to obtain provisions. I felt but little remorse, however, as the villagers had been paid for what they brought in small presents to the children, and would no doubt find an opportunity of rechanging the few pesetas we had given them into food in course of time.

Early on the morning of November 7 we left Agurzga, and proceeding, still almost due east, crossed a line of hills and descended some two hours later to the valley of the Ghresat. The highest point of this five or six miles of road reaches an altitude of 5800 feet, where a small watershed is crossed, from which the streams flow east to the Ghresat and west to the Agurzga. For a mile or two after striking the river the road follows its course, almost due south, and passing between some undulating hills, the large settlement of Ghresat, with its picturesque *ksor*, lies before one, and beyond it the wide plain that lies between the Atlas and the Anti-Atlas.

We had finished with the mountains, and with a sigh of relief emerged from the valley to the level country, feeling that at last the weary work of continual ascent and descent was done with, for a time at least.

# CHAPTER VI.

## GHRESAT TO DADS.

A FEW words must here be written regarding the country now about to be traversed—that is to say, from Ghresat, the spot where we emerged from the valley of the southern slopes of the Atlas Mountains, as far as Dads. Not only does my sojourn in the latter place make it a fit opportunity for my description of the road, but the physical features of the country before us also render it expedient, for it is immediately to the east of Dads that the watershed lies that separates the rivers flowing south and west to the Draa, more especially the Wad Dads itself, and those the course of which is east, and which form the basin of the western tributaries of the Wad Gheris. This river, after uniting with the Wad Ziz at Tafilet, is eventually absorbed by the desert at the marsh of Dayet ed Daura, to the south of that oasis. This long strip of country lying between the great

I

range of the Atlas Mountains and Jibel Saghru, or
the Anti-Atlas, consists of a plain some sixty miles
in length and averaging about thirty wide, rather
more at Ghresat and somewhat less at Dads.   This
plain, with an elevation of roughly 4800 feet at
Ghresat and 4700 at the southern extremity of the
tribe of Dads, near Aït Yahia, slopes slightly from
north to south and from east to west, the rivers
which leave the Atlas flowing mostly almost due
south until they meet either the Idermi or the Dads,
where these two streams have an easterly and westerly
course respectively, before uniting near Mesgita to
form the more important Wad Draa.

The soil of this plain consists for the most part
of sand strewn with small stones of almost black
colour, with here and there large boulders, sometimes
of limestone, at others of black igneous formation.
The peculiarity, however, of this strip of desert—for,
with the exception of the immediate river banks and
oases, it consists of little else—is the manner in which
the river beds are sunk below the level of the surrounding country.   Usually on approaching a river
one first perceives a flat-topped range of low hills
crossing the plain from north to south.   These hills
passed, one comes, generally from half a mile to a
mile farther on, to a steep descent, leading to the bed
of the river in question, the same formations being

found on the opposite side. At Dads and in other spots the cliffs that have to be descended before the bed of the river is reached are of considerable altitude, and the number of the population of all the districts hereabouts varies according to the breadth of the valleys between the cliffs, for on this depends the amount of land that can be put under irrigation and cultivated, and accordingly the quantity of life the soil can support by its products.

The effect is a curious one, for often when one is approaching a settlement on the river - banks, the fact that the watercourse and its cultivated surrounding land is far sunk below the level of the plain renders it invisible until one reaches the very edge of the decline. Up to that point one's eye ranges from the level plain on which one is to where it commences again beyond, its barren appearance and uniform colouring presenting the effect that both join, and it seems impossible that a large colony with gardens and irrigated lands can exist in the neighbourhood. It is easy to see that the whole formation of the country is due to the streams poured down from the greater Atlas, which, flowing south as far as the parallel range of Jibel Saghru, are there obliged to seek a common outlet by following the direction of the mountains as far as Mesgita, where the united force of the rivers has formed a passage through the range.

All the *ksor* of Ghresat are situated upon the east
bank of the river, and at some height above it, while
the west bank is occupied by a few gardens, where
fig and almond trees seem to thrive well. The stream
is clear, and even in this dry season we found a
couple of feet of water in the ford, which was perhaps
some sixty yards across. The river-bed is stony,
with larger boulders of limestone strewn here and
there, no doubt carried to this position from the
mountains above.

Several of the *ksor* are handsome buildings, one,
just above the ford, being particularly so, the decoration and turreted towers giving it a most imposing
effect. The inhabitants, like those of Agurzga, are
a subdivision of the Imerghan tribe of Berbers, who
are continually at war, not only with the surrounding tribes but also amongst themselves. Sometimes
a feud arises between neighbouring *ksor* within easy
range of one another, when a strict watch is kept
from the roof of each, and shots exchanged whenever
the opportunity presents itself. We were pointed
out two *ksor* where this unsatisfactory state of affairs
was progressing, both in a sad state of disrepair from
constant attack, and from the fact that no opportunity could be found to reconstruct the damaged
portions on account of the builders being fired upon
by their neighbouring enemy. The only parallel

case we can well imagine would be a blood - feud
between two houses exactly opposite one another
in a street. While a bullet from the tiles would
lay low the footman who answered the door on
the one side, the host returning from an evening
party would be struck in the back on the other, and
so on until possibly no male member remained in
either family.

After following the course of the river for perhaps
half a mile, the road takes a more easterly direction,
and one enters upon fifteen miles of stony desert,
which extends, without water at this period, as far
as the Wad Mdri, the easternmost of the rivers of
Askura. This strip of dreary country is known as
the " Sebaa shaabat," or " seven undulations," from
the fact that such exist. No vegetation was to be
seen but bunches of wild thyme, a few thorny bushes
—the *sidra* of the Arabs — and a little dry rank
grass, and the latter only where there were signs
of water collecting in the rainy season.

The absence of animal life was most noticeable,
and scarcely a bird was seen. From the summit of
the Atlas this had been so, and a few red-legged
Barbary partridge, a magpie or two, and a couple of
ravens, were all I had come across. Of four-legged
beasts still less, for though both gazelle and *muflon*
are to be found, we saw neither, and I can remember

having perceived no other signs of animals than a couple of jerboa.

Anything more dismal than the scene which presented itself could not be imagined. The two parallel ranges of mountains that bounded the plain on either hand were clearly visible, though here, I daresay, some thirty miles apart. The Great Atlas presented an appearance of grandeur certainly, but of little or no beauty, merely an unbroken line of immense limestone peaks, here and there capped in snow, while the Anti-Atlas, more broken and fantastic in character, loomed up to the south, a forbidding series of black and dark-red rocks. Nor did the country we were travelling through provide any relief to the eye, for what little vegetation there was to be seen was stunted and sun-dried.

A pleasure, indeed, it was to descend by a rocky path to the valley of the Wad Mdri, the easternmost of the rivers that water the large and important oasis of Askura, and enters the gardens that line the bank of the stream. Here the palm-tree, which we had not seen since leaving Morocco, again appeared, adding an additional charm to the scene, which boasted, against a background of blue sky and snow-peaks, a number of betowered and decorated *ksor* of great size, the largest and most ornamental we had as yet come across. The gardens, however, showed signs of being neglected, and the rough walls of loose stone had in many places half tumbled down. Again an ascent, and again another four miles or so of dreary stone-strewn desert; but over the latter portion of this we were cheered by the sight of the long line of palm-trees ahead, that marked the commencement of the larger portion of the Askura oasis and our night's resting-place.

We pushed on quickly, tired though we and our poor animals were, and an hour or so before sunset entered the groves of palm-trees, which commence quite suddenly, so that in a minute or two one has lost sight of the desert and is threading one's way amongst a forest of trees. For an hour we passed through the oasis before arriving at the spot where we were to camp. Often our road led us amongst gardens, above the top of the walls of which appeared palms, pomegranate, apple, pear, peach, and other fruit-trees, while clusters of roses and jasmine spoke of the love of the natives for flowers. A tree we had not as yet come across, and which I here noticed in large quantities, was the tamarix (*senegalensis*), which attains a very considerable size and has a handsome appearance. Large fields, skilfully irrigated, now and then took the place of the gardens, in which the natives rear crops of wheat, barley, and maize, the latter especially. Through these openings one could catch glimpses of the great *ksor* of the place, some of which are not only of great size, but also possess a most imposing appearance, with their decorated upper storeys and tapering towers. Everything seemed in excellent repair, which spoke not only for the agricultural character of the people, but also of their wealth—for, comparatively speaking, Askura is one of the richest, if not quite the richest, of the oases in Morocco south of the Atlas Mountains.

We forded two more rivers, the Wad bu Jhila— "father of madness," so called on account of its floods and swift current after rains in the mountains —and the large Wad Askura, from which the oasis takes its name. Both these rivers contained, at the time of our passing through, a plentiful supply of water, flowing in many channels over wide stone-strewn beds. In the centre of the easternmost— the Wad Askura—on what was at the dry period an island, a weekly market is held, which in winter is removed to another and more sheltered spot, for the island is often flooded. The object of its situation is that the spot is the only one clear from the forest, and therefore attack and fighting is less likely to occur than would be the case amongst the palm-groves ; for, ignoring their constant wars with the Berbers of the surrounding country, the tribes and even villages of Askura are continually fighting amongst themselves.

A steep bank brings one to the eastern bank of the second river, and a mile farther on, still amongst palm-trees and gardens, we pitched our tent for the night in a square *tabia* enclosure, used as a caravan-serai. But though tolerable immunity from plunder was secured by the walls around us, a number of the natives crowded into the place, and it was only owing to our continual vigilance that we did not lose articles of our baggage. I found the elevation of our camping-ground to be 4200 feet above the sea-level.

De Foucauld, whose extensive travels south of the Atlas did not bring him to Askura, merely mentions the place under the name of Haskura; but, as in the case of all names, I obtained the word written by native scholars in their own language, and I found none who placed an aspirate before the word, in all cases the spelling being identically as I write it here.

It is impossible to give any estimate, except the vaguest, as to the population of the place or the extent of the oasis; for on both points great divergence of opinion and universal exaggeration appeared to exist. Probably, roughly speaking, the total population is from 25,000 to 30,000 souls, and the extent of cultivated soil some 20 miles long—*i.e.*, north and

south—with an average of 10 wide, giving the result
of some 200 square miles, the whole of which appears
to be irrigated and under palm-cultivation. The
dates are not nearly so fine as those of Tafilet, but
are largely exported to Marakesh, as are also almonds.

Four tribes of Arabs inhabit the district; respectively—(i.) Kabyla el Ostia, (ii.) Kabyla Mzuru, (iii.)
Ulad Yakub, and (iv.) Ulad Magil. Each is governed locally by a sheikh, under the jurisdiction of
the Kaid of Glawa, Sid Madani, whose *kasba* at
Teluet we had so carefully avoided.

It is curious to find here, in a country almost entirely populated by Berbers, so large and important an
Arab tribe, and I could discover no tradition extant
as to how they came to have remained at this spot,
or whether it was conquered by them at any comparatively recent date. The most probable solution
of the question seems to be that they are the descendants of the original invaders of North Africa,
amongst whom the name of Ulad Magil, still a tribe
of Askura, is found. Certain it is that the deadly
hatred still existing between the two races is keenly
alive to-day, and were the Arabs less strong, or their
position more open to attack, there is no doubt that
they would have been ousted long ago from so fertile
and rich an oasis. However, being surrounded as
they are on all sides by desert has added much to

their security; added to the fact that every man
of means—that is to say, every man who can by

*A Village Scene.*

honest, or dishonest if necessary, labour scrape together the money — possesses a horse and a gun,
while almost without exception the Berber tribes

are mountaineers, and in this part of the country
own very few horses.   An attack upon the place is
thus almost an impossibility, the Berbers on foot
having no chance against the mounted Arabs, who,
by scouring the desert plains, can easily cut off all
retreat.

The inhabitants appear to be well-to-do, and many
were handsomely dressed in spotless *haiks* of wool.
The men are, as a rule, small of stature and wiry,
with keen hungry eyes and fine features, and form
a strange contrast in their appearance of cupidity and
rascality to the honest open countenances of the
Berbers.   The odds being so vastly unequal in open
warfare, the latter race have almost desisted from
attacking the place—though the innate hatred of the
two peoples finds ample scope in plundering one another's caravans.   Yet, rascals as are the Arabs of
Askura, one cannot help admiring the immense labour
with which they have dug the thousands of canals
that irrigate the gardens, and the excellent manner
in which these are kept in repair.   The love of gar-
dening is found all over Morocco; but the temperament of the race for sudden fits of economy, or lazi-
ness, puts a stop on all progress in this direction,
and on many occasions I have known Moors sink
wells and build irrigating canals, plant fruit-trees
and hedges, only to allow the whole to fall into a

THE VILLAGE OF DADS.

state of ruin as soon as completed; and where one
year I have seen flourishing gardens, the next the
orange-trees are dried up from want of water and
attention, and cattle are feeding on the leaves of the
young fruit-trees. But there is also another reason
for the constant ruined gardens one is continually
passing when travelling in Morocco—namely, the fact
that after the death of the owner the property is
divided, according to the *sherá* or native law, amongst
his heirs, who each singly wish to reap the entire
benefit without sharing in the expenses of keeping
the place in repair. I knew one most beautiful
garden, not twenty miles from Tangier, which was
once the pride of the neighbourhood, and which from
the above cause is to-day a barren field, with here
and there the dried trunks of what were once orange-
trees appearing from the soil. At Askura, however,
things are different, and the excellent state of the
gardens, the walls, and means of water-supply was
astonishing, and none the less creditable to the hardy
desert-people.

Our passage through the oasis, though I felt nervous lest amongst Arabs my foreign accent should
lead to my detection, was a delightful relief after the
weary days of barren mountain and still more barren
plain. Leaving the spot where we had camped before
daylight, we fell, just outside the caravanserai, into

the hands of thieves; and although the presence of
the old Shereef saved our personal property, the
caravan of Dadsmen suffered considerably, and we
left them behind trying to regain possession of their
stolen mules and merchandise.

Just as some fifteen miles of desert separate Askura
from Ghresat on the west, so some twelve miles more
intervene between the oasis and the next spot where
water is to be found—namely, Imasin. Like the
Wad Mdri, the Imasin, from which the district takes
its name, is sunk considerably below the level of the
plain, and bounded east and west by a low range
of flat-topped hills. Here again we were amongst
Berbers, the inhabitants belonging to the tribe of
Imerghan, a division of the same tribe as are found
at Agurzga and Tiurassín. This same people own a
large territory along the lower portion of the Wad
Dads, from the south-west corner of Aït Yahia almost
to Mesgita, near which the Dads, uniting with the
Idermi, becomes the Draa. Although entirely Shelha-
speaking people, the inhabitants of Imasin claim to
be Shereefs—that is, descendants of the Prophet
Mohammed, and therefore of Arab origin. One is
constantly coming across these so-called Berber
Shereefs, and a few words are necessary to explain
the incongruity. When first the descendants of the
Prophet reached Morocco, either at the same time as

the first invasion, or later with Mulai Idris, the
founder of the original dynasty of Sultans, they
spread themselves over the country, settling down
amongst the Berbers, who, with the exception of the
Arab invaders and their children, were the sole
inhabitants. These Shereefs, or " nobles," as the
word implies, soon became much respected, the more
so as Islam spread, though no doubt their superior
education and surroundings of civilisation had much
to do with it. However it may have been, they in
time became the arbitrators in cases of dispute, the
propounders of the new faith, and as such, with but
little difficulty and objection, married into the Berber
families. The result of this is apparent. Separated
from Arab people and brought up solely amongst
Berbers, their children and descendants forgot the
language of the forefather's country, and spoke solely
that of the people amongst whom they lived. Every
circumstance led to their living the lives of Berbers,
while still professing the religion of Islam. Their
wives were taken from the tribes-people of their
mothers, and to all practical purposes they lapsed
back into Shloh tribesmen. Still the blood of the
Arab ancestor had instilled into their veins the strain
of the Prophet, and the male descendants, according
to the rights of Islamic law, which recognises only
paternity in this respect, still continued—as they had

*A Berber Family at Dads: Woman mealing Corn.*

every possible authority to do—to call themselves
Shereefs ; and many of these " noble " Berber families,
to whom Arabic is an unknown tongue, possess probably no more than the original Arab blood of their
first Shereefian ancestor.   In the same way many of
the Berber tribes south of the Atlas are tainted with
Arab blood, and the most powerful of all, the Aït
Atta, are proud of claiming descent from the tribe of
the Koreish, which gave to the world the Prophet
Mohammed.

The principal and best known Berber Shereefian
families are without doubt the descendants of Sid
Ben Nasr of Tamgrut, on the Wad Draa, and those
of Mulai Brahim, and Mulai Abdullah Ben Hoseyn of
Tamslot, to the north of the Atlas, and some ten to
fifteen miles south of Marakesh.   In each, too, are
visible the traces of the effect their surroundings has
had upon them ; for both in appearance and dialect
the Shereefs of Tamgrut resemble the Haratin population of the Draa, amongst whom they reside, while
those of Tamslot bear a greater resemblance to the
northern Atlas Berbers.   The *zauias*, or sanctuaries,
of both attract a large number of pilgrims, that of
Tamslot being of course far more accessible, and
therefore much richer.   Mulai Brahim, who lies
buried on the northern slopes of the Atlas, above
Agorgoreh, shares with Sid bel Abbas, the local

K

saint of Marakesh, the title of patron saint of southern Morocco; and the present representative and head of the family, Mulai el Haj ben Said, is one of the best known and richest men in that part of the country. His palace at Tamslot is a large place, and though sadly wanting in repair, is still a building of considerable magnificence, while his stable of horses is certainly the finest in the south.

Probably of far purer origin than the Berbers of the trans-Atlas portion of Morocco are those of Aït Yussi, Ghiata, and Beni Mgild, on the northern extremity of the same range, to the south and east of Fez. They seem to have lost none of their pristine fierceness, and to have adopted none of the manners and customs of their conquerors beyond their religion; for the brown tent in which they moved from place to place long before the Arab invasion is still found amongst them, and their traditions, pre-Arab, are still handed down from mouth to mouth. Inhabiting the immense forests of that district, they live a wild gipsy life, at war with all men, and paying no more than the most nominal obedience to the commands and laws of the Sultan. In the south, however, it is different; and when, after having reached Tafilet, I found myself in the Sultan's camp, surrounded by Berber and Arab tribesmen, not only I, but natives of the country, often found it impossible to distinguish between them, so greatly did they resemble one another in feature and dress. In the other case, that of the northern Berbers, the type is quite distinct, the high cheek-bones and narrow eyes and reddish colouring distinguishing the Shleh from the Arab at once, and showing clearly his Hamitic origin.

Imasin is a poor little place enough. The few scattered *ksor* are all more or less in a state of ruin, and the gardens seemed uncared for and empty. Fording the river, we did not stop, but pushed on for another ten or twelve miles of desert, until a steep descent led us to the bed of the Wad Dads, at the point where the tribe of Aït Yahia is settled, and where the Imguna empties its stream into the larger river.

The tribe of Aït Yahia are a division of the Berbers of Seddrat, who, like all the other tribes, are much split up. The junction of the Wad Imguna and Wad Dads forms a triangular plain about two and a-half miles across, shut in on all sides, except on the actual course of the rivers, by high cliffs, on the summit of which stand numerous *äudin* or watch-towers. While the Wad Dads forms the base of the triangle, the Imguna bisects the plain, on which are to be found some four-and-twenty *ksor*, forming the district of Aït Yahia. The spot where the waters of the Imguna flow into the Dads is known as Tagnit bu Hammu. A few words must be said about the Wad Imguna. Rising on the southern slopes of the Atlas, near the snow-capped peak of Jibel Trekeddit, its upper valleys are inhabited by a small tribe called Aït Sakri. A few miles lower down the stream leaves the mountains, its banks at this spot being peopled by the Aït Ahmed, who in turn give place, as the river descends, to the tribe of Imguna, through whose territory for some twenty miles it flows, and from which it takes its name, or *vice versa*.

Choosing the village of Idu Tizi for our halting-spot, for the old Shereef had friends there, we pitched our little tent in a walled enclosure adjoining the *ksar* in which our hosts lived, for they had come out to meet us, and soon made us welcome. Poor though they were, they brought us an excellent supper of *kuskusu* and boiled turnips, the first hot food we had tasted for some days — and very welcome it was. In return we were able to entertain our host and his companions with sugar and tea, both luxuries far beyond the reach of ordinary man in this far-away part of Morocco—the carriage alone, with its physical difficulties of road, not to mention the constant plundering of caravans, rendering the price demanded for such luxuries exorbitant, even to our extravagant European ideas. The people knew but little Arabic, so I ran no fear of detection, and poured out the sweet green tea in true native fashion with great success.   Askura passed—the only Arab settlement between the Atlas and Tafilet—I began to feel far more certain of the success of my journey, and thought nothing or little of my disguise.   So accustomed was I becoming to my *rôle* that I found it no exertion to keep the part up, and became most orthodox and regular in saying my prayers, &c., with the rest of our little band.   It is only fair to state that I had lived for considerable periods of time in the interior of Morocco previously, and the various customs and habits of the people had gradually become part and parcel of my life, so that I performed the necessary duties without any anxiety or mental exertion.

The gardens of Aït Yahia have a poor appearance, and the irrigating canals in many places were dry, a sure sign, as was the case, that the people were constantly at war with outside enemies and amongst themselves.   The soil, too, is not suited for cultivation, for it consists entirely of patches of a poor yellow clay interspersed with rocks.   Fig - trees seemed to thrive best, and even these were small and wretched, while the date-palm was absent altogether.

Although up to now the direction of our road had been almost due east, we had gradually been leaving behind the main chain of the Atlas and approaching

Jibel Saghru,—the Anti-Atlas,—both of which ranges,
parallel to one another, take a slightly northerly
direction as they proceed east; and here at Aït
Yahia we found ourselves with only the river and
a few miles of sloping plain between ourselves and
the southern range. It is at Aït Yahia, in fact, that
the Wad Dads, having flowed south from the Atlas
across the plain, meeting the lower northern slopes of
Jibel Saghru, alters its course to a westerly one.

Anything more unlike the Atlas than this parallel
range could scarcely be imagined, for in place of the
long line of limestone cliffs there presents itself a
chain of peaks of no very great altitude and of
every colour and shape, the whole torn and twisted
by volcanic action, and of an alternately deep red,
purple, and black hue. Probably none of the peaks
of the range that I saw are above 2000 to 3000 feet
above the level of the plain, which would give an
altitude of from 6000 to 7000 feet above the sea-
level, for I found that we at Aït Yahia were at an
elevation of 4700 feet. In one respect only was any
resemblance noticeable between the two ranges—
namely, the utter absence of vegetation on each;
and anything more dismal than the intervening strip
of desert, shut in by grey limestone and snow-capped
mountains on the north, and dreary black hills on
the south, it would be difficult to imagine.

We crossed the Wad Imguna before daylight on the morning of November 9, and ascending the cliff to the level of the plain which we had left the evening before, turned slightly to the north, and for two or three hours travelled over the dreary barren plain. It was most curious to note the suddenness with which one comes into sight of, and loses again, the settlements in the wide valleys of this part of the country; for no sooner had we reached the summit of the cliff than Aït Yahia was entirely lost to view, the plain seeming to be one with the gradual slope of Jibel Saghru, on the farther side of the river. Ten minutes later not a habitation was to be seen, the *äudin*, or watch-towers, along the line of the valley being the only signs of any inhabitants in the dreary surroundings. Except for these we might have been in the centre of the Sahara, and even the half-ruined towers seemed the work of a long-departed people.

The news of the coming of the old Shereef and members of his family had travelled before us, and one forgot all the weariness of the landscape in the pleasant reception that awaited us. An hour or two before we arrived at Dads we caught sight of little bands of people, black specks in the bright sunlight, and as they recognised their relations they ran toward us. The old man dismounted from his mule

and proceeded on foot, the better to embrace the
ever-increasing flow of welcomers. It formed one
of those charming pictures which one now and again
comes across in travelling in Morocco,—the old man,
the centre of a little crowd of men, women, and children, all laughing and singing, being escorted after
years of absence back to the home of his ancestors.
I came in for my share of the welcome—for was not I
one of his party ?—and I shook hands with, and was
kissed by, a score of men and women and children,
before, just as suddenly as we had lost sight of Aït
Yahia, the wide valley of Dads burst into view.
Here at the summit of the cliffs more friends awaited
us, and as we descended, all happy that a stage at
least of our journey was over, our band formed quite
a caravan, the children laughing and tumbling over
one another in their glee, the men alternately singing
and crying out words of welcome, and the women,
with their hands to their mouths, uttering the shrill
cry of the *zakerit*.

So our little procession turned and twisted down
the steep path, every moment being met by more
people, one and all eager to welcome us, until, surrounded by a rejoicing crowd, we entered the narrow
streets of the village of Zauia Aït bu Haddu, and
reached the dwelling of the old Shereef.

.

# CHAPTER VII.

## DADS. .

IT seems so long since I have found an opportunity of writing of my personal experiences, and those of the good men who accompanied me upon my journey, that it is quite a pleasure to abandon for a time things geographical, and to enter for a chapter into the less important but interesting details of my stay at Dads, where a sojourn of five days in the Shereef's house, with innumerable kind but indigestible feasts elsewhere, allowed me to see much more of the Berber home-life than would otherwise have been the case.

The first new experience was to look upon the interior of one of these strange castles that the natives build themselves, the outsides of which had so impressed me by their size and the manner in which they are built. No sooner had we arrived at the Zauia Aït bu Haddu than the opportunity I had all along been wishing to find occurred, and on alighting from my donkey at the door of the Shereef's house, he bade me welcome with all the grace and rhetoric that the Arabs know so well how to use.

A stable-yard, a large enclosed space, divided the house from the street of the village, and, passing through this, a walnut-wood door, of roughly-sawn planks, gave entrance to the house. Within all was darkness, and it was only by striking a match that I could perceive we had entered a wide and dusty passage which seemed to lead nowhere. Groping along a gradual ascent, which took the place of stairs, we reached the first floor, on which most of the living apartments were situated, the remainder of the ground-floor serving as stabling, and opening by another entrance into the yard we had already passed through. Still ascending, we entered at length a large unfurnished room some 30 feet square, the whole black with smoke. Here we found a number of women, mostly accompanied by babies in arms, attending to the household affairs. Some were cooking the meal that was being prepared for our reception over fires of inferior and smoke-giving charcoal, while others were weaving on hand-looms a heavy woollen material, to serve eventually for the *haidus* or cloaks of the Berbers. The walls of the room were of rough *tabia* and the floor of plastered mud, while the ceiling consisted of trunks of walnut-trees supported on pillars of *tabia*, and covered with brushwood and clay above, the latter forming the floor of the next storey. A few huge copper cooking-pots and a rough unstained box or two formed all the furniture visible, together with a heap of dishes of considerable size, each a segment of the trunk of large walnut-trees skilfully hollowed out. Some of these were already filled with the steaming *kuskusu* and boiled turnips that were to form the staple *pièce de résistance* of the coming feast. Again an ascent of clay, supported on walnut beams fastened into the wall, led us to a second chamber of much the same dimensions as the first, only in place of the narrow loopholes which allowed a dim light to enter in the lower storey there were here round holes in the roof, serving at once for windows and chimneys, and decidedly un-successful at either, for the heavy smoke of fig-wood charcoal hung like a cloud in the air, obstructing what little light might otherwise have entered. In other respects the rooms were in every way identi-cally the same, the walls black with smoke, and covered with cobwebs near the ceiling, but with these exceptions tolerably clean. Again we ascended, this time emerging on to the flat roof, in the centre of which stood a highly decorated room built of mud bricks, with a door of the usual walnut-wood and two or three small windows with shutters. We were a great height up, probably some 50 to 55 feet from the ground ; but towers rose still higher, though their only purpose seemed to be the defence of the *ksar*, for they contained no rooms, but only galleries with narrow loopholes in the walls. The door of the room was thrown open, and we entered the clean and comfortable *minzah* and threw ourselves down on the rough rugs and carpets, delighting in being able to rest at last, and in a cool atmosphere, after the heat of our journey—and with every promise, too, of escaping the rigorous cold at night.

The old Shereef remained below in a small room, which in his younger days, when he resided at Dads, he had built himself, with plaster walls and some rough Moorish painting on the ceiling, and a horse-shoe window opening on to the street, some 20 feet above the roadway. Here, no doubt, he interviewed the members of his family that he had abandoned for so long, and doubtless, too, listened to the reproaches of the wives he had deserted for nine years or so. However, all the male relations and a number of friends of the house trooped up to our quarters, and as most of them knew Arabic well, the conversation flowed cheerily enough over the excellent hot dishes of food that they brought us. Then came Moorish tea, with quantities of sugar and mint, I presiding at the tray, in the seat of honour, for I was the stranger of the party, and therefore the most honoured. A splendid handsome group of men they formed, these hosts of ours and their friends, and clean withal, which added very considerably to the pleasure of their company.

What questions they asked !—not the rude personal questions the Arab pesters one with, but as to what was going on in Morocco, and how our little party had fared on the way; and even more general than their interrogations were their protestations of welcome. Very welcome they made us too, bringing from their various houses great dishes of food—plain stuff enough, but none the less acceptable — and keeping the day as a sort of holiday.

It may seem to the reader that almost every page of this book contains references as to what we obtained to eat; but on a journey in which one tasted meat only twice in a month, and when often we walked forty miles with nothing more than dates or inferior dried figs to dine and sup and breakfast on, it is wonderful how important a *souvenir de voyage* is the remembrance of the rare occasions on which we satisfied our hunger, or, as on our arrival at Dads, we did more, and actually had enough to eat and to spare.

I quickly made friends with the natives of the
place, and before our guests departed, so as to give
us an opportunity to sleep after our weary journey,

*Inside the Village of Aït bu Haddu, at Dads.*

we had arranged to meet again later in the afternoon, and walk about in the gardens which line
the river-banks.

Meanwhile, I think some description ought to be

given as to the appearance of the men I found myself among and their womenkind.

Certainly of all the tribes and peoples that I have come across in Morocco, those of Dads far exceed the rest in good looks and handsome build. As a rule, all the men are well above average height, gracefully and strongly formed, withal possessing an appearance of athletes. In colour they are fair, the eyes sometimes blue, but generally dark, while the eyelashes and eyebrows are black. The nose, contrary to the general Berber type, is aquiline, and the mouth finely cut and well shaped. Although they follow the rule of shaving the head, they do not, like the Arabs, allow the beard and moustache to grow, but entirely shave off the latter, and leave only a small pointed beard on the extremity of the chin, which extends to the ears in a fine line of closely cut hair on either side. Their hands and feet are small and well shaped, the former showing no signs of manual labour, all of which is performed by the women, the men being the warriors, as it were, and, unless employed as caravan-drivers, spending their time in idleness or bloodshed.

It is impossible in such a description as this to really reproduce the type of the Berber of Dads, for his charm, and undoubtedly he possesses much, is owing more perhaps to his manner and innate politeness

than to his outward form, though even in the latter
respect he is superb.   Fierce as they are in war, the
people of Dads are when at peace the gentlest of
creatures, extremely devoted to their children, and
living a home-life absolutely unknown amongst the
Arabs.   Just as in appearance, so in moral character,
do they excel, and the vices so common amongst the
Moors are unknown in the homes of the Berbers.
They seem to possess none of that uncontrollable
passion that is so large a feature in the Arab character, and its place is taken by affection and sincerity.
Seldom marrying more than one wife, prostitution is
absolutely unknown, with the result that the health
of the tribe is excellent, and one never sees those
horrid disfigurements of feature so common in other
portions of Morocco.   No doubt to a great extent the
moral character of the Berbers is due to the fact that
their women are allowed entire liberty, do not veil
their faces, and mix on almost all occasions with the
men.   One of the first things that struck me on my
arrival at Dads was the good-humoured and innocent
chaff that passed between the men and the girls of
the tribe, even in the streets of the *ksar*, and still
more when they brought us our food to the *minzah*
on the house-top.   The women are distinctly pretty,
with very fair skins and clear complexions; but they
detract much from their appearance by the strange

manner in which they adorn their features with *henna*
and *kohl*, the former a red dye, the latter antimony.
Usually five red streaks pass from the top of the
forehead to the eyebrows, while each cheek contains
a triangular patch of the same hue. The eyebrows
and lashes are darkened with the *kohl*, a black patch
is put upon the tip of the nose, another at each point
of the mouth, and still another on the chin. The
neck is often slightly tattooed in a narrow design
running from under the chin as far as the breasts.

The costume of the women of Dads consists almost
entirely of *khent*—indigo-blue cotton—the dress being
formed of two pieces, which fasten over the shoulder
and hang as if " cut square," back and front. Under
the arms the two strips of *khent* are sown together as
far as below the knees. A girdle—usually a cord of
red wool wound several times round the body, and
the ends hanging down in long tassels—takes the
place of the wide *hazam* of the Arab women, and is
infinitely more graceful. Often a second strip of
*khent* is worn as a shawl, being brought over one
shoulder and fastened below the other arm. Necklaces of silver beads and pendants with coral and
amber form the chief ornament; and often the head-
dress of *khent* is decorated in silver, while bangles
and a few anklets are worn. The women usually go
barefoot, a few of the richest only seeming to wear

shoes; while with the men the sandal—generally of raw hide—is almost universal.

The men's dress is picturesque. Over the long wide-sleeved shirt, or *chamira*, is worn a *haidus* of thick black woollen material, or else the same hooded garment in white wool, often varied with narrow stripes of cotton interwoven. On the head a small white turban, leaving the crown bare, is the customary covering; but many affect, too, the *kheit*, or soft wool string, and still more go bareheaded. As is usual with all Berbers, no belt or sash is worn, the long *chamira* hanging ungirdled from the neck to the ankles.

All sorts and varieties of hairdressing are to be found amongst the children. Some have the crown bare, and the hair on the sides of the head long, just for all the world like the babies of Japan, while others possess a regular patchwork design of hair and bald spots all over the head. They seem a happy good-natured lot these children of Dads, and spend nearly the entire day at play, seldom fighting or quarrelling. The principal occupation of the boys seems to be slinging, at which they are remarkably adept. The sling is formed of a small net of close-woven string, with two long cords attached, and even quite small urchins can send a stone to a great distance. Another amusement, absolutely unknown to the Arabs

so far as I am aware, is the modelling of little figures
out of clay. Some that I saw were excellent, principally men on horseback, and most creditable per-
formances for children who have nothing but their
fingers to work with. The horsemen were generally
stood up a few yards off and pelted with stones until
broken, the excited urchins meanwhile shouting, "The
Arabs! the Arabs!"—the common war-cry of their
tribe when fighting with the latter race.

In spite of the great size of the *ksor* of Dads,
with their castellated towers and fortified walls, the
place is an extremely poor one, and little or no
money circulates, except amongst the men employed
in caravan-work. Even in this case it is very few
indeed who possess more than a couple of mules, such
being considered a large capital, and the long and
wearisome journey to Morocco City and back usually
brings only some five dollars or so of profit per mule;
that is to say, an absence of a fortnight, with some
250 miles of desert and mountain, the latter often
snow-clad, may, if robbers be escaped and favourable luck be met with, bring in some sixteen shillings
of English money. But, as a rule, the population
of Dads subsist upon the dried figs and other scanty
produce of their gardens, which are poor enough little
fields, well irrigated certainly, but with inferior soil
and scanty products. The figs are plucked ripe and

laid out on to the flat house-tops to dry in the sun, and eventually stored for the winter. So hard do they become that we were obliged to crush them between stones before we were able to make any impression upon them with our teeth. Very few cattle are to be found, such as there are being entirely stall-fed, *fsa*—a kind of lucerne—being grown for the purpose. There being absolutely no grazing land, the cows seldom leave the yards of the house. They are invariably fed out of mangers, built of *tabia*, and raised about 12 to 18 inches from the ground. The women attend to the cattle as to everything else, it being their duty to fetch and carry water and firewood, in fact to do almost all the work with the exception of tilling the soil, and in a few cases I saw them even so occupied. As a rule, the cultivation is done by paid workmen, who take piecework, the digging of an acre of soil preparatory to its being sown with turnips bringing the labourer about two shillings English money. These labourers are not of the Dads tribe, for they think it below their station to dig, but usually come from the banks of the Wad Draa, and are known, both amongst themselves and all over Morocco, as " Haratin "—that is to say, " freemen," and not slaves. In type they form much in common with the negro, and seem too not unlike him in good humour and docility.

Their language is a variety of Shelha, called "Drauia," but is only partially comprehensible to the tribes

*A Woman of Dads.*

speaking the pure dialect. Numbers of these "Haratin" are to be found all over Morocco, where they usually pursue the calling of water-carriers, and thus

become members of the fraternity of Mulai Yakub, to
whose tomb, at the hot springs near Fez, they have
to make a pilgrimage before taking to the *guerba*
or "water-skin," from which they peddle the liquid
to the crowd.    They are usually an honest and trustworthy people and excellent labourers, talking and
laughing while they dig or ply whatever trade they
have taken to, but they seem incapable of skilled
labour of any sort.

Having now briefly sketched the character and
manner of life of the people of Dads, a few words
must be written as to the country their tribe
inhabits.

The division of the Berbers which takes its name
from the river Dads possesses the entire banks of
that river from the spot where it leaves the valley
of the main chain of the Atlas to where it changes its
course from north and south to east and west, a few
miles from the northern slopes of Jibel Saghru, the
Anti-Atlas, where the tribe of Aït Yahia, a division
of the larger Seddrat, commences.    The distance
thus in the hands of the Dads tribe is a narrow
strip of land on both banks of the river, some
twenty-five miles in length.    The fact that their
district extends from the Atlas range to the Anti-
Atlas gives them a power altogether beyond their
numerical strength amongst the Berbers of trans-

Atlas Morocco, for by their position they hold entire command over the caravan-roads from Marakesh to Tafilet and the intermediate places.    Whichever road be chosen—whether it be by the valleys of the Warzazat and Idermi, by the Glawi Pass, or by Demnat and Aït bu Gemmés—the traveller is obliged to pass through Dads, and in order that caravans may do so with immunity, it is necessary that alliances be made with the tribe by the surrounding people.    This, too, empowers the inhabitants of Dads to trade with far more security than those of the other districts, for the fact that they allow caravans to pass through without plundering them gives them the same right elsewhere ; and should another tribe rob or attack a Dads caravan, woe betide the next band of men of the tribe in question that passed through Dads.    Thus it was that I heard on my return from Tafilet that a small caravan from Askura, coming from the east, met with a reception that amply repaid the loss of the property of the mule-drivers who had accompanied us through Askura, and whose plundering we had witnessed.    Again, the strength of Dads is owing, no doubt, not a little to the fact that the tribe is undivided, and collected at one spot, whereas, I believe without exception, all the other Berber tribes are scattered over various parts of the country, none inhabiting one district, as is the case with Dads. Although continual blood-feuds are springing up amongst the inhabitants of the various *ksor*, the tribe unites in the case of attack from without, all intervillage quarrels being left until the enemy is driven off. But so firm a position have the people managed to obtain for themselves, and so renowned are they for their pluck and bravery, that nowadays attack from other tribes is uncommon. However, a few years since the powerful Aït Atta marched in force against the inhabitants of Dads, accompanied by a large number of horsemen; but the superiority in numbers, and the fact that the Dads people possessed no horses, did not suffice to give them victory, and they were, after a long struggle, eventually driven back to the east across the plain of Anbed. A few Aït Atta *ksor* which had formerly stood at Dads, inhabited by friendly tribesmen, were thereupon destroyed, and the Attauis driven out or put to the sword.

In all those wars and blood-feuds no quarter is given, any one old enough to carry a gun or dagger, the two weapons of the country, being considered fair game. Prisoners taken alive are stabbed to death with the curved dagger of the place, powder and shot being too valuable. Contrary to this barbarous custom, the women and children are spared, the former being permitted to go free, and a strict code

of honour prevents their being violated. Immediately
a *ksor* is besieged the women and children are allowed
to pass out untouched, and are even helped on their
way to safe quarters by the enemy. In many cases of
this sort strange incongruities are found amongst the
Berber people. In the case of the Arabs, prisoners
of war might be spared, but the women would be a
prize too tempting to be allowed to escape, and would
one and all be outraged, and the children as likely
as not sold.

The river flows through the centre of the valley,
flat gardens extending from its banks to where the
parallel cliffs rise to the level of the plain east and
west. The *ksor* for the most part lie immediately
below these cliffs, though in the upper portion,
particularly in Aït Iunir, they are found scattered
amongst the gardens, rising most picturesquely above
the tree-tops. These gardens are usually walled, and
contain little but figs, and these of a poor quality,
though they give large crops. The upper portion of
the valley seems to be far more fertile than near Aït
bu Haddu, for instance, for the fruit-trees reach a far
larger size, and the vegetation is richer altogether.
Apples, pears, plums, and apricots abound here,
though below few are found, and pomegranates are
not uncommon. The date-palm is absent altogether.

As at Askura, one is struck by the labour that has

been expended in ensuring a continual supply of
water for the gardens. This is done by means of
innumerable small canals. On account of the level
of the gardens being somewhat higher than that of
the river-bed, the water has in almost all cases to
be drawn off from the main stream far above the
ʼksor and gardens it is to supply, and this fact is a
constant cause of warfare; for when a village is
separated from the river by a couple of miles perhaps
of canal, on which it entirely depends for its supply,
the enemy soon take advantage of the fact and cut
off their water, which raises the siege at once, and a
sortie has to be made by the defenders. Nor is it
only during war, for, more often still, the original
commencement of the strife is the fact that some one
has drawn off the contents of some one else's canal,
and a feud commences. The water, however, serves
a purpose in warfare other than raising sieges by
being cut off, for the very opposite policy is often
resorted to, and water brought to play upon the soft
tabia walls of the ksar, a channel being dug right up
to the building. Strong as it is to withstand the
effects of climate, tabia is like blotting-paper before
water, and almost as soon as the walls are reached
the building commences to crumble away from the
foundations, imperiling the lives of all within, and
necessitating a sudden flight, and probably the falling

into the hands of the enemy waiting without. In
order to prevent their enemies from approaching the
*ksor* and cutting off or turning on the water, both
equally disastrous, watch-towers are built along the
banks of the canals. The *äudin*, as the natives call
them, are usually square towers some 30 to 40 feet in
height, and full of loopholes. In case of war they
are garrisoned with a handful of men who are supplied
with sufficient quantities of water and provisions to
stand a siege, and from them a guard can be kept
over the canal and its banks, while their position—
the summit, as a rule, of mounds—prevents the water
being turned on to their foundations. The whole of the
Dads valley is sprinkled with these towers, which add
a by no means unpicturesque feature to their scenery.

Looking down from the tops of the cliffs upon the
valley of Dads, the district presents an appearance
the like of which I have seen nowhere else in the
world. It is not that it is beautiful scenery, or that
its fertility calls for admiration ; rather it is the fact
that in its curious position and architecture it is
unique. The valley, with the river flowing through
its midst, is entirely shut in on both sides by high
cliffs of yellow soil. From amongst the gardens crop
up everywhere the *ksor* with their battlements and
towers, each one of which would be considered a large
building in Europe. As a frame to this strange scene

there is the barren desert, bounded on the north by the rocky snow-clad peaks of the great chain of the Atlas, and on the south by the irregular line of Jibel Saghru.

The district of Dads is divided into six portions, each of which contains many *ksor*. These subdivisions of the tribe are respectively, commencing from the south—

    (i.) Arbaa miya, "the four hundred";
    (ii.) Iutagin;
    (iii.) Aït u Allel;
    (iv.) Aït Hammu;
    (v.) Aït Iunir;
    (vi.) Aït Tamuted.

Of these the first-named, Arbaa miya, is decidedly the largest, strongest, and altogether most powerful. It contains some forty *ksor*. It is at the north end of Aït Tamuted that the Wad Dads leaves the valleys of the Atlas to enter the plain.

I spent five days at Dads, and very pleasant ones they were, while the rest after the weary tramp refreshed men and beasts wonderfully. During the heat of the day we would wander down to the banks of the river, and saunter through the gardens, or sit and talk under the shade of the fig-trees. So accustomed had I become to playing the part of a native that my life with the Berbers caused me no anxiety lest my identity should be discovered, and I even became lax in my attentions at prayers, attending merely the noon and sunset "services." The mosque of Zauia Aït bu Haddu was a small enough place, with a roof supported on heavy beams of rough walnut-wood, and a minaret in bad repair. Water for the purpose of ablutions had to be brought from the nearest canal, for the *zauia* stands above the level of the gardens, almost immediately below the cliffs. Being a sanctuary of Shereefs, it was not built on the same plan of defence as the generality of the *ksor*, though its entrances were mostly guarded with gates. No doubt the fact that most of its inhabitants are descendants of the Prophet renders it less liable to attack, and less likely to be embroiled in the inter-tribal feuds which are of everyday occurrence.

Close to the village was a "Mellah," or "Ghetto," of Jews, living by themselves in a separate quarter, which also was undefended, from the fact that they do not in any way participate in the wars. The Jews exist at Dads, as elsewhere among the Berbers, under the system of *debeha*, or sacrifice, so called from the fact that a sheep or ox is supposed originally to have been offered to the Berbers in order to obtain protection. The families of Jews here too live in a feudal state, each being dependent upon some Shleh family for immunity from ill-treatment and robbery : in return for this they pay a small yearly tribute to

their protectors. As a rule they are the skilled workmen of the place, being particularly renowned at
Dads for their guns, which are often gorgeously
decorated in silver. The
shops, too, are almost entirely in the *mellahs*, though
little can be purchased except indigo - blue cotton—
*khent*—candles, and sometimes tea and sugar. Money
is so scarce, however, that
the trade is very small,
though large quantities of
merchandise pass through

*Young Jew of Dads.*

Dads *en route* to Tafilet, and dates on their way
to Marakesh.

The cliffs that bound the river east and west are in
many places fretted with caves, but all tradition as to
their former use is lost. I was told that some copper
implements of agriculture were found in one or two
only a short time before my visit, but the manner in
which I was travelling prevented my making many
inquiries upon the subject. However, I was enabled
to enter many of these caves, and they appear to have
been used as dwellings by their inhabitants, a sup-
position much strengthened by the fact that farther
up the Wad Dads there are several settlements of

cave-dwellers existing to-day, known as Aït Iferi, "the sons of the caves." I did not enter these inhabited caves, though I passed them, but from all outward appearance they seemed to resemble those near the Zauia Aït bu Haddu, several of which I explored. These varied somewhat in size and shape, but three chambers seemed to be the average number. These rooms were all small, the largest I measured being some 13 feet by 7 feet, while the smaller averaged some 7 feet by 6. The walls are very rough, pieces of rock often projecting a foot or so, and in all respects they did not show nearly so much skill in their excavation as those I had previously seen at Imin Tanut, some two days' journey southwest of Marakesh, near the residence of the Kaid of Mtuga. Nor are the caves of Dads situated in the face of the precipices as are these others; for whereas at Imin Tanut it is impossible to enter any but a very few, those at Dads are easily accessible, being one and all placed at the bottom of the cliff. One larger than the rest lies at the back of the *mellah* of Jews near the *zauia*, and is used by them for a place in which to wash their dead, and here their corpses lie for a night before burial.

With the exception of these caves I found but little signs of antiquities, the ruins I had been told of before leaving Marakesh turning out to be merely the remains of "*tabia*" *ksor*, the age of which it was impossible to determine. Once allowed to fall out of repair, it takes a very short time for these buildings, constructed with such a soft material, to crumble away, though when properly attended to, and the rain kept off, they seem to last for a great time. One curious ruin exists near Dads, which I was enabled to visit, but I refrain from giving any attempt at a minute description here, as I was unable to take satisfactory measurements. Suffice it to say that it stands on a circular hill of bare rock, and is built of large blocks of stone, without mortar. I attach considerable importance to this ruin, and hope to be able to return on some future occasion and more minutely explore it. The hill is known as Jibel Korah, and is well known to every native of Dads. The ruin has a bad reputation, and is said to be inhabited by devils. A similar building exists near Todghrá, on a rocky slope to the south-west of that oasis.

As the roads ahead of us were reported to be infested with robbers, especially deserters from the Sultan's army which was now at Tafilet, we thought it best to leave behind at the *zauia* my two mules, and proceeded on our way with only a couple of donkeys, one belonging to the Shereef's nephew, the other mine. Our party, too, diminished in numbers.

The old Shereef had reached his destination, and was to go no farther; his son was a useless creature, and I decided not to take him; while our pilgrim, the devotee of the sect of the Derkauiya, turned aside to seek his home. A good fellow 'he had been, and heartily sorry I was to lose his company, though he seldom said much or intruded his presence upon us. Yet he was by far and away the most interesting of our little band, and exhibited the strange case of the fanatical devotee, all whose ideas had been overthrown by his pilgrimage to Mecca. His loathing for Christians had received a blow in the kindness of the captain of the steamer he had travelled on, and, in spite of his religious detestation of the "Nazarene," he confessed to a secret partiality for their character. Before leaving the Sahara, in fact, he had formed his judgment of the whole world on his surroundings and the traditions of his people; but now his eyes were opened, and he was sorely bewildered. Had I dared, I would like to have made a more careful study of this man's mind and opinions, but it must be remembered that I was passing as a Moslem, and therefore had to be guarded in my conversation.

Our party from Dads to Tafilet consisted of five —the Shereef's nephew, to whom no words of praise could do justice; my Riffi servant, Mohammed; the

M

miserable cur of a negro whose conduct caused us
so much anxiety, but who paid for it on our return
to Marakesh; a Dads tribesman, who went as our
*zitat*, or guarantee against robbery and murder; and
myself, still in my torn *chamira* and *jelab*, bare-
footed, browned by the cold and sun, and as hard as
nails : and a merry little band we were, as—our two
donkeys packed with our scanty baggage, only a
few pounds in weight—we shook hands with all the
friends who had been so kind to us at Dads, and,
receiving their blessing, set out. The last to leave
us was Hammu, my friendly caravan - man, and he
accompanied us some way up the valley, until, reaching a district with which his *ksar* had a blood-feud,
he bade us "adieu" and turned back. For a quarter
of an hour or so we could hear his voice rising and
falling in the strange cadence of the Berber songs
until it died away in silence.

# CHAPTER VIII.

## DADS TO UL TURUG.

ALTHOUGH we left the Zauia Aït bu Haddu on November 12, we spent that night in the province of Dads, our road having merely taken us some twelve miles up the river's course, as far as a *ksar* in the district of Aït Iunir, which I had promised to visit *en route*, as it was from near this point that the main road to Tafilet leaves the valley to cross the plain of Anbed. The path, for it is no more, winds about amongst the gardens and *ksor*, every few minutes crossing one of the small canals that irrigate the fields, &c. These, where not too deep, are forded, but in many places are crossed with little bridges— merely the trunks of trees laid across from bank to bank, and covered with stones and soil. Only two places of any note are passed on the way, the tomb and sacred groves of Sid bu Yahia, and close to it the *sôk*, or market, of the Khamis, or Thursday. The tomb

of the saint is built of *tabia*, and consists of two
rooms, in one of which the remains of Sid bu Yahia
lie, while the other serves as a mosque. A pointed
dome of green tiles covers the former. Near by is
the grove of trees, so common an adjunct to sanctuaries in Morocco. They are silver poplars, and of
great size. The market-place is only an open space,
and the day not being Thursday, it was deserted.
There is a second large *sôk* at Dads—the Arbaa, or
Wednesday—a little to the south of Zauia Aït bu
Haddu : we had passed through it when nearing Dads
on the day of our arrival.

Close to the Sôk el Khamis are the remains of
seven villages of Aït Atta, which were destroyed
when that tribe made an unsuccessful attempt to
wrest the valuable strategical position along the river
from its present holders. Up to that date the Attauis
had possessed these seven villages ; here they were
allowed to live in peace, but on the breaking out of
open hostilities their *ksor* were razed.

Sometimes our road led us close to the river's
banks, at others almost under the cliffs that rise to
the level of the plain. The water in the river is clear,
and of a brilliant blue colour. Fish abound ; but although the natives speak of three varieties, I was
able to see only one — the barbel. Nor do they
keep to the main stream ; for the canals, even where

only a few feet wide, often contain large shoals of them.

At a large *ksar*, with frowning towers and battlements, the very picture of the dwelling of a Berber chief, we stopped for the night. Our host met us at the gate and welcomed us, taking our donkeys to a stable, where barley was given them to eat, and then leading us within. We ascended innumerable steps until a small suite of rooms, opening on to a piece of flat roof, was reached; here we were installed. It was a charming spot, for far more care and art had been expended upon the building than in any other *ksar* we had seen; and the walls were clean with whitewash, while the ceiling consisted of a layer of canes, stained red and black, in strange designs, the whole supported on neatly cut beams of unpolished walnut wood. A few rough rugs lay strewn over the floor, and a semblance of comfort was given to the place by some shelves containing a teapot, some bright little cups and saucers, and a brass tray and kettle. Food was soon brought us, the usual *kuskusu* and boiled turnips, with the extra luxury of a chicken—no small honour in these parts—then tea and dates.

The view from the flat roof on to which the window of the room opened was a very charming one. The vegetation in Aït Iunir is far better than that of the lower districts, and big trees, especially cherry, pear, and walnut, abound. From the summits of the trees rose the surrounding *ksor*, one and all crowned with towers, and of very considerable size. The house in which we were must have covered a couple of acres of land. Yet even here were apparent the signs of the constant state of warfare in which the people of Dads exist, for the walls of the *minzah* were perforated with bullet-holes, shots from the next-door neighbour, whose castle stood only a couple of hundred yards away. It was on this account, that the feud was still proceeding, that our host made us sit down under the parapet of the wall to eat our meal, lest our appearance might bring down upon us a volley from the people over the way.

In this house I again noticed what I had already seen at the Zauia Aït bu Haddu—namely, the manner in which bees are hived amongst the Berbers. A hollow space is left in the wall of the house, opening into a cupboard within, from which the honey can be removed. A small hole, often only a hollow cane, on the outside of the wall, allows a means of ingress and egress for the bees.

Altogether, the *ksar* in Aït Iunir where we spent the night of November 12 showed far more signs of prosperity than any we had as yet visited. Not only was it very extensive, but the women wore far more jewellery, their necks being hung with large silver necklaces and coral and amber beads, while the clothes of the men were newer and of better material than usual. Added to this, the presence of such little luxuries as tea-trays and cups spoke of better living than the usual hard fare of the people.

In spite of the long march before us we sat up late, our host insisting on not leaving us until past midnight, and I was only able to snatch a couple of hours of sleep before we were told that it was time to be off.

Miserably cold it was when we girded up our loins and packed our little donkeys for the start, and at such moments as these I almost felt inclined to abandon my risky journey and turn back. The thought that all these hardships would have to be gone through on the return journey, and in far colder weather, was no pleasant one; but I felt I could face them rather than fail to accomplish my object, and so I persisted—until at length my efforts were crowned with success.

In the cold grey dawn we forded the river and ascended the steep slope on its eastern bank, reaching at the summit the commencement of the plain of Anbed, which forms the watershed between the rivers flowing east and west—that is to say, between the basin of the Wad Todghrá, which joins the Gheris

near Ul Turug, some ninety miles to the east, and
the Wad Dads, the chief tributary of the Wad Draa.
Not a vestige of vegetation was to be seen beyond
the few dried-up tufts of wild thyme, but a distant
view of gazelle and a flock of *muflon* show that there
must be some pasture, probably a little rank grass in
the hollows where water lies in the wet season.

The tramp across the dreary desert of Anbed is some
fifteen miles in length.  The whole way one proceeds
almost due east, parallel with the range of Jibel
Saghru, and distant from it some eight or ten miles.
The same dreary outlook presents itself as did in
crossing the strips of desert before arriving at Dads
—stone-strewn barren plain and verdureless moun-
tain-ranges on either hand.  The peep we obtained
of gazelle and *muflon*—Barbary wild sheep—was the
only time that, beyond domestic animals, we saw any
mammal, with the exception of a striped jerboa, and
of these only one or two, during the whole journey
from the foot of the Atlas to Tafilet.  Hyena I heard
of, however, and several of the graveyards we passed
were heaped with large stones to prevent their scratch-
ing up the bodies.

About twelve miles east of Dads a valley opens up
in the plain of Anbed, descending by which one reaches
the Wad Imiteghr, which crosses the end of the valley
at right angles.  There were appearances that the tor-

rent in the gorge must be large in the rainy season, or rather after heavy rainfall—for there is no regular wet season, rain being very scarce, but at this period it was quite dry. A few caves on the north side are used for housing sheep in, at such times as moisture allows of a little grass to grow. The road was very rough, and the bleaching bones of animals showed clearly enough that the boulder-strewn path had proved fatal to many a beast of burden. The descent from Anbed by this valley brings one to a continuation of the plain at a lower level, which extends, falling the while, as far as the valley of the Wad Gheris. On the farther (east) bank of the Wad Imiteghr are a few *ksor*, with an attempt here and there to raise a garden amongst the boulders. The most prosperous of the castles, and that a poor enough place, was pointed out to me as Ighir.

My road from this spot onwards diverged from that usually pursued by caravans between Dads and Todghrá, for while the principal track takes a slightly more northerly direction, we turned a little to the south and followed the course of the Wad Imiteghr, about half a mile from its north bank. The river was at this period tolerably well supplied with water, though the rains had been very scarce and not a drop had fallen since we had left Marakesh three weeks before.

During a long way we only passed two sets of habitations—the settlement of Imiteghr already mentioned, and a few miles further on the still poorer village of Timatruin. In this name, as in so many others amongst the Berbers, the prefix *T* is only a contraction of the Shelha word *Aït*—"sons of"—and therefore the literal spelling of the name of the place should be Aït Imatruin. The same fact exists in the word Tafilet, which, derived from the Arabic Filàl, a district in Arabia, has received from the Berbers the initial *T*—the contraction of *Aït;* while in this case the final *lt*, or *lat* as it should be spelt, is a feminine termination.

Ten miles after fording the Wad Imiteghr near Ighir, we reached a group of *ksor* lying under a spur of Jibel Saghru, which here juts out into the plain, although the river has worn a passage through it by a narrow gorge which divides it from the main range of the Anti-Atlas. The district is inhabited by Aït Mulai Brahim, descendants of the famous Shereef Mulai Brahim, whose tomb is a place of pilgrimage, and is situated above Agregoreh on the northern slope of the Atlas. The same family has given another great saint to Southern Morocco, Mulai Abdullah ben Hoseyn, who lies buried at Tamslot, a few miles south of Marakesh. These tombs, with their large offerings made by pious pilgrims, have much enriched this branch of the Shereefian family, and the present representative, living at Tamslot, Mulai El Haj ben Said, is perhaps the wealthiest man in Southern Morocco.

We were kindly received by the Shereefs, and shown into the mosque, a large building for so small a collection of *ksor*, with a tank for ablutions, and a domed *mihrab* or niche toward the east.

A few of the Shereefs spoke Arabic, and what with half a dozen other travellers who had sought the mosque of the *zauia* for a night's rest, we were a pleasant little party. Sunset prayers over, we sat down on the clean matting and passed the evening in conversation. The topic turned more than once on Christians—for such the natives call all the European peoples, though amongst the Berber the term *Rumin*, or Romans, is more common than *Nazarani*. The ignorance of the Shereefs on all questions out of their own particular sphere was astonishing. They seemed to lack all the brightness and rapidity of thought that I had noticed at Dads, and to have sunk into a sort of sleepy indifference to everything beyond their own immediate surroundings. They asked if Christians were like men and women, and I think doubted my men and myself when we told them they were. I could not venture to point myself out as an example, as not only would I have run a risk of getting my throat cut anywhere in the country, but here in the sacred precincts of the mosque death would have been a certainty, so I satisfied their curiosity by telling them that I had often seen Christians, and that they much resembled "true believers" to look at, but that their language was not the same, but sounded like the gibberings of apes. The conversation took many directions, and I was not greatly surprised to find these far-away Shereefs as ignorant of their own religion as they were of the Christians. I took the opportunity of giving a little discourse on Islam, a by no means difficult task, filling in the gaps with romances as to the doings of Moorish saints, whose histories, or rather, I should say, the traditions relating to whom, are nearly all known to me. Such a good reputation did I obtain for theological knowledge and religious devotion that the Shereefs felt bound to bring me supper from their *ksar*, and my men and I feasted merrily on boiled turnips, while several "true believers" went to bed supperless,—and the infidel and his wicked associates filled themselves with the offerings of the pious. This was by no means the first time on the journey that my knowledge—slight though it is—of Islam and its traditions stood me in good stead, and I am proud to say that wherever I spent a night I left behind me an impression of extreme religious fervour—which must have been sadly upset on my return journey, when, protected by a strong guard against insult or attack, I made my nationality and my disguise known. But of this I shall have more to say anon.

Leaving the *ksor* of Aït Mulai Brahim before dawn on November 14, we entered, close by, the gorge through which the Wad Imiteghr flows. It is only a mile and a half in length, and ends just as abruptly as it commences. No doubt its formation is owing to the river having forced its way through the projecting spur of Jibel Saghru, which is now separated by this valley from the main chain. The gorge is known by the name of Imin Erkilim—*imin* (Arabic *fûm*) meaning "a mouth," while Erkilim may or may not be Hercules, for on my inquiries as to who Erkilim was, I was told that Erkili was a great man, a sort of god, who did something no one quite knew when. From the name given me being Erkili, I presume the final *m* to distinguish the genitive case; but this is merely a surmise.

One emerges from the narrow valley, with its cliffs of rock on either hand, close to the village of Aït bu Kanifen, the inhabitants of which are celebrated robbers, often attacking any caravan that may chance to use this route in the valley the end of which their *ksor* commands. A few hundred yards of desert beyond and we entered the luxuriant palm-groves of Tiluin, or Aït Iluin, where is a large and flourishing *ksar*. These were the first palm-trees we had come across since Askura, for at Dads and the other oasis we had passed through they were entirely absent. Issuing from the pleasant shade of the groves, we crossed again a couple of miles of desert, at the termination of which we entered the southern extremity of the oasis of Todghrá, the immense palm-groves of which were clearly visible winding for many miles up the river of the same name. It is close to this spot that the Wad Imiteghr empties itself into the Todghrá at an elevation of 4250 feet above the sea-level.

We only skirted the border of the palms of Todghrá, and in half an hour were in the desert again, which extends from here to Ferkla, our night's resting-place, with the exception of the little district of Tabsibast, near which are some fertile gardens. From here on we trudged for sixteen miles along a weary road of stone and sand, black stone on yellow soil, with not a speck of anything green in sight. The road runs parallel to the Wad Todghrá, on the southern slope of a low line of hills, distant from the north bank of the river from one to three miles. Equidistant on the southern side rises the dismal black line of Jibel Saghru. This barren district is known as Seddat, and is said to be a favourite ground for the horsemen of the neighbourhood to pillage caravans upon,—nor could a more suitable spot be chosen, for not only was no habitation visible, but we saw no sign of life, beyond a few gazelle, the whole way.

The *wad* proceeds through the district of Seddat first directly east, but when rather more than half its length has been accomplished—say some ten miles —the track turns slightly more to the north, continuing this direction until the large and important oasis of Ferkla is reached.

Just at sunset, having been fourteen hours on the march, and on foot the entire time, we entered Ferkla. I was too tired, and too hungry, to admire the magnificent forest of palms, the walled gardens over the top of which showed up fruit-trees of many varieties, and jasmine and roses, and the multiplicity of canals that, confused as a spider's web, carried the clear sparkling water in every direction. The presence of these canals, however, was a relief, for from Tabsibast we had seen no water, and the heat had been very great during the afternoon. Although we carried enough in a stone jar on the back of one of our donkeys to assuage thirst, there was not a sufficient quantity to allow us to bathe our weary and blistered feet. The formation of the soil of this desert—in fact, of all the country from Ghresat to Tafilet—is

such as to render walking very unpleasant, though
the roads are nearly all level. Moorish slippers are
impossible, owing to the movement of the shoe on
the foot at every step that is taken, which, the shoe
being full of sand, quickly rubs the sharp grains into
the sole of the foot, causing most painful blisters at
once. On this account the natives never use the
shoe, preferring a sandal, which, consisting only of
a leather sole tied over the ankle and between the
toes with a narrow band of raw hide, does not hang
loosely on the foot, nor tend to collect sand. But I
found that this method was equally painful, owing
to the fact that the raw hide bands, unsoftened by
tanning, cut deeply into the skin. At length I was
obliged to abandon both and proceed barefoot, a plan
which, though it caused me much pain for a time,
eventually hardened the skin so that it became im-
pervious to the roughness of the sandy or stony
roads.

We wandered on for what seemed to me an interminable distance amongst the palm-groves, passing
many *ksor*, at each of which I hoped in turn we were
about to take up our quarters for the night, and each
of which we passed by without entering. I had
placed myself and my plans entirely in the hands
of the *zitat*—our guarantee—from Dads, and left
everything to him. He was an excellent fellow, and

his opinion of myself seemed to increase when he found I could trudge my forty miles or so a-day with an appearance—though by no means a true one—of little inconvenience. He was a typical Berber this latest addition to our party, some 6 feet in height, with a fair white skin and dark eyes and eyebrows. His face was clean shaven except for the small pointed beard on the end of his chin, and a remarkably handsome face it was. But his heart was better even than his looks, and more than once, as we tried to sleep of a night, our teeth chattering with the frost, he would cover me with his warm cloak, sharing it with me until I slept, when he would give up his half so that I might be warmer—and in the morning tell a dozen lies, saying that he had been so hot he had kicked it off, and it was only by accident that I had found myself warm and comfortable, and him half frozen.

I think the only qualms of conscience I felt at being in disguise were with this good fellow, for as yet he had not the faintest idea of my identity. So much did this trouble me that I took advantage of our lying huddled together under his warm cloak that night to tell him the whole story of my journey, whispered, lest we should be overheard. He said but little, but I knew full well that I could trust him, and in the morning I was warm, wrapped up

in his *haidus*, and he, only in his *chamira*, shivered
with the frost. If anything his attention to my
comforts increased after I had confided to him the
fact of my disguise; and every now and then he
would burst out into the merriest of laughs as we
trudged along, thinking the whole affair a tremendous
joke, and reiterating his approval of my venturing
where none had ever trod, and where my life if discovered was worth probably about half - an - hour's
purchase. Nor was his astonishment at my knowledge of Arabic—imperfect though it is—a small one;
for, himself a Berber, he too spoke it as a foreign
tongue, and if anything not so fluently as myself.

At length after dark we reached the principal *ksar*
of Ferkla—Asrir by name—where we put up for the
night. It was the largest village we had as yet come
across in the Sahara, enclosed in high *tabia* walls, and
boasting a number of well-built houses, and even a
few shops. It lacked, however, the picturesque appearance of many *ksor* that we had seen upon our
road; for the tall towers with their decorations and
battlements and turrets were absent, the style of
architecture resembling far more that found in the
towns of Morocco. In fact, Asrir may be more fitly
described as a town than a *ksar*, for within its walls
it is divided up into streets, many of them of the
same tunnel-like formation as one is so used to in

Fez, for instance, the houses meeting overhead. In
a large square near the gateway—for there is only
one entrance to Asrir—were collected a number of
soldiers on horseback and mules and camels, almost
the first signs we had as yet come across of the
proximity of the Sultan's army, which had a few
days previously reached Tafilet. These soldiers consisted for the most part of mounted messengers returning to Morocco, and it was piteous to hear them
asking questions as to the length of the road before
them, and the state of the pass over the Atlas; for
after their weary wandering of some eight months
in the fastnesses of the mountains and the desert
beyond, both they and their poor horses were well-
nigh starved. I came across one little party of five
or six men, all of whom were well known to me, servants of one of the Kaids, or governors, of a district
in North Morocco. The recognition gave me at first
a start; but I quickly realised that it was scarcely
likely to be mutual, and that it was by no means
probable they would discover under the dirt and
rags of a donkey-driver the man whom they had
known travelling with a large camp in European
costume. None the less I gave them a wide berth,
and was glad to hide myself away in the darkest
corner of a caravanserai, where we took up our
quarters for the night. The place consisted of an

open yard surrounded on all sides by a covered arcade, the roof of which was supported on pillars of *tabia*.    Quite a crowd was collected here for the night, for not only were there a number of soldiers from the Sultan's camp, but also camp - followers returning homewards, and Jews bound for Tafilet to see what they could pick up in the oasis, where Mulai el Hassen, the Sultan, was, accompanied by some 40,000 people.

Several tribes hold districts of Ferkla, a state of affairs that leads to constant warfare.    The principal divisions are members of the (i.) Aït Merghad, (ii.) Aït Isdeg, (iii.) Aït Yafalman, and (iv.) the Arab tribe of Alh Ferkla.    There are also several *mellahs* of Jews.

The oasis, which is very extensive, is watered from the Wad Todghrá, which flows through its midst, supplying innumerable canals.    Altogether it is said to contain upwards of forty large *ksor*, one or two of which, I was informed, can put as many as from 300 to 400 men into the field in time of war.    I found the elevation of Asrir to be 3260 feet above the sea-level.

Stowed away in the corner of the *fondak*, or caravanserai, I ran no risk of detection, and was able to watch the scene around me from a point of vantage offering not only safety from detection, but also some shelter from the frosty night-air. The crowd, illumined by the lanterns that many of them bore, passed and repassed, struggling for barley for their animals and food for themselves. Near us was a rough extemporised oven of earth, at which a number of half-nude Haratin, natives of the banks of the Wad Draa, were cooking *shua*—boiled mutton—in tiny, and none too clean, wooden bowls. We procured a couple of these for a small price, and enjoyed the luxury of real meat.

One fact that I had been noticing all along the road here thrust itself before me more than ever —namely, the entire absence of the camel. One would naturally expect to find him in this portion of trans-Atlas Morocco, but except for a few coming from the camp at Tafilet, I saw absolutely none. The fact is, the Berbers have never taken to the camel, and for some reason or other highly disapprove of him — why, I was unable to discover. However, on more than one occasion I have heard the Berber in chaff call an Arab a camel-driver— no doubt a term of reproach in his eyes. For beasts of burden the small mules of the district seem to have taken their place, and no doubt they are more economical with food. The camel, it is true, is easily fed where there is grazing to be found; but in these dry districts where all its fodder would have to be grown for the purpose, his keep would be far more heavy than that of the tiny mules in use, which scarcely eat more than a donkey, and subsist largely on dates.

We left Asrir at dawn on November 15, passing out of the *ksar* as soon as the gate was open, for it is kept closed during the night, a custom in practice all through these districts.

Our road lay for an hour through the palm-groves, ever crossing the little canals of clear water. We picked up a good supply of dates from beneath the trees for one day's provisions for the march, and a handful or two were given us now and again by the natives, many of whom were engaged in harvesting the fruit, and who, evidently attracted by the string of big wooden beads round my neck, mistook us for a party of wandering devotees of the sect of the Derkauiya. Whatever may have been their object in bestowing upon us charity, it was welcome enough, and for once we set out on our day's tramp with the certainty of a mid-day meal.

We forded the Wad Todghrá, first, at a spot where it flows over its wide bed amongst the palm-groves, and then again near where it issues from the oasis to pursue its course to the east. Then desert again, only here a scrubby bush covered the arid waste, thorny mimosas for the most part, called by the

Arabs *sidra*, with spikes all over it that tear one's clothes as one proceeds. To the north-east the horizon was bounded by a low line of yellow cliffs, close beneath which we could distinguish the oasis of Gheris, to which De Foucauld, after leaving Ferkla, pursued his journey of exploration. Our roads had been parallel, and in some places identical, from Dads to this spot, but from here on to Tafilet I had an untrodden and unmapped way before me. To the east again of Gheris the palm-trees of Tiluin—Aït Iluin—were to be descried. This oasis is said to be the original home of the tribe, which we had already come across near the southern end of Todghrá, and through another territory of which we were to pass the following day.

A few miles outside the limit of the palm-groves of Ferkla the road passes between two conical hills, of no great altitude, that on the right (south) being, however, the larger of the two. On the slope of the smaller one a ruined saint's tomb stands ; but I was unable to find out the name of the man whose bones lie in this desolate spot. On my return journey from Tafilet we followed another road more to the south, which passes to the farther side of the southernmost of these two hills, near the small settlement of Islef, a division of the tribe of Aït Merghad.

Half a mile to the east of these two hills is a

ruined *kasba*, or residence of a governor, who is said
to have shared the same fate as his castle—to have
been pulled to pieces.

*Saint's Tomb on the Road to Ul Turug.*

Ten miles from Ferkla the road takes a turn to the
south, and enters a valley of Jibel Saghru, to which
range, since leaving Dads, we had been travelling

parallel. Through this valley the Wad Todghrá flows, dividing the range into two parts, that on the east being known as Jibel el Kebir, "the great mountain," though why it is difficult to say, as both in extent and altitude it is considerably smaller than the hills of Saghru on the west and south. It was with no little pleasure that we entered the valley, barren though it was in most parts, for any relief was acceptable after the interminable arid desert we had been crossing for the last six or seven days of our journey. Two villages lie near the northern end, Igli and Maroksha, both inhabited by the Berber tribe of Aït Khalifa, representatives of whom we had not as yet come across. Igli is a most picturesque spot, crowning a knoll in the very centre of the valley, the summit surmounted by a huge tower. With this exception the village is not fortified, though its position above the level of the surrounding land renders it easy of defence. Maroksha lies on the level ground, half-hidden amongst groves of palms, irrigated from the stream of the Wad Todghrá. From Ferkla this river flows slightly to the north of east, the road being some miles on its south side, until almost due north of Igli the stream takes a directly southerly course to enter the valley between Saghru and Jibel el Kebir, half a mile perhaps to the east of the village.

A mile to the south of Igli we crossed the dry bed
of a tributary of the Todghrá, flowing from Jibel
Saghru, and, fording the main stream a few hundred
yards farther on, entered the groves of Milaab, which'
are protected on the west by a tower perched on a
rocky projection. The road at the ford resumes its
former easterly direction, the river flowing a little
more to the south. Although Milaab is but a small
place, I think I saw nowhere else such attention paid
to the cultivation of the soil and the date-palm. The
road for the mile and a half that it threaded the
groves was delightful. On either side of the straight
level track ran little canals of fresh clear water, beyond
which stretched away a forest of feathery palm-trees.
The whole scene resembled more a botanical garden
than a desert oasis, so evenly were the trees planted
and so well tilled the soil, which, green with *fsa*—
lucerne—resembled a level lawn. The exact distance
between each palm seems to have been carefully
measured, so that, look which way one would, one's
sight wandered down long avenues of the straight
stems and luxuriant leaves.

However, pleasant as was the half hour or so of
cool and shade, it was soon over, and once more
we issued into the barren glare of the stone-strewn
valley, not without many regrets for the fertile tract
we were leaving behind us, and much admiration for

the people who had raised so luxuriant a grove in so dreary a spot. The inhabitants of Milaab belong to the Berber tribe of Aït Iazzer.

The valley of the Todghrá here takes an almost circular form, being shut in on all sides by dreary black peaks, torn and scarped apparently by volcanic action. Away a mile or two to the south-east was visible the narrow gorge by which the river issues to the valley of the Gheris. The road does not follow the course of the Todghrá, but, maintaining its easterly direction, crosses by a weary track over the brow of a range of black hills, descending again into the wide open valley beyond near the immense fortified *ksar* of Ul Turug, the principal stronghold of the Aït Atta tribe of Berbers.

It had been a shorter march than usual, and though nearly some thirty miles had been accomplished, we were able to rest under the shade of some trees near a small stream before entering the *ksar*, which we did not desire to do until dusk, so as to run less risk of discovery; for we knew well that so near had we now come to Tafilet that the place was likely to contain a large number of Arab tribes-men from the Sultan's camp, to some of whom I might be known.

We feasted that afternoon, for we had dates in plenty, and our Berber who accompanied us fetched

us a few grains of green tea and a little sugar from
the *ksar*, with a kettle to brew it in and a tiny glass
to drink it out of, and we made merry in the shade
of the tree, enjoying our rest and the pleasant cool-

*Ul Turug.*

ness that precedes the bitter cold of the winter nights
in the Sahara.   Our journey was nearly accomplished
now : this one night in Ul Turug, a long march on
the morrow, and we would sleep on the soil of Tafilet,

if not actually in the Sultan's camp—and all our weary adventures would be over.

But there was yet another reason that made me desire to push on, and rejoice that the termination of our journey was so near. The bitter cold at night, want of food and clothing at all times, the scorching rays of the sun by day, and the long marches made barefoot over the hot sand, had sorely taxed my strength, and I already felt in my throat the sure signs of a coming illness, with which I had a couple of years previously lain long prostrate. Already, to swallow had become an exertion attended with pain, and I knew well what to expect. Yet I could not allow my spirits to sink, ill and weary though I felt, for there was so little now between me and success, and retreat was out of the question. So I laughed and talked as gaily as I could with my men, sipping the weak solution of hot green tea by turns, and promising ourselves no end of luxuries when once the great camp of the Sultan should be reached, and a day and a half of travelling at the most lay between us and it.

Between the spot which we had fixed upon to rest at for a while and the large *ksar* was the cemetery, a flat piece of ground covered with the low mounds which the Berbers raise over their graves, with here and there a high-domed building, or *kubba*,

marking the last resting-place of some Shereef,—for
Ul Turug is a *zauia*, or sanctuary, and many of its
inhabitants Shereefs. The *ksar* itself is situated
partly on the steep slopes of Jibel el Kebir and
partly on the plain, where the palm-groves commence, the whole settlement being surrounded by
a wall of considerable defensive powers. Every 50
or 60 feet along the wall is a large tower, of the
same height as the wall itself, but projecting slightly
from it. One gate alone gives entrance to the *ksar*,
situated under a heavy buttress in the centre of the
east side of the stronghold. Seen from where we
stayed for an hour or two before entering, the place
presents an appearance of great solidity and strength,
which is by no means belied by its interior.

Shortly before sunset we passed in, being scrutinised closely by a group of guards at the gate; but
a word from our Dadsi sufficed, and we entered
unmolested.

The gate, like so many others in Morocco, takes
a turn half-way, this form being the easiest in case
of defence being necessary. From the outside, as
well as from the interior, a dead wall meets the
eye when looking in or out as the case may be.
Within we entered a large square, surrounded on
two sides by buildings, while the two others were
faced with the outside wall, along which a covered

arcade had been built where animals and goods, as
well as human beings, could find shelter from rain—
whenever that rare event happens—or sun. From
this square streets lead between the houses to the
different parts of the *ksar*. Many of the dwellings
are extremely well and solidly built, one and all
of *tabia*, but with arched windows of wood, and
doors of the same material,—not the rough planks
we had seen at Dads, but showing considerable signs
of skilful carpentry. We found provisions obtainable, even eggs, a fowl, and some bread, and in every
respect Ul Turug resembles more a little town than
a desert *ksar*. We took up our position under the
high wall of a house, and, tying our donkeys to
a couple of tent-pegs, lit a small fire of wood we
had collected outside and supped.

Quite a number of people were passing the night
at Ul Turug. Not only were groups of Berbers to
be seen hurrying to and fro, but Arab soldiers from
the Sultan's camp, many of them with their horses,
and Jews and negroes, all either coming from or
going to Tafilet, a sudden impetus having been
given to trade by the presence of the Sultan and
the vast multitude that follows him in his marches.
Camels and mules laden with grain from Marakesh
there were too, all horribly lean and sore-backed after
the long march over the Atlas and the desert. In

the crowd our little band escaped observation altogether, and very few took any notice of us : one or
two Berbers, more friendly than the rest, shared
our little blaze of sticks, bringing us in return thin
strips of flabby native bread, which when toasted
became quite crisp and good.

A few words must be said as to the powerful
Berber tribe of Aït Atta, a stronghold of which Ul
Turug is.   Probably no division of the Shloh people
south of the Atlas is so well known as this tribe, and
deservedly so, for by their bravery and warfare, by
their constant extension of territory, and the fear in
which their name is held, they have become a byword
for all that is fierce or strong.

Professing an Arab origin—for they claim descent
from the famous tribe of the Koreish, that gave to
the world the Prophet Mohammed—they have lapsed
by time into essentially a Berber people, speaking
the Shelha tongue, and adopting the Berber manners
and customs, and to a great extent dress and appearance.   Almost the sole reminder of their Arab origin
to-day is the fact that they are great horsemen, and
still greater robbers and plunderers.   As a rule, the
Berbers seem to be constantly at war without the
idea of plunder, their feuds being far more often
matters of revenge.   With the Aït Atta, however,
this is different, and they seem to retain from the

time of their Eastern ancestors the love of going
afield for conquest and booty, with the result that
there is little land of the eastern portion of trans-
Atlas Morocco which has not at one time or another
been overrun, or at least attacked, by their hordes.
Not only to-day do they hold sway over the immense
wastes of Jibel Saghru, but even a large portion of
the Wad Draa has fallen into their hands, the natives,
Haratin, paying to their conquerors an annual tribute,
in return for which they are protected against attack
from other quarters. On the banks of the Wad Ziz,
the principal river of Tafilet, they hold the districts
of Ertib (Reteb) and Medaghra, and it is members
of their tribe who plough the banks of the Dayet ed
Daura, far to the south of Tafilet, the great marsh
formed by the rivers Ziz and Gheris. To the north
their influence extends as far as the southern slopes
of Jibel Ayashi, near where the caravan road from
Fez to Tafilet passes, and to the east they hold much
territory in the desert.

In appearance they differ much from the Berbers
of Dads, for instance, being, as a rule, men of short
build, thin and very wiry, with sunburnt complexions,
and lacking the handsome features and bearing of
many of the other Berber tribes. Although, like the
other Berbers, they shave their moustaches off, and
leave only the pointed beard on the extremity of the

o

chin, they resemble far more the Saharan Arab tribes than the kinsmen with whom they claim relationship. Their costume much resembles that of Dads, though generally far dirtier, and modified to suit horsemen. In addition to the *chamira* and *haidus*, they often wear the *haik*, the toga-like garment found throughout Morocco. Curiously enough, while the dress of the men has no particular points different from the other tribes, that of the women is unique in this portion of the desert, for they cover their shoulders with a shawl of red, black, and white stripes, closely woven of native wool and imported cotton. These shawls are longer than they are wide, and are held in their place by two short strings near the centre of one of the longer sides, the shorter ends being fringed in the same colours as the material is made of. With this exception, the rule is to find the rest of the costume of *khent*. The hair, too, is quite differently worn to the usual mode in vogue in these regions, being parted in the middle and drawn back under the ear in heavy plaits, held in position by a head-dress of *khent*. A few I noticed wearing silver ornaments on the front of their dark - blue head-dresses. The women offer none of the attractive features of those of Dads, being heavily built and clumsy, dirty and slovenly.

I had more than once been interested upon the

road at watching the various games practised by the boys of the different oases. At Dads *kora*, or football, was the general favourite, apparently identical with the game so common amongst the *tolba*, or "scholars," of Morocco. At Ferkla it had been a kind of hockey, one boy armed with a stick endeavouring to keep out of a hole in the ground a hard small ball which some half-dozen others were trying to hit in. For clubs they used the centre stem of the palm leaf, from which the fronds had been cut. Held by the thin end with the knob at the bottom, they formed an excellent weapon. Here, however, at Ul Turug we saw neither *kora* nor hockey, the whole youth of the place having taken to stilts, on which some were very skilful in getting about. The stilts resembled exactly the kind in use amongst boys in England, and one could not help feeling a sort of brotherly love with these desert urchins when one found them playing games identical with our own.

However, the tranquil state of affairs in Great Britain has not yet necessitated one practice, common amongst the youths of the Aït Atta tribe, which we saw going on outside the *ksar*. This consisted in practising escape from an enemy by holding on to the tail of a galloping horse, the rider urging his steed meanwhile to its full pace. It is marvellous what speed can be made in this manner, and it was a sight well worth seeing to watch an old ruffian of the tribe galloping about on his handsome desert horse, with a youth holding on to each stirrup, and another to the tail, and scudding over the ground beside and behind him respectively. This means of retreat is in common practice amongst the tribe of Aït Atta, and soon puts their foot-soldiers, no match against many of the Berber tribes in running, out of distance of their pursuers.

We spent the night of November 15 at Ul Turug, and though I found the elevation of the place to be only some 2850 feet above the sea-level, we experienced a sharp frost, and suffered not a little from the cold. In the grey dawn we rose, and, packing our little donkeys with their light burdens, left the *ksar* as soon as the gates were opened; nor was I sorry to get safely out of a spot that has the reputation of being one of the most fanatical in this portion of the Sahara.

# CHAPTER IX.

## OUR ARRIVAL AT TAFILET.

WITH light hearts we set out briskly upon the march, for although we had no hopes of reaching the Sultan's camp that night, we were determined, unless some unforeseen mishap occurred, to sleep in the district of Tafilet.   Our Berber from Dads, whose heart and soul were centred in my success, which I owe not a little to his good management and fidelity, sang loudly as we pushed on through the palm-groves that lie to the east and south of Ul Turug.   Pleasant enough the walking was in the cool of the morning with the shady forest of trees around us, but experience had taught us that these oases are never of any very great extent, and surely enough we had soon left cultivation behind and set out upon a twelve-mile trudge over barren desert.   It was just at the commencement of this arid plain of Maghrah that we forded the Wad Todghrá, and we could see the

spot where it issued by a gorge from the mountains
only a mile or two away on the west. Our road
lay almost due south now, the corner of Jibel Saghru
having been turned; for the track to Tafilet skirts
its northern and eastern slopes, where oases exist,
in preference to crossing the barren range where
water is scarce and food unprocurable,—for there are
no settlements in the northern part of Saghru, the
valleys only being resorted to after the occasional
rains by the shepherds of the Aït Atta tribe. Otherwise the mountains are free to the *muflon*—the Barbary wild sheep—which wander in large flocks over
the steeps, safe from molestation alike of sportsmen
and wild beasts—for, with the exception of a very
occasional leopard, there are none of the latter large
enough to attack them. The reason that the lion
is not found here is no doubt the fact that scarcely
any covert exists. However, were the region one
that could be reached by sportsmen, unlimited bags
of *muflon*, antelope, and gazelle could be obtained,
as the natives seldom if ever hunt. Unfortunately,
long before a European could obtain a shot of his
quarry, he would probably have fallen to the rifle
of some native sharpshooter; for so intense is their
hatred of Europeans, that a journey without disguise,
or perhaps the company of some great Shereef, would
be absolutely impossible. I believe, however, that

there are possibilities of much exploration being done amongst the Berbers if one could only get to know them personally; but of doing this they would scarcely give one time or opportunity, for they would probably make an end of one before learning to appreciate the fact that one's intentions in entering their country were harmless. So many traditions still remain of the *Rumin* and the treasure they have left buried in these parts, that one's actions would always be looked upon with suspicion, which it would need much skilful diplomacy to allay.

But to return to my journey. The plain of Maghrah is bounded on the west by the steep black slopes of Jibel Saghru, while to the east it extends across the Wad Gheris to the low line of cliffs and hills that separate the valley of this river from that of the Wad Ziz farther to the east. The plain is quite level except for one low barren hill about five miles south of Ul Turug. In spite of the absolute barrenness of the surrounding country, one was struck with admiration at one feature that presented itself as we proceeded—namely, the great subterranean aqueducts that carry water from the Wad Todghrá to Tiluin, the next oasis to the south, a distance of some eleven miles.

This vast labour deserves some minute description, in order that the extent of the work may be realised.

The aqueducts are formed by the sinking of pits at intervals of about 25 yards apart, each some 30 feet deep and 10 feet in diameter. Then from pit to pit a tunnel is excavated, through which the water flows. These tunnels appear to be sufficiently high in most parts to allow of a man walking upright to pass through them. Had there been but one row of these pits and connecting tunnels it would have been a work of vast labour, but I counted no less than *eleven*, all running parallel with one another, and no great distance apart. A very simple calculation gives the result, that to bring water from the Wad Todghrá to Tiluin no less than 9000 of these shafts have been sunk and the intervening channels excavated—and this with the most primitive of picks and spades. Their existence will remind the reader of the value of water in the desert.

Leaving the plain of Maghrah one enters the oasis of Tiluin, a branch of the tribe of Aït Merghad. Twice previously on the way hither we had seen other settlements and oases belonging to these people, once near the end of the gorge of Imin Erkilim, near Todghrá, and again to the north-east of Ferkla, not many miles from Gheris. Here, just on the northern extremity of the oasis, are the ruins of a large *kasba*, or possibly *ksar*, the bare high *tabia* walls of which wear to-day a melancholy appearance.

Opposite, on the top of a rocky hill, once apparently
stood a large village; now nothing but crumbling
heaps of stones and *tabia* mark its site. A few hundred yards only beyond this spot, and amongst the
palm - trees, stood some saints' tombs, the largest
whitewashed and in good repair. Nothing could
have been prettier than the picture they formed—
the white domes against the rich green of the trees.
At a stream of running water, on the very banks of
which the tombs were situated, were a party of
soldiers bivouacking. They had lit a small fire and
were cooking tea, the sunlight falling in bright spots
on their polished trays and brass kettle, the crimson
and scarlet saddles of their tethered horses, and
their bright clothing. The bit of colour was charming, for all through the desert one longs for something brilliant. It is quite a mistake to imagine
that colour is to be found in such countries—in fact,
the whole of Morocco is almost devoid of it. In
the desert especially the absence of anything bright
becomes almost oppressive in time. The sky takes a
heated white appearance, only a shade or two different
in colour from the white glowing sand. Any figures,
or life of any sort that may appear, but alters the
tones of the landscape; for so covered is everything
with the white dust, and so fierce is the glare of the
sun, that at a distance the shadows only appear, and

they as hard black patches. The natives, with the exception of the indigo-blue cotton of the women, wear no coloured garments, and even the women's costume appears black against so light a background. It may be imagined, then, how to our weary eyes the little group of soldiers formed a pleasing picture; but, tempting as it was, we did not dare accept their cordial invitation to join them in their meal, lest my disguise should be discovered; for it is a very different matter to deceive the Berber, who has never seen a European, and generally imagines him to be some kind of a wild beast in appearance, to attempting to do so in the case of Arabs of Morocco proper, who know well the Christian type, and would discover at once the presence of a foreign accent in one's speech. So with many regrets to be obliged to refuse the proffered drink of tea and hard-boiled eggs and bread, we pushed on, driving our little donkeys before us with sharp cries. Through the palm-groves we passed, until issuing again, we crossed the narrow strip of desert that separates the oasis of Tiluin from that of Fezna, and entered the palm-groves of the latter.

Fezna showed far more signs of prosperity than Tiluin, for whereas in the latter we passed only one *ksar* that was in good repair, the former boasts many, while, too, the cultivation of the palm is much more carefully attended to. Water flowed in tiny canals on every side, while the soil was green with *fsa*, on which the natives are entirely dependent for fodder for their few horses and cattle, the soil in the oasis being entirely cultivated, and without its limits all is sand, and sand capable not even in the rainiest times of bearing grass. The inhabitants of Fezna belong to the tribe of Aït Yafalman, members of which we had first come across in Ferkla.

Again only a narrow strip of desert divides Fezna from Jerf—"the cliff"—which owes its name to a low line of hills ending abruptly in a precipice, that extends from Jibel Saghru into the valley of the Wad Gheris. This point forms an excellent landmark from almost all directions, and was visible from the hill above Dar el Baida, where the Sultan's camp was pitched, to the east side of the oasis of Tafilet, in the district of Tanijiud. Jerf is a large and flourishing oasis, and the two *ksor* near which we passed were not only of considerable size but also strongly fortified. Very different were these *ksor* of the valley of the Gheris to those we had been accustomed to at Askura and Dads, for here there were none of the ornamental towers, but only the level walls of *tabia*, protected at intervals with flanking towers. In fact, the style of architecture resembled much more the walls of a Moorish city than the picturesque Berber residences of the country directly south of the Atlas Mountains.

We had now approached, and been travelling parallel to, the course of the Wad Gheris; but until after we had left Jerf some little distance behind we did not actually catch a glimpse of the river. From here on, however, to our night's resting - place, the Wad Gheris was continually coming into sight, whenever almost an open space presented itself in the long string of oases that line its western bank.

The first of these cultivated districts is Bauia, but the soil is poor, and though attempts at fields appear now and again, the sand has in places almost obliterated them. After Bauia one passes near the Kasba el Hati, where quantities of grain were being stored against the Sultan's arrival. Very little of this grain was the produce of the soil, for the crops of barley and wheat are very poor in this part, and far the larger quantity had been brought on camel-caravans from Morocco.

Between Bauia and Kasba el Hati we passed the only unwalled and unfortified village we had as yet seen—the only one I saw, in fact, during the whole of my travels south of the Atlas Mountains. I was told that it was only used in spring, and then only for herding cattle in, for the soil round yields, if rain happens to have fallen, some scant grazing for cows and goats.

A mile or two beyond Kasba el Hati one passes Ulad Hanabu, which, like all this string of oases, is inhabited by Arabs of Tafilet, though the name Hanabu is without doubt a Berber one, and probably the same as Hannibal.

Here at last we began to see signs of fields and cultivated land, and very attractive they were in our eyes, so weary were we with the everlasting desert. The country was green with turnips, maize, and lucerne, with intervals of long narrow strips of sand-dunes, running east and west, carried, no doubt, to their present position by the dominating east wind of summer, that, blowing across the whole area of the Sahara, comes up like the blast of a furnace, and laden with fine particles of sand. So far the desert we had been crossing had been principally composed of gravel and stones, but here we commenced to catch glimpses of the great expanse of sand-hills that lies to the east and south of Tafilet.

We were now following the immediate bank of the Wad Gheris, and a few words as to this river must be written here.

Rising in the main chain of the Atlas Mountains, it waters on its downward courses the following districts, commencing at the north: (i.) Mtrus; (ii.)

Aït Merghad, the main settlement of that large
Berber tribe; (iii.) Semgat; (iv.) Taderught; and
(v.) Gheris, whence it flows almost directly south,
watering the string of small oases we had passed
through between Jerf and the cultivated land on

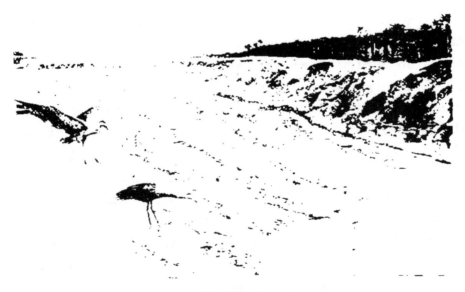

*Wad Gheris.*

the north-west of Tafilet, known as Beled el Unja.
Thence it flows through the two districts of Tafilet
proper, Sifa and Wad el Melha, and uniting with the
main stream of the oasis, the Wad Ziz, eventually is
absorbed by the sand at the great marsh of Dayet
ed Daura. The water of the Gheris is brackish, but

though very unpalatable, our donkeys drank it, as do also the cattle of the neighbouring district.

The river at this part flows some considerable distance below the level of the surrounding country, in a bed varying from 300 to 350 yards in breadth, while the actual ford where we crossed it the same evening at El Meharza was about 60 yards across. High banks of clay, the soil deposited by the river, line its bed on each side, the palm-trees above growing close up to the edge of these cliffs.

Descending to the course of the river, we waded across, and climbing the steep bank on the east side, found ourselves at the great *ksar* of El Meharza, the capital of the district of Es-Sifa, soon after sundown on November 16.

Tafilet was reached at last, and only a few hours' journey lay between me and the camp of the Sultan of Morocco, on the east side of the oasis. The illness I had felt coming on for the last few days was now well upon me, and not only did I find it impossible to eat, but even to swallow liquid was a process of pain, so large had the swelling in my throat become. However, this of all the nights of our journey was the one on which I could afford least to give way; for not only was my desire to reach Tafilet accomplished, but there were still weightier reasons why I should keep all my wits about me. We had left the Berber country now and had entered amongst Arabs, and though most of them little knew the looks of a European, for nearly thirty years had elapsed since the last traveller had visited Tafilet, yet they would be sure to recognise my foreign accent, and though it might not necessarily lead to my identity, it would at least cause an unpleasant amount of questioning as to whence I came. We had therefore invented a pretty little story about my coming from Syria to pray at the tomb of Mulai Ali Shereef, who lies buried at Tafilet; but, happily for the sake of our consciences, we were not obliged to make use of it, though I rather regretted not being able to address the little crowd with the speech, every word of which I had prepared, and which not only showed my great religious zeal, but was poetically expressed, and I am sure it would have pleased my hearers equally well. But, as I said, we were spared this, for no question was put to me directly, and our men did all the talking that was necessary in order to obtain admittance into the *ksar*—for so constantly are the Berbers and Arabs at war, that no stranger is allowed to enter unless he can give a satisfactory account of himself to the gatekeepers, and this custom is general throughout the oasis. However, it was dusk when we entered, for the sun was already set, and a few words explaining that we had come from the north—a vague term generally used of all Morocco north of Fez—and were on our way to the Sultan's camp, sufficed to gain our admittance.

Nor was my presence the only difficulty that might have caused us to come to grief, for the company of our Berber from Dads might by no means have aided us, and he was really nervous of entering into an Arab stronghold, lest some inhabitant of whom a relative had been killed by a Berber—a by no means uncommon occurrence—might think right to revenge himself upon an innocent passer-by merely because he happened to be of the same race. Guiltless as our Dadsi was on this occasion, I had gathered from his remarks on the road that he had by no means neglected opportunities when they presented themselves of putting Arabs out of the way.

However, all our fears were needless, and with but the shortest of delay we found ourselves within the great double gateway that protects the *ksar*—for so constant is warfare in the district, that the natives have thought it necessary, or at least expedient, to have two gates, one within the other, and separated from one another by an open piece of ground, surrounded with high walls, so that should their enemies force the outer gate, there would be every chance of annihilating them from the ramparts as they assailed the inner one.

P

Proceeding by a wide street with high houses on either hand, we at length found a large *fondak*, or caravanserai, where we took up our quarters under an arcade that ran along two of its sides; and to commemorate our safe arrival in Tafilet, we bought some tea and sugar and a candle, hired a kettle, and enjoyed ourselves as far as was possible in the cold.

Travel had left its mark on all of us. I felt ill and weak, and my throat gave me much pain. Poor Mohammed had a most unbecoming cold in his head, and no pocket-handkerchiefs. The negro—upon whom many curses—worried us by his constant demands for more food, and enraged us by insisting on riding our little donkey the whole way, while Mohammed and I walked. The old Dadsi Shereef's nephew, too, was thin and tired, and one and all were begrimed with desert sand and with our clothes torn by desert thorns, while our bare legs and feet were fretted over with scratches. Yet we thought of none of these things that night; we merely huddled together in the cold and laughed and chatted, and congratulated each other that now, at long last, after some seventeen days' weary march, and often from thirty to forty miles a-day, our goal was reached and success attained.

I little thought then that the greatest hardships

of my journey were yet to be borne, for I imagined that the Sultan and his Viziers, though doubtless not pleased at my coming, would extend to me some small form of hospitality, and at least not refuse to me the only request I had to make to them,—a few yards of canvas, the smallest of the soldiers' tents, as a place where I and my few faithful men could rest in. But I was wrong.

Near us, spending the night in the *fondak*, were a few Haratin of Wad Draa, short in stature, of deep copper colour, and with faces showing much of their negro origin. Cheery fellows they were, and we invited the three or four of them to our dinner-party; and though they spoke but little Arabic, their laughter added to our amusement. They, like myself, were travellers, wandering apparently for no particular object, though the principal cause of travel amongst these Draa natives is, that the cultivated banks of the river produce only sufficient to support a certain number of lives, and thus the excess population, for it is a largely increasing one, seeks its livelihood elsewhere. This no doubt accounts for the large number of Haratin, &c., found throughout the entire country of Morocco.

We were up before dawn, and, loading our donkeys by the light of the remains of the little candle we had bought overnight, set out on the last stage of our journey. Entering the thick palm-groves, we presently joined a larger track than usual, and, taking a south-easterly course through the district of Es Sifa, forded the Wad Ziz, the principal river of Tafilet, some four miles from El Meharza. The water of the Ziz, unlike that of the Wad Gheris, is fresh, and it is on it, therefore, that the natives are principally dependent for their supply for irrigating purposes. The actual course of the river, and the flow of water, was by no means equal to that of the Gheris at this period; but this may have been owing a good deal to the fact that a large quantity is drained off from above, for so deep does the river lie below its banks, that water for cultivation of the land immediately adjoining any part of its course has to be brought from many miles higher up.

The district of Es Sifa, through which we had been passing between the Wads Gheris and Ziz, except in the immediate vicinity of El Meharza, does not show any great fertility, though palm-groves exist in comparatively large quantities. The soil is sandy and the gardens ill-cared for and almost untended, most of the *tabia* walls that we saw being more or less in a ruined condition. From where we forded the Ziz, entering just to the north of the ruins of Sijilmassa—or, as it is more generally called now, Medinet el Aamra—far more attention is given to the cultivation of the palm and other trees; while the carefully walled gardens of Wad Ifli, for so this district is called, show signs of much care and attention on the part of their owners. Canals of water run in every direction, the largest and deepest we had as yet seen, especially the one which flows to the north of Sijilmassa, and which no doubt supplied that once great city. Even to-day the channel is in good order, with carefully banked walls of bricks, and crossed in many places by arched bridges. Of Sijilmassa I shall have more to say anon. Then on through the thickening palm-groves, by bewildering tracks that turn first in one direction and then in another, over innumerable fast-flowing streams of water; past the great *ksar* of Rissani, the seat of whatever government can be said to exist here, with its strongly fortified walls; then in sight of the market of Mulai Ali Shereef, with its beehive-like domed stalls in which the natives sell their goods; then again in sight of Abu Aam, the trading centre and seat of learning of the oasis, where the merchants of Fez reside, until at last the ending of the palm-trees brought us into open desert again.

Issuing almost suddenly upon the great waste of sand, a strange but welcome sight met our eyes.

Stretching away for a couple of miles along the edge of the desert, white against white hills, the whole dancing and shimmering in the heated air, lay the great camp of Mulai el Hassen, the late Sultan of Morocco. It was a welcome sight indeed, for whatever reception I might meet with from the Sultan and his officials, I knew this at least, that my life was safe.

We stood still in silence and gazed upon the imposing scene before us. Amongst the white tents, many decorated in designs in blue, passed the soldiery, mounted and on foot, and the crowds of camp-followers and natives who accompanied his Majesty upon his last fatal expedition into the desert. Horses galloped here and there, many of the riders engaged in the picturesque sport of *lab el barud*, or powder-play. The smoke of hundreds of camp-fires curled almost imperceptibly into the air, and above all was heard the dull hum of human life.

We had not breakfasted, and already we had been marching some three or four hours, so we sat down in the shade of a few palm-trees and cooked the last drops of our little packet of green tea, and rested for a while. Then a little later I sent my Riffi servant into the camp to announce my arrival to the Sultan's Minister of Foreign Affairs, Sid Mfdhul Gharnit.

# CHAPTER X.

## WITH THE SULTAN AT TAFILET.

MOHAMMED the Riffi was a long time before he gained an interview with Sid Gharnit, the Minister of Foreign Affairs, and when he did so it brought no promise of a pleasant reception for myself. In fact, my un-looked-for arrival caused that elderly gentleman no little concern, for though I was well known to him personally, and bore a firman from the Sultan to travel in his dominions, he seemed much upset. There was, however, one item of news that my man brought me on his return that cheered me much. Kaid Maclean, the English officer attached to the Sultan's suite, was in the camp. Had he not been there, it is difficult to say into what straits I might have fallen, but, fortunately for me, he was; and with everything else against me, his pleading, as will be seen, eventually much bettered my condition.

A few words must be said here to explain the presence in this remote corner of the Sahara of the two European officers who were accompanying the Sultan ; and I am sure that Kaid Maclean will forgive my meddling in his affairs and writing a few words about him.

Some seventeen years ago Mulai el Hassen asked the then British Minister, the late Sir John Drummond Hay, to find him a young English officer to drill his troops. Maclean, then a lieutenant in a line regiment, had previous to this applied to Sir John for some such post, and was speedily appointed. Entering upon his work with much zest and spirit, he soon discovered what good stuff was in the Moors as soldiers, and they in turn began to appreciate cleanliness and smartness, so that in a year or so the men placed at the Kaid's disposal reached a stage of competence in drill, while he gained their respect and admiration. But jealousy at Court put an end to the disciplined army, and with little exception drill was discontinued. Meanwhile, however, Maclean had become a trusty servant of the Sultan, useful to him in a thousand ways ; while his British moral standard, so different to that of the Moors, had forced his Majesty to perceive his probity in all matters, and he bestowed confidence and affection upon the British officer. From that time Kaid

Maclean has continued in the Sultan's service, and is perhaps as well known as, and certainly more popular than, any official at Court. His position throughout has been a difficult one; but so carefully has he avoided entering into any duties beyond his own, so skilfully and openly has he shown no desire to encroach upon the prerogatives of others, and so steadfast throughout has been his wish to do nothing that did not further the interests of the Sultan and the Government he has allied himself to, that he has been able to keep himself free from the jealous quarrels that are of everyday occurrence at the Moorish Court.

On the Sultan's leaving Fez in April of the year in which I made my journey, 1893, he took with him as far as Sufru, a small town some few hours' journey south of the capital, all his European staff— that is to say, the military missions of France and Spain, some three officers of each, attached to his Court. But from Sufru, for reasons which are not quite apparent, he ordered the Europeans to return to Fez, with the exception of the French officer, Dr Linares, who was commanded to accompany him throughout his journey. Kaid Maclean returned with the rest; but shortly before my leaving Saffi, he, without my knowledge, had proceeded to Tafilet to join the Sultan's camp, as usual accompanied by

his guard of troops.   Yet in spite of the fact that he
was in his Majesty's service, wore the Sultan's uniform, and was accompanied by troops and bore a
special firman from his master, he was several times
roughly treated, and was more than once in danger
of his life upon the road.   He had arrived some ten
or twelve days previous to myself at Tafilet, and I
look back to the fact that he was there to urge my
cause with the Sultan and the Viziers with no little
feeling of thankfulness and pleasure.   To Dr Linares,
too, I owe a word of thanks.   Had not he been
present to perform an operation on my throat, in
all probability this book would never have been
written, nor I have returned to tell the tale of my
journey.   Fortune, which has never deserted me in
any of my long journeys, stood by me then, to
ease my suffering and, I think I may almost say,
save my life.   But I have progressed too far.

At length Mohammed returned with the welcome
news of Kaid Maclean's presence, and a couple of
soldiers to bring me into the camp, where some
shelter would be afforded to me until the Sultan's
opinions and wishes as to myself should be known.
Meanwhile I was told to " lie low," and that no communication must pass between myself and either of
the European officers, or even the native officials.   In
a few hours' time, when Mulai el Hassen should leave

the privacy of his tents for his office, my fate would
be known.

So I followed my guides into the great camp.

It was a sight well worth seeing—worth almost
the long journey to Tafilet; for, though not the first
time I had intruded my presence in the camp of the
Sultan of Morocco, I had never previously witnessed
a following of so large a number of troops and others,
or so vast a quantity of tents.

Threading our way through the camp, we at length
arrived at a spot near which I recognised the European encampment of Kaid Maclean. There, with a
few words of welcome from my guides, I was shown
into a small and much-dilapidated bell-tent, of the
fashion in use in the Moorish army for the soldiers,
of whom it was already half full, and a place was
made for me by its occupants—a rough set of men, it
is true, but none the less ready to make me as comfortable as the circumstances would allow. In that
little tent I spent five days, of which I shall have
more to say, and I learned that the Moorish soldier,
be he never so ill paid and ill clothed, be he dirty
and rough in his language, can when he likes show
a solicitude and kindness far greater than one would
ever expect from such; and my five days of illness
and watchful care from the handful of men who.
shared my little quarters—or rather, I shared theirs

—was an experience gained in the strange character of the Arab people. Scanty as were their rations, the best of everything was specially cooked for me, notwithstanding the fact that I could not even swallow water for the greater part of the time; and these great rough fellows, brought up and trained to every crime and brutality, became like nurses in a sick-room. With voices lowered lest they should wake me when they thought me asleep, with no noise in setting their tiny tea-tray or stirring the little fire of charcoal, they spent their time in trying to amuse me and stir up my wretched spirits. I met two of them this last summer in Fez, whither I had proceeded to meet the young Sultan on his way thither, a month after his accession, and we spent a riotous night of revelry, laughing over the hardships we had shared in the camp of the late Sultan at Tafilet, and amusing ourselves in a way than which we ought to have known better; for so pleased was I to be able to repay in a small degree their kindness to me, that we must have kept the neighbourhood of my residence awake all night with music and singing.

Soon after my arrival I received a message from Kaid Maclean saying he could not see me until the Sultan's wishes were known; but that if I wanted anything I could send to him surreptitiously, for he had received strict orders to have nothing to do with me at present. Meanwhile I made a written request to Sid Gharnit that a small tent might be found for me and my men to lodge in, and that was all I asked. Toward evening I received a reply. The Sultan had been informed of my coming, and was very indignant, absolutely refusing to give me a tent or anything else, and I was to remain where I was until further orders.

There was nothing to be done, so each hour growing sicker and sicker, I lay down in the dirty little tent, unable to eat or sleep. Hearing that my health was bad, the French doctor was sent to me, and prescribed a gargle, which, though it temporarily relieved the pain, did not prevent the swelling increasing. Then four days of great suffering, often struggling for breath, unable to lie down for fear of choking, or to swallow even a drop of water to quench my thirst. What clothing I had was insufficient, and the cold at night was as intense as the heat of the sun, beating through the thin and tattered canvas of the tent, was by day. Kaid Maclean had received orders not to see me, and he knew better than to disobey them, yet he did everything in his power to ease my suffering, and constantly saw my servant, Mohammed Riffi, as to my condition. At length things grew serious; at times I became unconscious for short periods, and the indignation of my men and the soldiers in the tent knew no bounds, for nothing was done to relieve me.

Poor Mohammed at length broke through every law of Moorish etiquette, and with a burst of expostulation—and I doubt not a little abuse—forced his way into the Viziers' tent, and let them know not only what he thought of them, but what would be thought of them at Tangier should I die.

This changed matters. The French doctor was hurriedly sent to me, accompanied by Kaid Maclean, and at sunset on the fifth day the quinsy in my throat and the enlarged uvula and other swellings were lanced.

The relief was instantaneous; but even greater than the relief was the change in the bearing of the Moorish officials toward me. Accompanied by Kaid Maclean, Dr Linares had an interview with the Viziers, and made my condition known, asserting that he would not be responsible for my life if I was not at once moved to other quarters, and that I was in a most precarious state of health.

Terrified at what might be the results to themselves should I die, and my death be laid at their door, they gave permission for me to be removed at once, and a few minutes later, with the doctor supporting me on one side and Kaid Maclean on the other, all of us rejoicing at the turn of events, I was half carried, half led, into the comfortable tent of the Kaid. A wash and a change of clothes, a little wine, and an egg and milk, and I turned over to sleep for the first time for four days and four nights.

It may be thought that I have spoken at too great a length on my own illness; but I have felt, uninteresting as my personal case may be, that it might serve as a warning to any other traveller who, like myself, might think that in reaching the Sultan's camp the end of his sufferings had come, and that he would find, if not hospitality, at least no hostility. What would have happened had I been in good health I do not know, nor do I like to repeat the rumours which were given me on the best of authority; but there is no doubt that I would have been quickly despatched to the coast, and that in a manner neither pleasing nor flattering. However, enough; I have long ago forgiven those to whom I owe that period of suffering. The Sultan died from the effects of his journey; the then Grand Vizier lies in chains in Tetuan prison, together with his brother the Minister of War, who throughout, owing to Kaid Maclean's entreaties, had shown every possible desire that my condition might be bettered. Sid Gharnit and I have talked the matter over, and he protested, as

I have no doubt was the case, that he was unable
to do anything for me against the Sultan's order.
Personally, he remarked with a smile, he would
have lent me a tent, if for no other motive, that
he thought I should probably have brought him
some little present from Europe next time I visited
the Court; and with this touch of humour we
buried the hatchet and supped together, talking
over the great changes that had come to pass since
then, and ever and anon referring to the turns
of fortune that the Moors look upon as predestin-
ation. The great men of that day were dead or
in prison, while I had returned to health, — and
all in the short space of some six months.

Ay! "How are the mighty fallen!"

I recovered more quickly than I had fallen ill,
and in a day or two, under Kaid Maclean's care,
was able to leave my bed and sit in one of his
easy-chairs and watch the ever-changing scene that
presented itself to me in the heart of the Sultan's
camp.

No one who has not seen the great *mahalla* of
Morocco on the march and pitched can form any
idea of the strange mixture of boundless confusion and perfect order that succeed each other in
such quick succession. A few words as to how the
Sultan travelled and how he lived cannot but prove

KASBAH OF SEKOURA.

interesting, and my stay in his camp at Tafilet allowed me to see much of both.

First of all, in order that some idea of the size of the expedition which Mulai el Hassen led to Tafilet may be obtained, let me begin by stating that there were nearly 40,000 persons in his camp at the time of my visit, including the members of the surrounding tribes who were attending the sovereign on his march through their country, and this entire crowd was living under canvas. But in order that the manner in which the huge camp is arranged may be realised, it will be easier to commence with its pitching, which, as far as the ground allows, is regularly repeated upon every occasion —and at Tafilet the absolute level of the edge of the desert showed off the system to perfection. Allowed that all the baggage-animals carrying the immense number of tents and quantities of baggage have arrived at the spot chosen for the night's encampment, the site where the Sultan's enclosure is to be placed is chosen, and until his tent is erected none other can be. At length the golden ball that crowns the great *kubba* is raised into the air, and a moment later from all sides rise up a multitude of tents great and small, each one of which has its regular spot,—for from the time of choosing the situation of the Sultan's encampment

Q

men have been employed in marking out the sites. This is done by a soldier pacing the diameter of a circle, with the Sultan as its centre, and from this diameter a complete circuit is made of the camp. This outer line of tents is divided into various lengths, a certain part of the circumference being allotted to the soldiers of each tribe—that is to say, the conscripts of each district of Morocco—for the regular army with the commander-in-chief form a separate camp.

A large open square space is left to the east of the Sultan's tents, which is surrounded by the field-guns and other artillery, and leading from this square to the outer line of tents is left an open roadway. Between the circumference of the circle and the Sultan's tents spaces are allotted to the governors of districts, the officials of the army and the Court, the Viziers, and the Shereefs and relations of the Sultan.

His Majesty's encampment is in itself a large camp. Surrounded entirely by high walls of white canvas decorated in patterns of dark blue, it is divided into two portions, in one of which the women are kept, while the other contains his Majesty's private tents, which are many, and some of huge dimensions. At Tafilet I counted from the hill above the camp no less than between fifty and sixty tents within the canvas walls. None but the most trusted servants and slaves enter the enclosure at all, and then not the women's portion while they are present. The entrance into the Sultan's quarters is formed by the two ends of the walls overlapping for a considerable extent and running parallel to one another, and curved as they proceed, so that there is no possible chance of any one seeing within, while the height of the canvas prevents anything but the tops of the tents being apparent from without.

Immediately outside, and within the square formed by the cannon, is pitched the office-tent in which his Majesty transacts his business. It is a small square tent of red and green cloth, supported on four poles with gold tops. One side is left completely open. Within it boasts no furniture but carpets and matting and the divan on which the Sultan sits to transact business. Close by is another large tent, of dark canvas, and of the form of a *ghima*, the common dwelling of the Arab. This serves the purpose of a mosque, and there the Sultan, surrounded by the Shereefs, Viziers, and *tolba*, leads the prayers at the regular hours.

It was Mulai el Hassen's custom to leave his private camp at sunrise, and, walking to his office-tent, give audiences to the Viziers, &c., and transact business until nine or ten, when he would retire to the privacy of his own quarters, to reappear again during the cool of the afternoon, generally from four to sunset; and often of a night I could see him sitting there, with members of his Court standing before him taking down his commands. Tiring, indeed, must be the work of a Vizier, for he must always stand in his master's presence.

Mulai el Hassen may be said to have transacted the entire business of his country himself; for although the different Viziers are known by such titles as Ministers of War, and Foreign Affairs, &c., &c., they were in reality little more than private secretaries, and the actual organisation and welfare of his country, as well as its relations with the foreign Powers, rested with the Sultan alone.

The course usually pursued is as follows. Long strips of paper are prepared with a *précis* of all the matters of importance written upon them, in as few words as possible. On having an audience the various Viziers hand these to the Sultan, who scans them through, asks questions on any point on which he may wish to learn further particulars, and pencils the answers on the margin. I have on several occasions seen these slips after they had left the Sultan's hands, and they are masterpieces of *précis* writing, often a few inches of narrow paper containing a list of pending affairs that would necessitate many meetings of a Cabinet Council in London. Even more precise were the Sultan's answers — the pencilled " Yes " or " No," or the short questions affixed.

The camp once pitched, a matter of but a short time for so many men, the regular routine of camp-life begins. Fires are lighted, and the cooking, &c., commences. A large number of traders accompany the camp, who set up their tents, where tea and sugar —such necessaries to the travelling Moor—can be procured by the rich, while *kiff*, the chopped hemp-leaf, appeals to the soldiery, if they happen to have anything to buy it with. Bread, too, is sold, the ovens being built upon the spot of stones and clay, or mud-bricks, as the soil suits. Sheep are slaughtered, and *shua*—boiled mutton—can be procured, each bringing his own dish or basket to take the meat away in. Usually it is principally the mounted tribesmen, serving only for a few months, and bringing some money of their own, who indulge in these luxuries. The richer classes, the Shereefs and Viziers, procure all their provisions from the Government, which in turn procures them from the district if in a rich portion of the country ; but at Tafilet nearly all the grain, &c., was brought from Marakesh and stored beforehand. These provisions, supplied by the tribes through which the army is passing, are called *mona*,

and often amount to such a quantity as to cripple
that portion of the country for a year or more, so
large a drain is made upon their wheat and barley,
their sheep, oxen, and fowls, to say nothing of their
pockets,—for the governor of the district, as well as
provisioning the Sultan and his troops for as long a
period as they stay in the country under his jurisdiction, has also to make handsome presents. The *mona*,
too, includes quantities of tea and sugar, no light tax
in far-away parts, where long transport has added
very considerably to the price. The soldiery receive
pay—irregularly—and with this have to purchase
their own rations, for which it is usually quite insufficient. At Tafilet the pay a private was receiving
would procure about a quarter of a small loaf of bread
per day; but with a few hundred square miles of palm-
groves, each tree richly laden with fruit, they did not
fare so badly, though on the journey back, where
nature did not offer them such assistance to the
pittance the Sultan paid them, their sufferings from
cold and hunger were extreme. Only the riding and
baggage animals of the Sultan and his immediate
officials receive fodder from the Government, the
various Kaids and the auxiliary troops—a kind of
yeomanry—that they bring with them being dependent upon their own means; and as on a part of the
Sultan's route from Fez to Tafilet barley cost no less

than 5s. a feed for a horse per night, the poor brutes fared ill. The camp at Tafilet, after three weeks' stay in one spot, though grain here was tolerably cheap, was literally surrounded with dead mules and horses. The quantity of baggage-animals was enormous. I was told by one who ought to be well informed that no less than 9600 horses and mules were fed by the Government each night, and there must have been 3000 or 4000 more belonging to the Kaids of districts and their retinues. A rough calculation gave the result that the Sultan must be paying some 3000 dollars — £500 — per night for fodder, or rather the cost of bringing it to Tafilet would have been as much as that ; for the merchants, who looked after their affairs far more keenly than his Majesty could afford time to do, were able to sell it, and make a small profit, at a price that gives this result, and no doubt the Sultan was charged far more. Even if the transactions necessary for purchasing it and bringing it this great distance were absolutely honest, it could not have cost him less than the sum mentioned. When one calculates the total amount spent on barley, averaging rather less over the whole time, on an expedition of nine months' duration, and when one adds to this the pay of the soldiery—for though often they do not get it, the Government invariably pays it out—and the food for the regular troops and the Sultan's immense retinue, not forgetting the presents that have to be given on the road, and then to the total the vast amount of swindling that takes place on every side, one will gather some idea of the cost of such an expedition. As a rule in the more adjacent portions of Morocco, so large are the levies of provisions, and so much of the *mona* is supplied by the governors of the districts, that the summer march of the Sultan affords a profit to the treasury, besides offering many opportunities for private pilfering. So poor are these districts of the Sahara, however, that few of the spots at which the army rested, with the exception of Tafilet and Askura, could have afforded to keep them supplied for more than one or two nights — and at Tafilet alone the Sultan remained three weeks.

A word of praise must be said for the organisation of, and order maintained amongst, so large a number of men as are collected in these vast camps. It must be remembered that every tribe and every district is represented by a certain number of members, conscribed by the Sultan previous to his setting out. These are often at open warfare with the surrounding tribes, members of all of which are also in the camp. Yet in spite of the fact that the men who have been at war with one another for genera-

tions perhaps become neighbours in the camp, few
or no broils occur, and the general behaviour, to
the onlooker, is excellent. At night the stillness
and quiet were remarkable, considering the class of
men, and the camp seemed almost deserted, few
moving about, though no doubt this is owing as
much to the fact that any man not carrying a
lantern is liable to be shot by a sentry as to anything else—for the price of a lantern is beyond the
reach of the ordinary soldier. From gun-fire at sunset to that at sunrise one can rest in absolute quiet,
except for the band that plays at nine o'clock outside
the Sultan's tent, first on the native *ghaita* and then
on European instruments — very badly it must be
acknowledged on the latter.

By day it is more lively : soldiers hurry hither and
thither, bright specks of colour in their gay, though
often ragged, clothing ; horses and mules, kicking up
the suffocating dust, gallop to and fro ; bugles sound ;
guns fire ; and there is all the stir and bustle of town-
life. I never tired of sitting in front of Kaid Maclean's tent, under its awning, and watching the
scene around me. As far as the eye could reach
in any direction extended the tents, some the great
circular *kubbas* with their gilt globes and patterns
in blue, some two-poled *utok*, and many resembling
the ordinary regulation tent of our own army. From

my vantage-ground I could watch the Sultan himself, a white figure seated under the tent of red and green cloth, and even recognise the Viziers as they stood before the open tent listening to his commands. I could see him, too, as he left and entered the private enclosure, and it was an interesting sight to watch how the whole life of the camp depended upon that one figure; how, when the time arrived for him to appear, the bodyguard ranged themselves into long line and bowed their heads as he passed them, crying, *"Allah ibarek amar Sidna!"* — "God grant blessings and his 'fulness' to our Lord!" It was easy to perceive how one and all, from the greatest of the Viziers to the least of the soldiery, lived in terror of, and with it almost adoration for, their Sultan. For of all autocrats there is none who holds power as does the Sultan of Morocco. Life and death, imprisonment and confiscation, as well as advancement and wealth, are all in his hands. A nod of his head, and a man rises from poverty to riches; another nod, and he dies secretly in prison. Yet in spite of the immense power wielded by Mulai el Hassen, he was a man of justice far above the general order of his people—a man who hated blood-shed, yet brave and cool in danger. Now and again his acts were cruel, but his cruelty was often justified by the crimes that had been committed by his victims. Tolerant to an astonishing degree, no people mourned his death more than the Jews, who, when he commenced his reign, were harshly persecuted in Morocco, and to-day possess a liberty far above that enjoyed by his Moorish subjects; and I doubt not that their mourning was far more sincere than that of the Moors, though, to tell the truth, *they* did not mourn to any very great extent, being either too busy getting in their harvest, or else too glad to pay off old debts and settle old blood-feuds without fear of immediate punishment, to make many signs of grief. Yet those who held the country's welfare at heart must have sincerely felt the loss, for it will be long, no doubt, before Morocco can boast as capable a ruler, taking everything into consideration, as the late Sultan.

One curious custom in vogue in the law of Morocco came under my notice while at Tafilet. This is the question of property left at death by officials in the native Government—everything becoming the property of the Crown. Unjust as this law may at first seem to be, there is no doubt that there is at bottom a certain amount of reason for it. A man, when appointed Kaid of a district or town, is usually possessed of no wealth of any sort. The Sultan it is who gives him his appointment, and any treasure or loot made out of his office is all owing to the fact that the Sultan put the man into the position to make it. It is, moreover, illegally made, for the extortions of governors are supposed to go to the treasury, with an allowance deducted for the maintenance of the Kaid and his family and retinue. Of course it would be far more just if the residue were handed back to the people from whom it had been extracted; but in Morocco such a course would not be, to say the least, considered at all a satisfactory method. During my stay in the Sultan's camp the Kaid of Shragna died, and before he had quitted this life more than a few hours a cordon of soldiers was drawn round his encampment and the entire concern brought into the Sultan's treasury—slaves, horses, mules, tents, furniture, and a large sum of money. However, Mulai el Hassen behaved with his customary leniency, and returned all the property with the exception of the money, at the same time expressing his regret at the death of so old and trusted a servant. There is no doubt the Kaid had been a good governor—for Morocco—and the return of his valuable women and slaves and horses and mules showed that his Majesty could appreciate obedience to his word when combined with a general system of justice and kindness to the tribe under him, and could reward in the manner he did, as an example to others, the men who practised it.

Very different was the fate of Kaid Ben Bu Shaib,` one of the governors of the tribe of Dukála, who owned a great castle not far inland from Mazagán, on the Atlantic coast. The goings on of this man's sons had become a byword throughout Morocco, and no young girl in the district was safe from their molestation. The old man himself may have been innocent enough of all crime; but the native Government very justly remarked that a man who could not govern his own sons could scarcely be trusted to look after a tribe of his fellow-men. So troops were despatched secretly to Dukála for fear of his treasure being carried away by members of his family, and the same day as he was seized at Tafilet his house was surrounded and his property carried off. One of his sons, I believe, escaped; the other was taken prisoner. The old man in the camp was seized by a guard in the presence of the Grand Vizier, Haj Amaati—who himself, only some six months later, was to share a like fate—and received some rough treatment before the irons were adjusted to his legs. It is said that during the years he had been governor he had amassed a large fortune, and that 120,000 dollars were discovered in his house; but for this I cannot answer for certain. He was taken a prisoner to Marakesh and there incarcerated, much to the joy of the people he had governed, for his extortion and

the worse crimes of his sons had drawn the hatred of
the whole tribe upon them. The law of responsibility for one's relations' doings is by no means a
bad law in Morocco, though in cases it may come
hard upon individuals. So largely do the Arabs
congregate in clans, and so easily can a single member of a clan escape after crime, that if it were not
that his relations were held responsible, no punishment could ever be meted out. But to take an
imaginary case. A village contains one or more
separate families — that is to say, the village may
be divided into two or three small clans, as the
case may be. A member of one commits a murder,
and steps over the boundary into the tribe governed
by another Kaid. He thus escapes the jurisdiction
of his own governor, who is incapable of seizing him,
for fear of trespassing upon the prerogatives of his
neighbouring official. It is only the relations in this
case who can accomplish his capture, and wherever
he goes he will probably be in touch with them.
Therefore when the Kaid puts a couple of his
brothers, for instance, in prison, it stirs up the remainder of his clan to obtain their release by handing
over the culprit to justice. They set off and catch
him and bring him a prisoner to the Kaid, who
probably lets the innocent men out of prison with a
fine. At this they are so much exasperated that

they take good care to confiscate amongst themselves the real culprit's property, and when he is freed from prison drive him out of the village, lest any more of his goings on should bring them into the same unhappy circumstances on a second occasion. Though not a very direct way of dealing out justice, this interfamily law of responsibility answers its purpose extremely well.

I had not intended to enter at all into the ways and manners of the natives of Morocco in this book; but the case of Kaid Ben Bu Shaib suffering for his sons' sins—as well, no doubt, as for his own extortions—an example of the system in common practice, was more or less forced upon me.

The sight of all others that I witnessed in the *mahalla* at Tafilet was the Sultan's procession, when he went to pray at, and returned from, the tomb of Mulai Ali Shereef, his ancestor, who lies buried near Abu Aam, and of whom I shall have more to say in my chapter on the oasis of Tafilet.

I have often witnessed the great pageants of Morocco; and since this very one, which took place at the end of November 1893, I have seen two others—the last entry of Mulai el Hassen into Marakesh the following month, and the first entry of Mulai Abdul Aziz, his successor, into Fez in July 1894. But for picturesqueness neither approached the procession that accompanied the Sultan from the camp to the tomb of his ancestor at Tafilet, for here there was every feature to add to the oriental appearance of the scene. The background of palms and desert, the thousands of tents, the gay uniforms — though the word is ill applied to costumes of every hue and colour — of the foot-soldiers, the long white robes of the cavalry, the gorgeous velvet saddles and still more gorgeous banners of gold brocade and embroideries, — all formed one of those strange scenes that one can witness now and again at the Court of the Moorish sovereign, so much in contrast to the usual dull colouring of the country and its inhabitants.

Nothing more beautiful could be imagined than the long procession of cavalry and infantry, of wild Berber and Arab tribesmen. A gentle wind unfurled the banners to the breeze, and raised the dust under the horses' feet just thickly enough to cast a white glamour over the whole scene, through which sparkled and glistened the flags and the golden globes of their poles, the bayonets and rifles of the infantry, and the heads of the spears of the guard. Then, mounted on his great white horse, saddled and trapped in green and gold, with the canopy of crimson velvet and gold embroidery held over his head, rode the Sultan, while huge black slaves on either hand waved long scarfs to keep the flies from his sacred person. In and out of the city of tents, for such the *mahalla* is, wound the procession, the line of march guarded by troops on either side.

Another example of the kindness and solicitude of the Sultan was manifested that day, for, on account of the heat, he countermanded personally the order that the infantry were to accompany him on his ride of two hours or so, and sent them back from a couple of hundred yards beyond the limits of his camp.

Quantities of slaves were on sale in the *mahalla*, and it was a pleasure to witness their absolute indifference to what was going on. They were free to run about round the slave-traders' tents, and merry were the pranks they played upon one another and on the Moors. Just opposite Kaid Maclean's tent, where I was installed, was a man who possessed seven, most of them young girls and boys, and a happier band I never saw. They laughed and gambolled from morning to night, and in their mischief often came and had a peep at me, running away again half frightened at their temerity. No doubt the freedom of the camp and the many strange sights it presented formed a delightful contrast to the desert journey they had so lately accomplished, for none of them had as yet learned to speak Arabic. Poor little

R

things! they had yet much to suffer in the cold
Atlas before they reached their various destinations
in Morocco.

At last, after nine days, my fate was decided upon.
I was to return to Marakesh in the company of Kaid
Maclean, and nothing could have met my wishes more
completely than this did. It was by the Kaid's own
entreaties that this had been decided upon, and now
that I was sufficiently recovered in health to travel,
we were both anxious to start. The cold weather
was setting in, and already we were experiencing
sharp frosts of a night, and we dreaded that every
day's delay would increase the probability of our
being snowed up in the high passes of the Atlas.

Dr Linares dined with us our last evening, and
he envied much the fact that we were leaving the
desert behind so shortly, with every chance of making
a quick journey, while he was to remain with the
Sultan and travel back by the short stages by which
the *mahalla* proceeded.

We could no longer claim the glory of being the
only three Europeans in Tafilet, for the camp had
received an addition, in the persons of seven French
deserters from the " Legion étrangère," who had
tramped all the way across the desert from Algeria,
a march which had taken them some two months
to accomplish. They arrived robbed of everything

but their ragged uniforms, and half-starved, to find but poor consolation in the Sultan's camp, although, in hopes of gaining employment, they became Moslems. Arabic names were given to each; but possessing no knowledge of the language, they could not remember them, or who was who, much to the amusement of the native soldiers, who, ill-fed though they were, spared whenever they could some trifle of food. On their arrival at Marakesh they were sent to Mogador, and handed over to the French authorities to suffer the punishment they had merited for their desertion. There was still another Frenchman in the camp, a Mons. Delbel, who to all intents and purposes was a Moslem, and was everywhere received as such. He has since published his notes upon the journey in the journal of the Geographical Society of Paris.

At length the day arrived, and long before dawn, by the light of lanterns, we struck camp, and in the bitter cold turned our horses' heads to the north and set out for Marakesh.

# CHAPTER XI.

### TAFILET OR TAFILELT.

TAFILET, Tafilelt, or Tafilalet, is said to derive its name, as already mentioned, from Filàl, a district in Arabia, and to have obtained its present form by the prefix *Ta*, a Berber word we know better in the form *Aït*, corresponding to the Arabic *Ulad*—"sons of." The final *t* is again of Berber derivation, and is also found under the form *at* or *ta*, which appears to be a feminine termination. Thus the whole name may be said to signify "The sons of the Filàl (district)," the feminine noun being used instead of the word "district" or some such term. This addition of the prefix *T* and the feminine termination I found to be in common use amongst the Berbers.

The fact that the root of the name owes its derivation to Arabic sources naturally tends to convince one that the oasis must previous to this time have borne some other, and Berber, title—that is

to say, before the invasion of this portion of the
Sahara by the Arabs in 707 A.D. In seeking for
an earlier name, one is at once led to think of
Sijilmassa, an undoubted Amazigh or Shelha word,
and which, even after the name Tafilet came into
general use, existed as the name of the capital of
the district until that town was destroyed toward
the end of the last century. It was this double
nomenclature, no doubt, that originally gave rise to
discussions on the part of geographers from the middle ages until the latter half of this century as to
Sijilmassa and Tafilet; for with that haphazard way
in which natives use the name of a district for a
town, and *vice versâ*, the two became hopelessly
confused, until the visit of René Caillié to these
parts in 1828 set matters somewhat at rest, although
over and over again since that date the discussion
has been revived. There is but little need nowadays to say much on that point. Caillié's and Rohlf's
notes, scanty though they are, yet valuable as being
the only records we have of the visits of Europeans
to Tafilet, have satisfactorily decided the question;
and it is now well known that Sijilmassa, though the
name often implied the district, was in reality the
capital of the oasis of Tafilet, or, as it is more properly spelt, Tafilelt. Such geographers as Marmol,
who in his 'Africa,' published in 1575-1599, speaks

of Tafilet as a great city of Numidia, must have
referred to Sijilmassa. Yet the question only last
year was revived in Tangier in connection with the
late Sultan Mulai el Hassen's expedition to the
Sahara.

Still, except from what we gather from medieval
geographers, and their evidence was mostly hearsay,
there is not one atom of proof which tends to show
that such a *town* as Tafilet ever existed, nor could
I during my stay there gain any information to that
effect, my informants one and all stating that Sijilmassa, or, as it is now called, Medinat el Aamra,
was the sole and only large town that ever existed
in Tafilet. Although many of the *ksor*, as the fortified villages are called, are of very considerable size,
there is none to which the term town can be aptly
applied.

Before offering any description of Tafilet as I saw
it, a few words as to its history may not prove out
of place.

Thanks to oriental historians, we are from time
to time able to obtain a glimpse of what was passing in this remote corner of the dominions of Morocco, although Tafilet was until comparatively lately
a separate kingdom, and to - day figures as such
amongst the titles of the reigning Sultan of Morocco,
who in summing up his dominions styles himself

"King of Tafilelt." Originally a settlement of the Amazigh or Shloh people — both terms signify "noble"—it was not until the year 88 A.H. (707 A.D.) that the Arabs appeared upon the scene, under the leadership of Musa ben Nasr, who, according to Ibn Khaldun, founded the town of Sijilmassa, though there seems every reason to believe that the name at least had been in existence from a much earlier period. In all probability the Berbers were dwelling there in thatch huts, and it was not until the Arab invasion that buildings of *tabia*, or native concrete, were raised, the sole material at hand at Tafilet, where stones are not to be found. We find that the divisions of the Berber people at this time (88 A.H.) inhabiting that and the surrounding district were the Beni Mgil, who to this day are a powerful tribe on the plains of the Wad Muluya, and the Dhu Mansur, though the second name is distinctly Arabic, and is probably a translation into that language of the Berber name, now unfortunately lost. Tafilelt itself was in the possession of an *ahlaf*, or confederation, the principal families of which were the Monabat and Amana. "At this time," says Leo Africanus, "the oasis was a great emporium of trade, a number of Moorish and European merchants being settled there, while a king governed and took taxes at the *douane*." It would be interesting to learn more of the European merchants, and one is inclined to think that *foreign* would have been a more appropriate term, possibly meaning Turks, Algerians, Tunisians, and Egyptians.

With varied local history, of which there is no need to make particular mention here, Tafilet maintained its trade importance throughout the middle ages, its rulers reigning under the title of Sultans of Sijilmassa. It was no doubt owing to the caravan-routes that so inhospitable a spot became so important a trading-place, for the extremes of heat and cold are cruel.

In 1536 the then King of Fez captured Tafilet for the Beni Merins, his own dynasty. In 1620, however, Ali Shereef arrived upon the scene from Yembo, in Arabia, bringing no doubt with him such a store of oriental knowledge and such a holy reputation from his life in Mecca that in a very short time he became a great man at Tafilet, and was appealed to as arbitrator in all questions. On his death his son, Mulai esh Shereef, succeeded to the holy birthright, styling himself King of Tafilet. Both lie buried near Rissani, in the district of Wad Ifli in Tafilet, and their tombs to-day are held in great reverence as founders of the present Fileli dynasty.

The third of the line, Mulai Reshid, in 1668 seized the throne of Morocco and became the first Fileli

Sultan, Mulai Abdul Aziz, who commenced his reign on the death of his father, Mulai el Hassen, in June last (1894), being the fifteenth ruler of this same dynasty.

Affairs in Morocco necessitated the residence of the Sultans being fixed there; but we hear of Mulai Ismail having made a journey to Tafilet, founded the still important *ksar* of Rissani, and rebuilt Sijilmassa; while in later times the Sultan Sidi Mohammed ben Abdullah visited Tafilet (in 1783 - 84). Curiously enough, the two Sultans who made this long journey, Sidi Mohammed ben Abdullah and Mulai el Hassen, lie buried in the same tomb at Rabat.

In local wars that occurred at the end of the last century Sijilmassa was destroyed, and nothing remains to-day of the great town but acres, almost miles, of shapeless ruins, with a mosque still in tolerably good condition. These ruins extend for some five miles along the east bank of the Wad Ziz.

Tafilet may be said to consist of a long strip of irrigated land extending along the parallel beds of the Wad Ziz and the Wad Gheris. Although the northern districts of Ertib (Reteb) and Medaghra are often included under the name of Tafilet, they seem in the eyes of the natives to be in reality separate districts, and as such I shall treat them.

Before discussing the actual oasis, some words
ought to be written describing the means by which
this portion of the desert is rendered capable of cultivation.    I have elsewhere briefly described the
course of the Wad Gheris; it now remains to briefly
trace that of the Wad Ziz.

The Wad Ziz rises in the Atlas Mountains, near
that portion of the chain to which the natives
apply the name Jibel Ayashi, near the Zauia Sidi
Hamza, situated close to the pass of Tizi'n Telremt,
where the trade-road from Fez to Tafilet crosses the
main chain of the Atlas.    Thence the Wad Ziz takes
a southerly course, which it pursues with but the
slightest deviation throughout.    This upper district,
the slopes of the Atlas which form the basin of the
river, is known as the province of Wad Ziz.    Some
thirty miles from its source ("one day's journey") it
is joined by the Wad Guers, flowing from the Atlas,
and rising some twenty miles to the west, on the
western slopes of Jibel Ayashi.    The Berber tribes
of Aït bu Hadidu, a division of the Aït Atta, and the
Aït Ishak inhabit these slopes.    The united rivers,
flowing south and passing through Tialallil, drain
the district of El Khanek, south of which the Wad
Ziz irrigated the oasis of Medaghra, then Ertib, and
finally, *via* Tizimi, Tafilet is reached, where by a
wonderful system of irrigation some 400 square miles

of desert are put under cultivation. It is only after rains that the Wad Ziz and Wad Gheris, which unite at the southern end of the Tafilet oasis, ever reach the great lake, or marsh, Dayet ed Daura, where the sand exhausts the water.

The Wad Ziz at Tafilet, although so large a quantity of its waters is drained off to irrigate the oases of Medaghra and Ertib, was at the time of my visit in November 1893—after a very hot and dry season —still well supplied with water. The channel is deeply sunk between high clay and sandy banks, the actual stream occupying perhaps one-third of the river-bed, and averaging from 60 to 100 feet in breadth ; the depth at the ford where I crossed it, at the north end of the ruins of Sijilmassa, being some 2 feet. The water is transparent, and very fast flowing, the river often splitting up into a number of small streams in the course. That the fall in altitude as the river proceeds must be large is easily perceived, as otherwise the water, drained off no very great distance above, could not be brought, except by artificial means, to the level of the high river-banks, which must be from 30 to 40 feet above the level of its course. With regard to the system of irrigation, I shall have more to tell farther on.

If one asks a native where he is going, and he replies to Tafilet, one may generally make certain

that he is on his way to one of the seven districts
of the oasis which I am now about to enumerate,
and *not* to either Ertib or Medaghra, which both
lie farther north, though it seems that by Europeans
they are included in the district of Tafilet.

These seven provinces are—

    (i.) On the north, Tizimi.

    (ii.) On the west, Es Sifa.

    (iii.) On the south-west, Wad el Melha.

    (iv.) In the centre, Wad Ifli.

    (v.) On the south, Es Sefalat.

    (vi.) On the east, El Ghorfa.

    (vii.) And to the north-east, Tanijiud.

To attempt to correctly estimate the extent of
ground under cultivation would be too hazardous
to be of any value, for the oasis varies so much in
width from place to place, according as the irrigating
canals are taken far afield or not, that nothing short
of a careful survey could give a satisfactory result.
Again, it is impossible to state with accuracy the
southern limits of the oasis, for much of the land
situated south of the junction of the Wad Ziz and
the Wad Gheris is only capable of cultivation after
exceedingly heavy rains, when natives of the Aït
Atta tribe till the banks as far as the Dayet ed
Daura. From the northern limit of the oasis of
Tizimi to the junction of the rivers Ziz and Gheris

may be safely estimated at from forty to fifty miles, the average width of this portion of the oasis being about ten miles. All this district of, say, 450 square miles, is under dense palm cultivation. By this, however, one must not understand the whole oasis, for I have purposely ignored all that lies south of the meeting of the two rivers, a district which depends greatly upon floods and the melting of the Atlas snows for its varied supply, and what might be true of one year might be a gross exaggeration or underrating for any other season.

I have above enumerated the seven districts into which the oasis of Tafilet is divided. It now remains to make a few notes about each of these divisions. To take them in geographical order.

(i.) *Tizimi*, or Aït Izimi, is a large district extending along the west bank of the Wad Tizimi, as the main channel of the Wad Ziz is called at this part of its course, from the name of the district it passes through. The inhabitants of Tizimi are Arabs, though the name is essentially a Berber one, leading one to think that the original Berbers must have been displaced by Arab tribes. The present inhabitants are the Tizimi branch of the Ahl Subah Arabs, though one or two *ksor* belong to Shereefian families. Constant fighting is occurring in this part, owing to the proximity of the

Berbers at Medaghra and Ertib. Tizimi contains a great number of palm-trees and several large *ksor*, the principal being Kasbat el Barania, Kasbat ben Ali, and Ksar bel Hassen. To the north-west of Tizimi, a mile or so across the desert, is the oasis of Mulai Brahim, where is the tomb of the saint so named, a place of pilgrimage. The oasis properly belongs to Tizimi, and is in the hands of the Shereefs and the Ahl Subah. I saw the tomb when passing through Tizimi. It is a large, domed, square building, painted white, and surrounded by a few smaller tombs of less important Shereefs.

Separating Tizimi from the two nearest districts, Es Sifa on the south-west and Tanijiud on the south-east, is a strip of desert varying in extent from two to five miles, through which the Wad Ziz flows in a sandy bed, a few oleanders and coarse herbage being the only signs of vegetation on its banks.

(ii.) *Es Sifa* is the next district, forming the west side of the oasis. It lies between the Wad Gheris and the Wad Ziz, which are here some four to five miles apart, their courses being almost parallel. The district is, however, irrigated almost entirely from the Wad Ziz, the Gheris being too salt for the purpose. This part of Tafilet is poor enough. The palms do not flourish well, the irrigation canals are in ill repair, the water-supply is very poor, the garden walls are broken down, and the *ksor* are few and far between. The immediate surroundings of El Meharza, in which I spent a night, and of which I have already given a short description, appear the best kept portion of this district of the oasis. El Meharza lies high above the Wad Gheris on its east bank, and is a place with pretensions to size and importance.

(iii.) *Wad el Melha*, or salt river, so called from the Wad Gheris, which forms its western boundary, is the next district, forming the south - western province of Tafilet. Like Es Sifa, it lies between the Wad Ziz and the Gheris, and though a smaller district than this last, it is more fertile and better irrigated. Taghranjiut is its principal *ksar*, situated in a portion of the district known as Beled el Riad, or " garden - land," about equidistant from the two rivers.

(iv.) *Es Sefalat* forms the southern boundary of the oasis proper, and is a large and fertile district, bounded on the west by the Gheris, while it extends to the east considerably across the Wad Ziz, which almost bisects it. This district possesses the largest *ksar* in the whole oasis—namely, Tabuassamt, which lies on the west bank of the Wad Ziz. Although so large, the *ksar* is of no great importance, though it

forms a caravanserai for the caravans going to the
Sudan and Draa valley.    However, little or none of
the merchandise which passes through it is exposed
for sale there, the caravans usually arriving late at
night and leaving before dawn.

(v.) *El Ghorfa*, or Ghorfa, lies to the east and
north-east of Es Sefalat, and extends from that district to the desert.    Although its western portion
is well watered and cultivated, the east seems to have
suffered from the drifting sands, and boasts no great
fertility.    It contains many *ksor*, but being subject
to attacks on the part of the Berbers and Arabs of
the Sahara, no great trade is possible.    The southern
boundary of El Ghorfa is the Sebkhat Aamar, a large
salt lake, the monopoly for working the deposits of
which rests with the Shereefs, who send most of the
salt to the great market near the tomb of Mulai Ali
Shereef in the district of Wad Ifli, some fifteen miles
distant.

(vi.) *Tanijiud* is the north-east province of Tafilet,
and, like Ghorfa, is bounded on the east by the desert.
Its water-supply, like that of the last-mentioned district, is brought by canal from the Wad Ziz, diverging
from the main channel of that river at Iniyerdi in
Medaghra.    The cutting off of this water-supply by
the Berbers higher up the valley is a constant cause
of warfare.    Several other small channels from the

Ziz reach Ghorfa and Tanijiud, all eventually becoming exhausted in cultivation or in the desert. The principal *ksar* of Tanijiud is that of Ulad Yusef, who are, as their name implies ("sons of Joseph"), Arabs. This *ksar* is situated on the extreme edge of the oasis, and almost in the desert, amongst the bare stony hills found on this, the north-east portion of Tafilet.

(vii.) *Wad Ifli*, the sole remaining district to be mentioned, forms the centre of the oasis, and is surrounded by the six others of which I have just given a brief description. All the religion, trade, and interest of Tafilet centres in this district. Its position, surrounded as it is by friendly people, ensures safety against attack from without, and it is no doubt as much owing to this cause as any other that Wad Ifli forms the most prosperous part of Tafilet. No attack could be made upon it until the outlying districts had been passed, and these, if not to protect the centre state, at least for their own safety, would offer a very stubborn resistance. It was no doubt largely on this account, and also as its position allows of its being easily and well irrigated, that the ancient Amazighs founded there the city of Sijilmassa, on the banks of the Wad Ziz, which, to judge from its ruins, must in its most flourishing days have extended some five miles along the river-bank. It is in Ifli, too,

S

that nowadays, when Sijilmassa has ceased to exist, the life and soul of Tafilet are found. Here is interred Mulai Ali Shereef, founder of the Fileli dynasty, while near by is the domed tomb of Mulai Esh Shereef, his son, King of Tafilet. In Abuaam, the richest of its many *ksor*, congregate and live the merchants of Fez, in whose hands is practically not only the entire local trade, but also that of the Sudan beyond. It is the influence of these merchants that has brought about improvements in the building of the houses, and luxuries within. Close by is the large *ksar* of Rissani, the official residence of the governors of Tafilet, where some fifty soldiers are permanently quartered, though any attempt to interfere with local affairs would cost them their lives. Here too in large *ksor* live the Shereefs, existing in luxury compared to their neighbours, for they receive a subsidy in money and kind from the reigning Sultans. The great market, too, of Tafilet is there, the Arbaa, or Wednesday market, of Mulai Ali Shereef, which I shall describe anon. In fact it is in Ifli, with its well-kept canals and limitless supply of water, with its bridges and walled gardens, its large *ksor* and saints' tombs, that all that is prosperous and wealthy in Tafilet is to be found, and it is little wonder that the inhabitants of this quarter of the oasis give themselves airs above the rest of the population. Gurlan, which Caillié mentions as the capital at the time of his visit to Tafilet in 1828, no longer plays a part of any importance in the oasis, though it still exists as a large *ksar*.

Having briefly described the differeut districts of the oasis, meution must now be made of the system of irrigation employed in the cultivation of so large an extent of soil. Fortunately the lie of the land is such that water has not to be raised by artificial means, the gradual slope of the valley allowing of the drawing of inexhaustible water-supplies from the Wad Ziz. Innumerable canals and conduits pierce the oasis in every direction, some of them as much as 15 or 20 feet in width and of considerable depth, while the water is pure and transparent, and flows very fast.

Near the ruins of Medinat el Aamra, or Sijil-massa, is the largest and deepest canal I saw, the channel bricked and bridged wherever the road or a track crosses it. This channel must be from 20 to 30 feet in breadth, and although my visit was made after a long and exceptionally dry summer, the water was some 4 to 6 feet in depth, flowing very swiftly. Although Sijilmassa stood on the actual brink of the river, the banks are so high that no water could be raised to the level of the town except on donkey-back, or by women in jars, and this canal,

which draws off so large a quantity of water from
much higher up the river, was no doubt built on this
account.   So numerous and so connected one with
another are the canals and conduits of the oasis,
that one crosses them almost at every 50 yards or so.
These watercourses are usually raised above the surface of the surrounding ground by banks at each
side, so that by cutting away a foot or so of bank
the stream can be turned on to the level of the soil,
and quickly floods the ground to be irrigated.   The
land between the canals — that is to say, the plots
of cultivated soil — are usually divided into square
beds, varying from 10 to 20 yards in length and
breadth, and divided from one another by low banks
of earth, so that one portion can be flooded without
wasting water unnecessarily on the ground or crop
that may not require it.   Often small channels are
cut on the top of these low earth-banks, so that
the stream can be carried here and there in every
direction, and turned on just where it is needed.
Except to the western side of the Wad Gheris, the
crops are all grown under the palm-trees.   In El
Unja, however, as the land in question is called,
there are but few palm-groves.

It is seldom in the oasis of Tafilet that one's
view extends to more than 100 yards or so in any
direction.   This is owing to the extraordinary thick

growth of the date-palms, which rise on all sides a
bewildering forest of straight stems. In Ifli, too,

*In Tafilet.*

the high walls of the gardens obstruct one's vision
in every direction. These walls are built of the

native concrete, *tabia*, and are often so high that only the tops of the fruit-trees within appear above them. The water from the irrigating channels finds ingress into these gardens by subterranean conduits, while small bridges cross the roads, generally formed by palm-trunks laid from side to side and covered with sand. One comes quite suddenly upon the high-walled *ksor*, which, until one has approached them nearly, are entirely hidden by the gardens and palms. The outer portions of the oasis are less thickly grown over with palms, but the line between the desert sand and the alluvial soil and irrigated oasis is clearly defined. One walks out of a green field of palm-trees ankle-deep into soft yellow sand, and one's vision stretches away over undulating white hills the very glare of which is painful to the sight. Here and there throughout the oasis are large open spaces, usually for the purpose of drying the dates in, and now and again for local markets, or *sôks*. The walled villages, too, often have a clear space surrounding them of 20 yards or so of open ground, to allow the sight of the attacking force in their continual intertribal wars.

Nothing more bewildering can be imagined than the roads, or tracks, that thread the oasis. Owing to the great value of land they are as narrow as is practicable, and turn and twist in every direction amongst the gardens. In going from El Meharza in Sifa to Dar el baida on the east side of the oasis on the borders of the desert, although the general direction is south-east, one is often travelling due north or due south, owing to the extraordinary turns the path takes amongst the walled gardens of the district of Wad Ifli.

The *ksor* of Tafilet all follow much the same design of building, and though I entered several and saw many, they were so alike one to the other that a general description will be sufficient, and answer equally well for all.

These villages are usually square or oblong, surrounded by high *tabia* walls of great thickness, protected at intervals by towers, sometimes the same height as the walls, and often considerably taller. One gate alone gives entrance to the *ksar*, and this is always closed from sunset to dawn. These gates are often double, there being a turn half-way through, so that from without one is not able to obtain a view of what lies within. At times, surrounding the whole *ksar*, is a deep ditch, often formed by the digging out of the soil for material for the walls, but nevertheless of great use in time of war. A common practice in warfare, as already mentioned, is to bring, by means of a canal, water to the foundations of the walls of the *ksar*. The action of the stream upon the soft *tabia* is quick and sure, and in an hour or two a breach is formed. These ditches, therefore, prevent the immediate application of this plan, and are generally drained into the surrounding fields, so that before the dangerous element reaches the wall it is carried off elsewhere.

A guard is placed at the gate, and a stranger entering is questioned as to his business and scrutinised. I myself went through this process on entering Meharza at Sifa, when in disguise ; but my men were quick in answering the questions, and we hurried on, so that I was not suspected for a moment. Few or no windows look out from the outside walls of the *ksar*, but loopholes are common in case of attack from without.

Within the walls a certain amount of regularity and good building is to be found. One generally, after passing through the gate, enters a large court, or square, from which the streets lead into the more thickly inhabited portion of the *ksar*. These squares are usually surrounded on three sides by houses, the fourth side consisting of the outer wall, in which the gate is situated. The houses are solid and very large, often several storeys in height. Windows open out into the streets, which is seldom found in the private houses of the large towns of Morocco. As a rule, the windows and doors are small, wood being a valuable commodity, as it has to be carried from a long distance, generally from the Atlas slopes of Beni Mgild and Aït Yussi to the north of the basin of the Wad Ziz. Palm-tree trunks are used as rafters and ceilings, though I was informed that in some of the houses of·the wealthier Shereefs handsome ceilings in decorated plaster and painted wood are found, the artists and workmen having been brought from Fez for the purpose of decorating them. The use of lime is uncommon, and only the better-class houses are whitewashed within, and very few indeed on the outside, the ordinary population being content with a plastering of light mud, which, when well applied, has by no means a bad effect, much resembling our plaster walls in colour and surface. The streets of the *ksor* are usually narrow, and in many cases the houses are built above them, forming dark tunnels, in piercing which, if one does not wish to fall into some hole or bang one's head against a low beam, one has to light a match or candle. *Fondaks*, or caravanserais, are common, usually consisting of large open squares, surrounded by a colonnade supported on rough *tabia* pillars.

The local markets are not held within the *ksor*, but in the open. There are several large weekly *sôks* in Tafilet, but that which is by far the most important is the Arbaa, or Wednesday market of

Mulai Ali Shereef.  It lies close to the tomb of
that saint, and within a short distance of Abuaam and Rissani.  Although, as a rule, the natives

*A Corner of a Sôk —Early Morning.*

bring their small tents—*gaitons*—in which to expose their goods, there are, as well, a number of
small domed huts built of clay and mud bricks,

much resembling beehives in appearance, the dome being rather more elongated. In this the native can sit protected from the fierce rays of the sun and vend his wares. Little rain falls at Tafilet, and these mud hovels are therefore of a permanent nature : so often are the goods displayed for sale perishable from heat, that they are of great benefit to both buyer and seller. Such articles as vegetables, fruit, sugar, candles, matches, &c., would be useless after an hour or so of exposure to the sun in Tafilet in summer.

Some mention must here be made of Sijilmassa, or, as it is now called, Medinat el Aamra, which for so many centuries formed the capital of Tafilet. Mulai el Hassen during his visit to Tafilet, and only the day before my arrival in that place, made an expedition to the ruins of the old city and camped for the night there, praying in the half-ruined mosque. Little can now be traced of the place : immense blocks of *tabia* lie scattered in every direction for some five miles along the east bank of the Wad Ziz, but rank vegetation covers a considerable portion, while in other places the land is cultivated in such spots as render cultivation practicable. Several *ksor* of more or less modern construction exist amongst the ruins. A great amount of reverence is still paid to the spot; and the yearly prayers on the Eid el Kebir and Eid Soreir are held in the *msala* adjoining the mosque, the minaret of which still remains.

I found the natives loath to talk of Sijilmassa, for after my arrival in the Sultan's camp I made no pretence of being a Moslem. At the same time they were greatly surprised that I had ever heard of, or knew anything about, the place, and not a little proud that such was the case. Their reticence I put down to the fact that there is a tradition of untold gold buried in the city—a tradition that exists about every ancient site in Morocco. The inventive genius of newspaper correspondents caused to be circulated in the English newspapers a report that Mulai el Hassen, the late Sultan, had recovered this treasure and built an immense fortress to conceal it in; but I fear, as I was present during nearly the entire visit of the Sultan to Tafilet, and saw his Shereefian Majesty every day, that the story must be discredited. So far from obtaining treasure, I estimate the expense to his Majesty of his stay at Tafilet of twenty days at a sum of nearly a million of dollars.

Of the foundation of Sijilmassa the natives seem to know but little. They, as is nearly always the case, connect its origin with the *Rumin*, or Romans, a term the Moslems use for any nation not professing Islam, and which is far more likely in this case to mean the

Amazighs or original Berbers than any one else; for, as already mentioned, it is quite clear that the Romans never reached as far as this, though I am inclined to believe the Carthaginians, if never actually in Tafilet, approached it very closely.

No discoveries of any great importance in the way of buildings are likely to be made in Sijilmassa, though bronze implements are reported to be found there, for apparently all the buildings were constructed of *tabia* or a poor form of brick. A bridge of arches crosses the Wad Ziz at one portion of the ruins; but unfortunately I was not able to see of what it was constructed, as I only caught a distant view of it, and it appears to be coated with yellow plaster. Probably it is built of brick and covered with cement, or· possibly stone was brought from Jibel Saghru for the purpose.

The inhabitants of Tafilet consist of both Arabs and Berbers, with a considerable number of Jews.

The Arab population, which is considerably the largest, is divided into four tribes or divisions—

1. The Shereefian families;
2. Ahl Subah Arabs;
3. Beni Mohammed;
4. Tafilet Arabs;

while the Berbers consist almost entirely of members of the large and powerful tribe of Aït Atta; and there are as well the Haratin, or free blacks, who may be classed as Berbers, their language being Amazigh in character, though their blood is largely tainted with negro strain. They come from the Wad Draa, and are employed as labourers in the fields. I have spoken in the earlier portion of my book of these Haratin, and little remains to be said here. In colour they are very dark, but the features usually incline more to Berber than to negro. Considered as a lower class, the Arabs and Berbers never inter-marry with them, though they themselves are proud of the fact of their freedom, which their name of Haratin implies.

The Shereefian families, inhabiting large *ksor* of their own, are principally the descendants of Mulai Ali Shereef, who came from Yembo in Arabia. They live and marry principally among their own class, the first wife of a Shereef nearly always being a Shereefa, though after that they will marry from the better native or Fez people. The children, no matter who the mother may be, are Shereefs, though the child of a Shereefa whose husband is not a Shereef has no claim to the title. Even the sons of Shereefs by purchased slave-girls are Shereefs. It is from these families that the reigning Sultans choose a governor or arbitrator to be their repre-sentative at Tafilet. At the time of my visit to

the oasis this post was held by Mulai Reshid, a
brother of Mulai el Hassen, whom I saw upon
several occasions. He was slightly younger than
the Sultan in appearance, of vivacious and pleasant
manner, and seemed justly very popular.

The Ahl Subah are a powerful Arab tribe of desert
propensities, always fighting with their neighbours or
amongst themselves, great horsemen, and apparently, like their steeds, indefatigable. Their warfare
with the Berbers is unceasing, and at the time of my
stay in the Sultan's camp a skirmish took place between the two in the very presence of Mulai el
Hassen, several on both sides being killed, altogether
some fifteen it is said. The Sultan promptly imprisoned the ringleaders of each party; but such
force was brought to bear upon him by the prisoners'
fellow-tribesmen that he was obliged to release them
in the course of a few days.

The Beni Mohammed are an Arab tribe much resembling the Ahl Subah in character and appearance.
They live in *ksor* of their own. The Tafilet Arabs
consist probably of a mixture of tribes, and have
unmistakable signs of Berber blood. Gentle, of
kindly nature, but fierce when roused, they are an
excellent people, and have a certain charm of manner
which is indescribable, due not a little to their mel-
odious voices and the beautiful Arabic they talk.

Their colour is usually dark and their faces rather expressionless, though lacking the coarseness often found in those of the other Arab tribes.

Of the Aït Atta I have already spoken in the earlier portion of this book. They are a fierce tribe of Berbers, intent upon the annexation of everybody else's country and property, and have extended their conquests in every direction, from the Draa to the Ziz basin. The oases of Medaghra and Ertib, often included in Tafilet, are in their hands, the only Arabs being a sprinkling of Shereefs. The Aït Atta are said to have captured these lands at the beginning of this century.

The Jews exist in Tafilet under much the same conditions as in Dads, of which a full description has already been given—that is to say, each Jew family lives under the protection of some Moslem, be he Arab or Berber.

The costumes worn by the Berbers and Arabs of Tafilet are almost identical : in the former case the long linen *chamira* is never belted at the waist, the Berbers, for some reason which I was unable to discover, objecting to this. The *jelab*, or hooded garment sewn up the front, is unknown, the *haik* and *haidus* forming the costume of both peoples. The *khenif*, or black cloak with its strange red mark on the back, is seldom seen, except in cases of Shloh from the mountains who come with caravans; while the embroidered short brown *jelab* of the Riffi who accompanied me was considered as a marvellous curiosity by the natives.

The women wear either indigo-blue dyed cotton or jute, called *khent*, or else coarse woollen *haiks* of native manufacture. Leo Africanus mentions in his notes upon this district that large quantities of indigo were grown there, but nowadays all the blue *khent* is imported from London or Bombay. Amber beads, silver and coral necklaces, silver anklets and bracelets, are worn, according to the wealth of the families. The women are usually short and coarse in appearance, dirty and loud voiced. No doubt the harems contain better specimens, but those we saw in the open could be safely, one would think, permitted to go abroad with uncovered faces. The children are sometimes pretty; but soap is an expensive luxury in Tafilet, and washing seems to be an annual affair, if practised as often. However, I saw men bathing in the Wad Ziz as I forded that river on one occasion. The women are a great deal tattooed, the nose, forehead, and chin being often highly decorated by this process. They perform all the housework, fetch water, mind the cattle, collect firewood, and take vegetables, &c., to market—in fact every duty except that of fighting seems to fall to their lot.

T

The men are armed with guns and swords. Every
youth, as soon as he reaches a certain age, is obliged
to purchase a gun, all his earnings being saved for
this purpose. Although the most common weapon
is the flintlock of the country, a quantity of cheap
double-barrelled guns, all muzzle-loading, are to be
found. The native of Tafilet has a hankering after
bullets that fit a No. 12 bore, and a charge of loose
buckshot and nails he looks upon as a most estimable
way of attacking his enemy. Little quarter is given:
in the case of fighting between Arabs and Berbers,
all males taken prisoner who are able to carry arms
are mercilessly killed, usually stabbed with knives,
—powder and shot, as already mentioned, being
expensive.

The saddlery is of native design, but the bridles
are usually brought from Algeria, being of the style
used by the Franco-Arab cavalry of that country.
This the Filelis find stronger than their own.

The food of the common people consists principally
of gruel and *kuskusu*, the latter at times garnished
with vegetables, and on rare occasions with meat or
fowl; but it may be safely said that so great is the
poverty in Tafilet that the poorer classes, although
never wanting for absolute food, do not taste meat
two or three times in the year, mutton on the Eid
el Kebir being often the sole occasion.

The coinage to-day in use in Tafilet consists almost entirely of the Moorish money struck in Paris, and although in Morocco City all kinds of damaged Spanish silver is in use, at Tafilet it is not accepted. The rates in use at Tafilet are quite different to elsewhere. All sums of money are calculated in *mitkals* and *okeas*, neither of which exist in coin, being only verbal terms. In Morocco 12½ *mitkals* go to the Spanish dollar, and 10 *okeas* to the *mitkal*, which gives 125 *okeas* to the dollar; but at Tafilet, although 10 *okeas* compose a *mitkal*, 5 *mitkals* complete the dollar, so that 50 *okeas* is the value of a Spanish dollar there, instead of 125 *okeas*. However, as the same coins are in use all over the country, and the *okea* and *mitkal* are only expressions, the result is the same, though at first confusing. This change in calculation begins at Dads, and is found in the districts east of that country.

With regard to the products of Tafilet, the most important without doubt are the dates, and it is from this culture that the inhabitants are enabled to exist at all. Not only are they sent by caravan all over Morocco, but there are merchants of Fez who ship large quantities to London, and we often eat here in the centre of civilisation dates that are grown in this far-away and little-known oasis, and which have been carried on mule or donkey back over the hot

arid desert and the snowy passes of the Atlas Mountains. To realise the enormous quantity of dates
grown at Tafilet one must see the oasis. The palms,
planted so thickly and so closely together as to
obstruct one's vision in every direction, form a
gigantic forest, to pass through which, by the
narrow lanes, is bewildering. I have explained elsewhere by what means the system of irrigation is
carried on, and the scanty crops of vegetables and
lucerne grown amongst them. The groves of the
finest date-palms are in the vicinity of Abuaam in
the district of Wad Ifli, and here they are nearly
all enclosed in high walls. It is these dates, the
*Bu Skri* and *Bu Kfus*, that are most prized, and
luscious they are indeed, though they spoil by
travelling. The commoner varieties are eaten in
the country, or given as fodder to the cattle, goats,
and horses. In the outer portions of the oasis the
palm-groves are not walled, and the expense of
building walls would not be repaid by the price
realised for the commoner varieties of dates. Between the Wad Gheris and the Wad Ziz, in the
province of Es Sifa, but few walls are found in
repair, and the want of proper irrigation has caused
the date-palms to deteriorate; but near Abuaam
and Rissani the gardens are nearly all in the possession of the Shereefs, and are kept in a state of ex-

cellent repair. The dates were ripe at the time of
my visit (November), and I was able to see not
only the plucking but also the drying process. The
labourers, principally the Haratin, are very skilful
in climbing the palms. When the summit is reached
either the entire bunch is cut off or else shaken, in
either case the dates falling to the ground. Here
they are collected into panniers, which are placed
upon the backs of donkeys and taken to the drying-
grounds. They are always plucked slightly unripe,
as otherwise they fall to the ground themselves, and
are rotted by the irrigation. At the drying-grounds
—large open spaces, sometimes surrounded with walls
—the dates are laid in the sun, a guard, often of
women, being placed over them ; for although they
never object to one's picking up a handful for one's
own consumption, the fruit would probably be stolen in
far larger quantities were they left absolutely without
watchers. These guards usually live in brown *ghiem*,
as the hair tents of the Arabs are called, but sometimes build themselves huts of palm-leaves. The
dates are poured in great heaps upon the ground,
being turned over by the women every now and
again to allow of the sun reaching them. The sight
of acres of great heaps of dates is a most curious one.
There are various processes of treating the dates.
Some kinds are merely sun-dried and left single ;

others are crushed into solid masses, which are sewn
up in basket-work for transport; while others again,
used by the poor natives when travelling, are crushed
into the shape and size of turkeys' eggs, and are easier
to carry in this manner. On one occasion, travelling
in Morocco, I was given one of those solidified date-
balls by a native of Tafilet, who was journeying to
Tangier on his way to take ship to Mecca. Its
appearance and feel was that of a stone, its weight
that of lead! I kept it for some time in my house,
and visitors used to take it for a fossil. What became
of it I do not know, but I never found any native of
North Morocco brave enough to attempt to eat it.
Yet by the donor it was considered a great luxury.

Besides the dates, crops of wheat and barley are
grown at Tafilet, especially in the land to the west
of the Gheris, called Beled el Unja. Millet and
maize, however, are more common, and form the
principal food of the people. In the gardens
cabbages, onions, peas, beans, grapes, pomegranates,
apples, pears, gourds, and melons flourish, but are
only cultivated by the richer classes, turnips being
the favourite vegetable of the poor. Large quantities
of lucerne are grown in the shade of the palm-trees,
and stored away for winter fodder for the horses
and cattle.

The only export of manufactured goods from

Tafilet are the prepared skins, famous all over Morocco as *jeld el Fileli*, and fine *haiks*, the fleece of the native sheep being very fine.

Gunsmiths and silversmiths, the latter principally Jews, are to be found in numbers, but the weapons are of coarse manufacture; while such trades as the making of sandals, universally worn by the poorer Arabs and Berbers, flourish. All good shoes are brought from Fez, those made in Tafilet, in spite of the fine leather, being very inferior. Bags for *kiff*, the chopped hemp which the natives smoke, are made in considerable quantities and sent to Morocco. These bags are generally some 6 inches in length by 3 in width. An outside cover or shell, open at one of the narrow ends, allows the bag with its several pockets to be drawn out. The whole is worn round the neck on a string, which, passing through the two upper corners of the outside bag, is made fast to that inside, so that to get at the *kiff* the outer cover is slid up the two strings.

Antimony and lead are both found in the vicinity of Tafilet, and the former, known as *kohl el Fileli*, was once famous, but it can be imported into Morocco nowadays from Europe at a cheaper rate than it can be worked and sent from Tafilet. The lead worked is only used for bullets, and is obtained merely in small quantities.

The aromatic gums which reach Fez from Tafilet are not products of the oasis, but are brought thither to the Fez merchants in small quantities from the different tribes, a good deal from the Sudan.

The imports into Tafilet exceed very considerably in value the exports. Most caravans travel from Fez, the road being better and safer than that from Morocco City. Cotton goods, shoes, *khent*, silk belts and handkerchiefs, iron bars, candles, sugar, and green tea, form the principal imports, a good deal of the whole being sold at Abuaam to other merchants and tribes, who send it farther afield into the Sahara and Sudan. The return caravans take away dates and Sudan produce.

The slave-trade flourishes at Tafilet, the slaves being brought direct to that spot from the Sudan. At the time of my visit they were being freely hawked about the Sultan's camp. The girls of the Hausa country fetched the best prices, being considered more cheerful and neater than those from farther west. The prices averaged from 30 to 40 dollars for boys, and up to 100 and 120 dollars for young girls.

The great veneration bestowed by the Moors and Arabs upon deceased saints is as noticeable at Tafilet as elsewhere. Although the founder of the present ruling dynasty of Morocco and his son lie buried in

the oasis, their tombs are reverenced more by strangers
than by the inhabitants, though the name of Mulai
Ali Shereef is continually upon their lips. But Mulai
Ali Shereef never founded a brotherhood, and this
has to some extent detracted from the esteem that
would have accrued to his memory, these societies
of devotees doing more to keep up the reputation of
their founders than any number of stray pilgrims
could do. The love of belonging to some particular brotherhood is extremely noticeable amongst
the superstitious people of the Sahara, who are
far more religious than their brethren in Morocco
proper. Some follow the sect of the *Taiebiya*, or
followers of Mulai Taieb of Wazan; some are
*Aissoua* and practise the rites of Sidi ben Aissa of
Meknas; some again *Hamacha*, devotees of Sidi
Ali ben Hamduch; some of Mulai Abdul Kader
el Jilani of Baghdad. But the most favoured of
all in this portion of the Sahara is the sect of the
*Derkauiya*, or followers of Mulai Ali and Mulai el
Arbi el Derkaui, whose patrons lie buried, one in
the Sahara, the other in the tribe - lands of the
Beni Zerual to the north - east of Fez. The *Der-
kauis* are distinguished by carrying a long stick,
and by wearing round their necks a string of large
wooden beads, often of preposterous size. Often,
too, a green turban decorates the head, a sign in

the East of the accomplishment of the pilgrimage
to Mecca or of holy descent from the Prophet, but
here meaning neither, being merely a sign of ex-
ceeding devotion to the sect. Mulai Suleiman, who
reigned as Sultan of Morocco from 1795 to 1822,
was a devotee of this sect, which no doubt then
became fashionable. The brotherhood possesses
*zauias*, or holy houses, all over the country, where
offerings are taken and meetings of the sect held.
These *zauias* are in the hands of chosen *Mokadmin*,
elected for the purpose. One of the little party who
accompanied me as far as Dads was a *Derkaui*, and
I took the opportunity of questioning him about the
sect. The original idea was "revivalistic"—that is
to say, it was the desire of the founder to cause the
world to return to the pristine purity of Islam, and
to do away with any worship except of the One God.
However, so impressionable are the minds of Arabs
that, instead of turning them from the reverence of
earthly saints, he only added his own name to the
long list. So firmly convinced was Sid el Arbi el
Derkaui of the unity of God, and that to Him
alone must be paid reverence, that he ordered his
followers in repeating the *Shedda* — There is no
god but God; Mohammed is the Prophet of God
—to only mentally mention the second half of the
sentence, so that Mohammed, holy though he was,

should not be spoken of in the same breath with the Almighty. A constant repetition of prayers and attendance at the mosque was also enjoined.

With regard to the animal life to be found at Tafilet a few words must be said.

With the exception of domestic animals, little or no wild varieties are to be found in the oasis. These domestic animals consist of camels, cattle, horses, mules, donkeys, goats, sheep, and dogs. Poultry and pigeons are also found in the villages. The camel is the ordinary large heavy variety found throughout Morocco, though the oasis is from time to time visited by desert tribesmen riding the lighter and swifter camel of the south. Cows and oxen are found in considerable quantities, but are all stall-fed, being only turned out to graze in the spring, when scanty grass is to be found on the outskirts of the oasis. Their fodder consists of dried lucerne and the commoner varieties of dates. The fertile and irrigated land is of too great a value to allow of its being used for grazing purposes. However, there are large flocks and herds of goats and sheep which find sufficient to eat amongst the more deserted portions of Tafilet, and I noticed great numbers feeding amongst the ruins of Sijilmassa and on the outskirts of the oasis on the east side near Dar el baida. At times of drought they are given lucerne and dates.

The sheep are of a curious desert variety, called by the natives *dimaan*. They are hornless and with large loose ears. The wool on their backs is curled, but their sides, stomachs, legs, necks, and heads are smooth. Usually they are of two colours, either black and white or brown and white. The wool, as much as there is of it, grows close to the skin, and is very lightly curled and fine in texture. The goats, too, are peculiar to the district. Goat and sheep milk is largely used for butter.

Of the larger varieties of wild animals the oasis is said to be void. Jackal are likely to be found, and a few hyena in the more deserted parts, though probably the latter are visitors from the mountains, and come in search of food. Large quantities of rats exist, but I saw no voles. Gazelle are found in numbers in the desert, but appear not to approach the oasis; while the *muflon* seldom, if ever, leave the vicinity of the mountains. In Jibel Saghru they are very plentiful. Ostriches are hunted only a day or two's journey to the south, and are said to haunt the vicinity of the Dayet ed Daura, into which the surplus waters of the oasis of Tafilet eventually run.

The horses of Tafilet are a small wiry breed, often very handsome, and capable of standing a great amount of fatigue. Many of the tribes ride entirely mares, on account of the fact that an ambush can be formed with these, whereas entire horses would neigh on the approach of a mounted enemy. They are also more docile, and can be left standing with their bridles on their necks, without fear of their running away or joining other horses. Their heads are small and legs fine, while their tails are better set on than those of the usual barb. Very large prices, comparatively to those in Morocco, are paid for them; but it must be taken into account that their rearing is much more expensive, as there is no grazing-ground, and they are fed entirely on lucerne and dates. Owls seemed to be the most plentiful of all the birds, but I saw large flocks of doves, several varieties of birds of prey, and a number of herons.

There remain now only a few words more to be said to complete these notes upon Tafilet—namely, regarding the trade-routes which lead to and from the oasis.

I have in the earlier part of my book given a detailed account of the road from Morocco City to the oasis—the route by which I travelled, which may be ranked as the second most important, a far larger trade being carried on with Fez.

As I have not myself, nor has as far as is known any European, travelled over this trade-road, I will only give briefly its principal features, preferring to be on the safe side rather than put too much trust or belief in native authorities who, though their general description may be true enough, have no idea of time or distance beyond that certain spots can be reached in one day.

The actual distance and time employed in the journey from Fez to Tafilet is about a day shorter than from Morocco City—that is to say, ten or eleven days, the *r'halat*, or stoppages, being, when possible, made at stated points where security for man, beast, and goods is be found.

The first stoppage after leaving Fez is Sufru, some six hours' caravan-travelling from the capital, a short march necessitated by the difficulties and delays in leaving the city and the security to be found within the little walled town, one of the most picturesque in all Morocco. Here the Berber tribes are entered, and the following day's march is the ascent of the northern slopes of this portion of the Atlas, a halt being made for the night at Tagharzut in the tribe-land of Beni Mgild. Here there is a large *ksar* built *tabia*. From Tagharzut to Njil forms the third day's journey, where there is a *Kaid*, or tribal governor. Njil lies on the borders of the Beni Mgild and Aït Yussi tribes. The latter are said to be one of the wildest Berber tribes, but are more trustworthy and a simpler people than usual. From Njil to El Kasabi, the fourth day's journey, the road ascends the valley of the stream which eventually, after receiving the drainage of the surrounding valleys, forms the Muluya, which flows into the Mediterranean between Melilla and Nemours. El Kasabi itself is on this upper reach of the Muluya. At the pass over the Atlas, Tizin Telremt, on the east of Jibel Ayashi or Ayashin, another watershed is crossed, and the basin of the Wad Ziz and Wad Guir reached. A halt is made for the night at a *ksar*, or *nzala*, as villages or buildings erected for the purpose of resting-places for caravans are called. From this *nzala* to the district of Gers, where the river of that name joins the Wad Ziz, constitutes the sixth day's journey, from which, by following the valley of the Ziz, Tafilet is reached in four days, the halts being made in any villages which can be trusted as friendly toward the caravan-men.

A few words must be said as to the trade-routes from Tafilet to Algeria, though no very great quantity of produce is brought that way, owing to the desert that has to be crossed and the wild tribes inhabiting it.

From Tafilet a number of tracks run almost parallel across the Hamada el Kebir to Es Saheli, El Megren or El Barka on the Wad Guir (95 miles), thence *viâ* Ain Shair to the north, or Kanadsa to the south, to Figig (130-150 miles). At Ain Sefra, 58 miles from Figig, is the termination of the French railway from Oran. The distance, therefore, as the crow flies, from Abuaam in Tafilet to Ain Sefra is about 260 miles.

Of the roads to the south of Tafilet but little need be said, as proportionately only a very small amount of the Sudan trade comes into Morocco by this route, the greater portion being taken *viâ* Tenduf and the Sus to Mogador. From Tafilet, however, a road across a corner of Jibel Saghru and *viâ* Tamgrut leads to the Wad Draa, and thence, *viâ* El Feija, Tatta, and Akka, communication exists with Timbuctu ; but little water is found between Tafilet and Tamgrut, and this portion of the Anti-Atlas is only inhabited by a few shepherds of the Aït Atta. The distance to Tamgrut is some 95 miles—three days' good travelling for caravans.

Two other roads are sometimes followed to Timbuctu—namely, (1) *viâ* Wad Igidi or Igidin to the south-east of Tafilet, and (2) *viâ* El Harib to the south-west ; but in both cases large sums of money

U

have to be paid to the tribes to secure a safe journey, and, especially on the latter, water is very scarce.

A road leads to Tuat *via* the Hamada, El Kebir, Ghrlnema, and Fum es Shink—fifteen days' travelling.

I have not dwelt at any length upon these trade-routes, as no very reliable information can be obtained from the natives.

# CHAPTER XII.

## THE RETURN JOURNEY.

At dawn on Saturday, November 23, Kaid Maclean and I had left the Sultan's camp some way behind, and were hurrying as fast as our sturdy mules allowed in the direction of home. A long march lay before us, over some 300 miles of desert and mountain, and winter had now set in. I had purchased a pony and native saddle at Tafilet; but riding was by no means a pleasure, for I was yet weak and ill. The cold was intense, and we longed for sunrise, even though we knew that in a few hours we should probably be complaining of the heat.

We did not follow the same road as I had pursued in coming, but struck more directly to the north from the Sultan's camp at Dar el baida, passing through the low range of barren hills near that spot. Then a few miles of desert, and the main stream of the Wad Ziz, here known as the Wad Tizimi, from the oasis it has just left at this spot.    The sun rose, and in the bright morning our spirits increased.    The scene was pretty enough; for although we were in sandy stony desert, only a mile or so away to our right lay the palm-groves of Tizimi, and here and there the yellow walls of a *ksar* were visible.

Our party was a large one; for quite a number of soldiers accompanied Kaid Maclean, some of whom were mounted, while others rode the pack-mules on the top of the baggage, and it was evident from their chatter and laughter that one and all were overjoyed at escaping from the dust and dreariness of the *mahalla*, to say nothing of the fact of the scarcity of food there.    Kaid Maclean was the bearer of special letters to the various Governors and Sheikhs on the road, and we looked forward, if not to luxury, at least to being able to obtain food enough.

From Tizimi we skirted the southern end of the small oasis of Mulai Brahim, and caught a glimpse of the white-domed tomb of the saint amongst the palm-trees.    Then desert again until we struck my old road near Fezna, having crossed the Wad Gheris shortly before.    The river here presents a very different appearance to what it does near Tafilet, for there are none of the steep cliffs of clay or wide channels at this portion of its course, as it hurries along over stones and boulders in a shallow bed through the desert valley. A few reeds and scraggy oleanders line its banks. The stream was strong, and we had to get the mules across with care, lest they should be carried off their legs by the current and soak our luggage.

Then on again, until, leaving Tiluin behind, the weary plain of Maghrah opened out before us. We pushed on fast, for the afternoon was well on, and at dark arrived at Ul Turug, weary with our twelve hours' ride.

We pitched the tent outside the *ksar*, and sent a soldier with the Sultan's firman to interview the young Kaid, who had recently been appointed. He met with no happy reception, and came back hurriedly and in considerable fear with the message that they had no provisions to give us, and that a "Christian's" portion was powder and shot, and not food. However, later on the young Kaid came in person, and was tolerably polite, though the aspect of his retinue was by no means friendly, and we were glad of the protection afforded us by an old hag of a Shereefa, very dirty and in rags, who declared that a divine mission had been ordained her to guard our persons. She seemed much venerated in the place, and was altogether a good old soul, though quite mad; and so friendly were her attentions that she raised a sheep from somewhere and

brought it to the Kaid—much to the joy of our
hungry men.

As soon as the natives had retired she announced
that we were by no means safe, and also that it was
her intention to sleep in our camp, as her presence
would protect us from danger.  This she did, under
the flap of the tent; and very glad we were of the
old lady's presence, for the reports the men brought
us were by no means reassuring.  Our guard, sufficient to protect us on the road and well armed,
would have been of no use in a general attack of the
natives, and we were grateful indeed to the old lady
whose insanity had taken so useful a direction.

In our conversation with the young Governor,
when we hinted to him the results that would ensue
if he refused to take notice of the Sultan's commands
that Kaid Maclean should rest in peace and security,
we discovered the reason of his altogether neglecting
the terms of the firman, or *daira* as it is called in
Morocco.  He, it appears, had paid a visit to the
*mahalla*, and been presented by the Sultan with a
suit of clothes, the customary gift of the country—
and the *kaftan*, or coloured garment of cloth, had
been missing.  For this oversight in his Majesty's
gift he had almost turned rebel, and although Mulai
el Hassen himself only a few nights later was to
camp at this very spot, he absolutely disregarded

his written orders. The fact of the *kaftan* is worth narrating, as it gives an insight into the turbulent character of these wild Berber people. Yet in carriage and manner, though by no means friendly, they were gentlemen all over. We struck camp about 3 A.M., and the sun rose upon us after we had crossed the bleak hills, and were proceeding west towards Ferkla. Once more I admired the palm-groves of Milaab and the picturesque situation of the village of Igli, dominating the mouth of the valley where the Wad Todghrá enters Jibel Saghru from the plain.

On issuing from the hills our road varied to that I had already taken, and we passed to the south of the conical hills I mentioned in describing my journey, near the settlement of Islef, a picturesque little place of a few *ksor*, with some gardens and running water in the vicinity. The natives all turned out to see and talk with us, and the presence of the soldiers, and the fact that we were ready to purchase a few of their red, black, and white *kanderas*, or shawls—part of the costume of the women of Aït Atta—kept them in a state of tolerable politeness, though their curiosity was unlimited, Kaid Maclean's mackintosh cloak receiving enormous attentions, being stroked and pinched and examined and ejaculated on by the whole crowd.

At Ferkla we were well received, the Governor, who expected the Sultan in a few days, knowing better than to disregard his lord and master's orders, for the oasis was already in bad odour at Court on account of the murder of a couple of soldiers who had been sent there as Imperial messengers only some few months before. More than this, it was at Ferkla that the tent and property of the Sultan's uncle, Mulai Othman, had been found. This old Shereef, who had been sent to settle some intertribal warfare, and collect taxes due, a year or two before, from some of the Berber tribes nearer Fez, had been treacherously murdered, and his guard annihilated by the tribe of Aït Shokhman, whose chief, Ali ben Yahia, a sort of king amongst the Berbers, had been equally treacherously captured by the Sultan a month earlier and sent a prisoner to Marakesh. The very day that I had left that city he had arrived in chains. It was no doubt for these reasons that the Governor of Ferkla received us with a show of welcome, and supplied us with ample provisions from the store awaiting the arrival of the Sultan and his army. We camped on a level piece of ground near one of the canals that, running from the Wad Todghrá, supplied a portion of the large oasis with water. This canal near here more resembled a swamp, and when, before dawn,

we were obliged to ford it, was covered so thickly
with ice that my donkeys took several steps before
the coating broke under their weight. Yet it was
running water, and well sheltered by palm-trees.

From Ferkla we crossed the weary plain of Seddat;
but on reaching the Wad Todghrá near the south of
the oasis of that name, forded it there, about a couple
of miles north of Imin Erkilim, and continued up its
right (west) bank, camping for the night near the
large village of Taurirt. The latter part of the ride
along the river's banks was a charming one, and presented as picturesque scenes as could be imagined
anywhere. Amongst the groves of palms ran the
river, and its fall being steep, it had in many spots
been banked up by the natives, in order to raise its
waters to the level of their irrigating canals. In
these places it formed large deep pools, out of which
it tumbled in no mean waterfalls to the level of the
stream below; and the entire route was enlivened
with its splashing and the groaning of the mill-
wheels it turned as it passed on its way.

We reached our destination before sunset, having
passed almost immediately before a market-place,
with the same beehive-like domed stalls as I had
seen at the great market of Mulai Ali Shereef at
Tafilet. We found the Kaid of Demnat, under
whose jurisdiction this portion of the Sahara nom-

inally is, encamped quite close to us, and we had no difficulty in obtaining provisions. Although there are nominal Kaids and Governors over all this portion of trans-Atlas Morocco, it must by no means be thought that they hold any jurisdiction, nor would the above-mentioned Kaid have even been able to visit Todghrá had not the Sultan been approaching. Even in his little town of Demnat, on the other side of the Atlas, his position was never secure, and on the death of the late Sultan last June (1894) his house was razed and he himself murdered.

The cold of a night was intense, and our men suffered much. Even in the excellent tent of Kaid Maclean, with every possible invention to keep out sun and frost, we had the greatest difficulty in keeping warm. The early mornings, too, were miserable, when, while the camp was being struck and the mules laden, I would crouch over the remnants of a small fire and try to warm myself. It was always too cold to ride, and we used to give our horses to the men to lead while we stepped out as fast as our legs would carry us over the level plain. At sunrise matters mended, though even at noon the heat was not severe, and on one if not two occasions we saw ice in exposed positions unmelted at mid-day, though no doubt the temperature then was above freezing.

Yet the rays of the sun were sufficient to warm our chilled bones, and the process of thawing as he rose higher into the sky was indeed pleasant.

This was the longest march we made, for after going continually — with but half an hour's rest for lunch — for thirteen and a half hours, we drew rein near the *zauia* of Aït bu Haddu at Dads. I at once sent Mohammed to the *zauia* to announce my return to the old Shereef, and collect the baggage and mules we had left behind.

Here it was colder than ever. The fig-trees, which had all been in leaf on my previous passing through, were now bare, and even before we could get the tents up they were coated with white frost, while every canal, no matter how fast it flowed, became ice.

I saw nothing of the old Shereef, for no doubt it would not have suited his purpose to be seen visiting Europeans, especially when I was one of them. Happily so dark was it when we arrived, and so cold, that our camp attracted no attention, and as we left before dawn my presence was never discovered, so that probably to - day at Dads I am remembered as a pious Moslem. There were no signs of Mohammed and my mules when we left the next morning, but we could not delay, so leaving them to follow, we set off.

Soon after noon we camped at Imasin, making only a short stage, as our animals and men required rest, and to allow of my mules overtaking us, which they did before the camp was fully pitched. Very glad I was to see my scanty baggage again, and my two good mules, that we had passed off on the roads as the property of the old Shereef; for my strength was still sufficiently shaky to render riding, especially on a Moorish saddle, no pleasure, and I could now look forward to a comfortable seat on a good strong mule. My poor pony, too, was none of the best. I had found but scant choice at Tafilet, and the poor thin little fellow was all I could procure. In spite of every care and attention, he died a few weeks after my arrival in Marakesh; as did one of our poor little donkeys, on the very day we arrived at Saffi, whence he had started some four months before. The end of the latter was most pathetic. He was ill, and I hired a special man to lead him quietly to Saffi; but within a few miles of the town, just at the spot where he could obtain his first view of his native city, he was taken with violent hæmorrhage and dropped dead. A good little beast he was, and we mourned his loss, and had him buried with every decency. My other donkey I left in good hands, for the missionaries in Marakesh took him from me, and I knew no better home could be found for him than in their care. It was with many regrets that I parted from him, though at our last interview, so young and full of corn was he, he did his best to put an end to my existence with his heels. I forgive him, for he had accompanied us, sharing with us the lack of food and the heat and the cold, for nearly 700 miles of weary mountain and desert. The poor one who died at Saffi, having started from that point, had almost completed 1000 miles when death overtook him.

We found Imasin a poor enough place, and had no little difficulty in purchasing our provisions, though here we found a luxury in quantities of walnuts, which our men as well as ourselves enjoyed. So poor were the people that when Kaid Maclean gave them some of the very walnuts they had sold us to eat, they were most grateful; and the fact that we did not bargain over the price, but gave them what they asked — it was small enough —gained us their friendship, and good fellows these wild Berbers seemed to be. They came and guarded our camp at night, and sat there in the cold, though even they, who seemed scarcely to feel either that or heat, shivered.

It was here I said farewell to the Dadsi who had been my *zitat* from Dads to Tafilet. No words that I could write would do him justice. Honest, faithful, adventurous, and sympathetic, he had been the

cheerer of our spirits when we were weary with
marching, the diplomat who had guarded me from
discovery as we passed along, and had helped to
nurse me when I was sick. Good, trusty soul,
may you meet with all the blessings you deserve!

From Imasin to Askura was again a shorter march
than usual, but there was no choice of where we
were to stay, for beyond Askura lie some fifteen
miles of weary desert—the Sebaa Shaabat—before
reaching the next inhabited district, Ghresat. We
camped near some large tamarisk-trees, a few hundred yards from the palatial residence of a Sheikh,
who sent men to guard the camp at night.

Passing Ghresat at mid-day the following day, we
reached Agurzga before dark, and pitched below one
of the great *ksor* that crown the eminences of rock
high above the river. Here, too, much poverty exists;
but the people were good, kindly souls, with apparently no thoughts of murder or robbery, and intent
only on selling us almonds and walnuts, and examin-
ing our weapons, a few shots from a revolver fired
in quick succession causing almost a panic.

Great was their amusement in recognising in me
the poor ragged Shereef who had passed through a
month or so before, and heartily we laughed together
over the deception. I was of course still in Arab
dress, and they had not failed to remember my

face. They showed no signs of annoyance or anger, nothing in fact but intense amusement, and a certain amount of admiration for my venturesomeness. Only one or two spoke Arabic, the rest nothing but Shelha. One old man, the wit of the party, could not get over the fact of my returning in a new character, and remarked, "I have always heard Tafilet was a terrible place. How bad it must be when it changes Shereefs into Christians!" and then added, fearful that his joke might offend, "After all, the Christians are the best; they buy our walnuts and our almonds and pay for them, and Shereefs want everything for nothing." There is no doubt we created a good impression in Agurzga, the few cups of tea the men drank with us being a luxury some of them had never tasted before; and when I absolutely sought out the poor people who, when they had believed me to be a Shereef, had brought me supper, and paid them for it, their surprise and joy knew no bounds. Their last words were, when we left the next morning—spoken in broken Arabic— "*Arja; Allah ijibna er Rumin.*" ("Come back some other time—God bring us Romans "—*i.e.*, Europeans.)

From Agurzga we followed the old road, obtaining the glorious view of the Atlas peaks, which I have already described, as we crossed the mountains above Tiurassín. But we did not stop there, pushing on

over the ford of the Wad Marghen, to the great
*kasba* of the Kaid of Glawa at Teluet.   It had long

*The Kaid of Glawa's Residence.*

been my desire to see this celebrated stronghold of
the Atlas, which evokes such expressions of astonishment from the natives who pass it ; but even my

ideas—formed on local descriptions—underrated what
I saw, for not only is the building of enormous extent, but is constructed of large blocks of well-
squared stone, which give the place at once an
appearance of great strength, and render it unlike
any other *kasba* or palace I have seen in Morocco.
The castle consists of a group of centre buildings of
great height, and not unlike the Tower of London
in form, while around it cluster a number of castles
and dwellings of every shape and size, but all big,
the whole being surrounded by high walls, guarded
with towers. Unfortunately I obtained no measurements of the building or its great courtyard within,
for though we camped outside I ventured to enter
its precincts, for its courts are common to all who
care to do so.

Evening was fast approaching, and already the
sun was hidden behind the mountains that shut
in the valley on the west, and a bitter cold wind
blew over the little plain of Teluet. Nothing more
dreary or majestic could be conceived than the
great castle, frowning with its towers and buttresses,
seen against a background of torn mountain-peaks
and snow.

What an awful spot to live in! for the Kaid's
house and the surrounding villages are snowed up
in winter, and in summer the heat in the little

x

valley, encircled as it is on all sides by high
mountains, is said to be intense.

The Kaid himself was absent, but we were entertained by his *khalifa*, or deputy, who came to
the tents with a little retinue of men and drank
tea with us. Hardy fellows they seemed, these
Berber mountaineers, with their tall thin figures
and handsome weather-beaten features, and good-
natured enough too, one and all ready to laugh
when we abused their climate and their mountains.
They seemed to feel the cold but little, if at all,
and scarcely wore an atom more of clothing than
in summer-time, and even then it is scanty enough.

The *kasba* is said to contain some marvellously
good Moorish work, one chamber of the Kaid's,
we were told, being particularly beautifully decorated, but owing to his absence we saw none of
this.

The night was a stormy one, the wind howled
and roared down the valley, and though we were
a little sheltered by the *kasba* walls, it found its
way in bitter gusts into the tent. At sunset it
was freezing hard, and this low temperature, with
almost a hurricane as well, at an altitude of only
a few feet under 7000 above the level of the sea,
was no joke. But we kept our spirits up. Only
a slight descent to make, and a stiff climb of 2000

feet, and we would reach the summit of the pass, to descend to civilisation and warmth.

By daylight we were well on our way, and the sun had not risen very high in the sky when Kaid Maclean and I had clambered to the top of the mountains. Contrary to all expectation, it was quite warm, for the wind had died away, and the bright sun and our exercise had thawed our bones. Far below us we could see our caravan toiling up, the men shouting to the mules to urge them on the difficult path.

I lay down near the same rock as I had rested under on my journey two months before; and as I looked upon the desolate scene of range after range of barren mountain, that had stretched out before me unknown and unexplored, and over and through which I had now threaded my way, and returned safely, I confess I felt some elation at my success, but no regret at leaving these inhospitable regions. Yet I feasted my eyes on the grand surroundings, for it was my last look of the wild country that lies south of the Atlas.

Our mules caught us up, and in a minute—merely half-a-dozen steps—we began to descend, and the view was hid. Far more cheering, however, was that before us; for, although rugged and barren and snow-scattered in our more immediate neigh-

bourhood, beyond lay the richly wooded valley of
Zarkten, and far away in the distance—a peep between the mountains—the open plains beyond.

We hurried on, stopping nowhere, and reached
Zarkten at sunset, after a long and weary march.
So intense was the cold that in one sheltered spot
a waterfall had frozen, and hung from the edge
of the cliff above in a wonderful fantastic collection
of immense icicles.

At Zarkten we found the temperature higher,
though it froze during the night, and it was bitter
enough when we rose by candle-light and set off upon
our way. There was much less water in the Wad
Ghadat than when we had ascended the valley, and
we were able to make our way for some considerable
distance along its course, thereby saving frequent tedious ascents and descents. We lunched at the ruined
bridge of Tugana, and instead of turning to the left,
continued to follow the course of the river. Signs of
a warmer climate were everywhere visible. Vines,
pomegranates, and olives peeped up from over hedges
of aloes and prickly-pear and canes, while the laurustinus, arbutus, lentiscus, and several kinds of firs
were welcome indeed after the bare peaks of rock.
The river flowed quickly on its course, here in rippling eddies, there in deep green pools, and nothing
could be imagined more charming than our road.

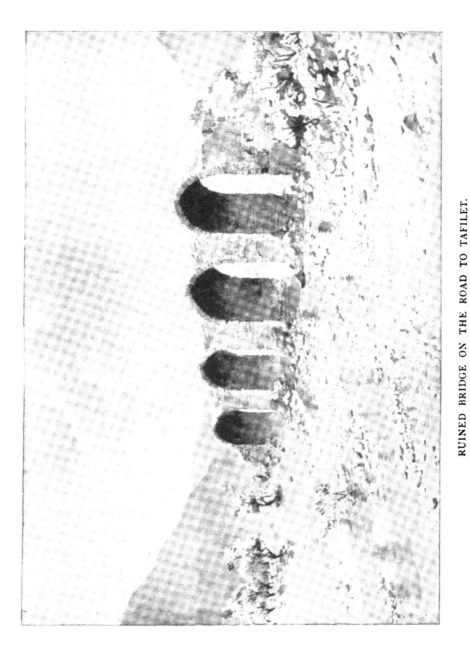

RUINED BRIDGE ON THE ROAD TO TAFILET.

The warmth revived us; our men sang and laughed as they strode along, and every one was in the best of spirits. Nearing Sid Rehal, our destination, we turned to the right from the valley, and pursued a shorter road. With what pleasure it was that from the hill-tops we looked down upon the little white Moorish town, with its mosque and tomb, its gardens, and the white house of the Governor of the district, can be imagined, for it meant so much—safety, warmth, and food, all three of which had been absent over the entire road. We finished up with a gallop, for I had mounted my pony to make a more respectable entrance, and a few minutes later we were drinking tea in our camp, which had preceded us while we lunched. How warm it was, and how plentiful were chickens and eggs, and green tea and sugar, and everything the heart of man could desire in Morocco, to say nothing of the fat sheep the Kaid sent us!

But one recollection that is not one of pleasure do I have—that it was my last camp in the company of Kaid Maclean, for his way lay north across the plains of Shauia, while mine diverged to the west to Marakesh, and it was a sad moment when the next morning I said good-bye—happily not for very long—to the man who had so befriended me. With the cold we experienced I could never have tramped the long road home from Tafilet alone and without shelter, ill as I was; but fortune had favoured me, and in my hour of need I had found unexpectedly the kindest and best of friends. I doubt if he, any more than myself, will ever forget our meeting at Tafilet, and our long journey back together.

Some nine hours' travelling the following day brought me to Marakesh, and that night I spent feasting and listening to music in the house of my old friend Sid Abu Bekr el Ghanjaui; for he made my safe return the excuse for a dinner-party, on such dimensions that I was almost as likely to come to grief from excess of food as I had been of dying of starvation. Seated in the pleasant warmth, on great piles of cushions, with steaming dishes of every luxury that the city can furnish or skilled cooks prepare, it was little wonder that I enjoyed myself, or that we laughed heartily as I narrated to my kind host and his genial guests my adventures on the road.

I remained some three weeks in Marakesh, for I was still weak from my illness, and much needed the rest. A pleasant time it was, spent in idleness, strolling in the bazaars, or picnicking in gardens.

Meanwhile the Sultan was approaching, leading his great army by the same route as we had followed, and in cold still more intense. No pen could describe what must have been the suffering of man and beast, nor can any reliable account of the loss of life be obtained, except that it was very large. Snow fell as they reached the Glawi Pass, and men and mules and camels died in numbers, frozen to death, while the Berbers stripped the bodies of clothes and rifles.

*Shops at Bab Khemis, Marakesh.*

I saw the Sultan's entry into Marakesh—his last entry into any Moorish city—and for days after half-starved men and beasts crawled into the town, lame and sick, the remnants of the great camp I had seen at Tafilet. I questioned many of those who came in, and their tale of suffering and hunger brought tears to one's own eyes as well as theirs. Yet in justice be it said, the Sultan and the Moorish Government did all in their power to alleviate their sufferings by doling out supplies of food ; but with a disorganised commissariat, of which probably a third of the baggage-animals had been frozen to death, fallen over precipices, or broken their legs on the bad mountain roads, it was but little.

From Marakesh I returned to Saffi, where again I was most hospitably entertained by Mr George Hunot, H.B.M. Vice-Consul, and a few days later found a small steamer going direct to Gibraltar.

Three days later I was back in Tangier again, after an absence of four months, to be laid up there for weeks in bed, my health temporarily completely giving way after the strain I had put upon it. But kind care and skilful nursing brought me round, and I no sooner recovered than the spirit of travel came upon me again, and I spent March and April in a most pleasant journey to my old haunts of Wazan, Fez, and Meknas. A couple of months later the news arrived at Tangier of the Sultan's death, and I left hurriedly for Fez, travelling day and night, and in that city, with the exception of a week or two at Meknas, I stayed until August. Of the events that took place during that period a short description must be given ; for although the account of my journey to Tafilet is now completed, the death of Mulai el Hassen and the succeeding crisis owe their origin to the Sultan's expedition to that spot, for it was the effects of his long and weary journey that caused his end.

# CHAPTER XIII.

## THE ACCESSION OF THE NEW SULTAN OF MOROCCO.

A BOOK dealing as this does, not only with my own travels, but also with the presence of the Sultan of Morocco at Tafilet, would not be complete, as already stated, were it not carried on for the space of the few months which succeeded that journey. For although the narration of my adventures in the regions south of the Atlas Mountains is already terminated, I was present during not a little of what I am now going to describe, the affairs that took place in June or July, when Mulai el Hassen was no more, and Mulai Abdul Aziz had succeeded to the throne. In order to render clear what follows, a few words in recapitulation must be said as to the Sultan's journey to the desert.

We have seen that in 1893 Mulai el Hassen led his summer expedition from Fez to Tafilet, and thence returned to Marakesh, crossing the Atlas Mountains in the middle of winter. The journey in every particular was a dangerous and trying one. Such wild tribes as the Beni Mgild and Aït Yussi had to be passed through, and when safely traversed the Sultan found himself in the desert surrounded by the most ferocious of the Berber tribes, who had to be appeased with presents of money and clothes. Although, as a matter of fact, no opposition was put to his progress, he must ne-cessarily have been during the whole expedition in a state of great anxiety, for had the Berbers amalgamated to destroy him and his vast army, they could have done so with the greatest ease. Food was only procurable in small quantities; barley in the camp reached a price that rendered it unprocurable except by the richer classes; while added to this the summer heat in the Sahara caused havoc among the soldiers.

Tafilet was reached in October, and a halt of three weeks made there. It is needless here to enter into any details, for I have already described the camp; suffice it to say that Mulai el Hassen's camp was pitched on the desert sand near a spot called Dar el baida, to the east of the oasis of Tafilet, and that he was surrounded by an army and camp-followers numbering probably 40,000 men. I saw the Sultan several times during his residence in the camp, and was struck with the remarkable change that had taken place in his appearance. His bearing was as dignified as ever, but his black beard was streaked with grey, his complexion was sallow, and the lines of age showed themselves under his eyes. For over two years previously I had not seen him, and when last I had watched him he was still a young-looking man : now old age had set its indelible mark upon his countenance. The fire of his eye was gone; his head drooped slightly upon his chest; he looked like a man tired and weary. No doubt he was. Anxiety was always present. News had reached him that fighting, and most serious fighting, was occurring between the Spaniards and the Riff tribes at Melilla ; there was a constant fear of assassination, and a still more constant dread of his whole camp being eaten up by the Berbers. Added to this his health was ailing, and winter fast coming on. Affairs delayed him at Tafilet, and before he left that spot at the end of November, although during the day the sun still beat down with almost tropical heat, rendering life in a tent insufferable, by night the cold was extreme, and frosts of almost nightly occurrence. Before the army lay a three weeks' march to Marakesh, over desert and mountain, through wild tribes where dangers were many and food scarce. What wonder that Mulai el Hassen suffered! Yet the worst trials were before him after he left Tafilet : as he approached the Glawi Pass over the Atlas—the lowest there is, and that at an altitude of over 8000 feet above the sea-level—the cold increased, soldiers, mules, horses, and camels died of exposure. Snow fell and covered the camp, and only by forced marches were the remnants of the great horde dragged out from the deathly grip of the rocks and snows of the Atlas Mountains to the plains below.

I saw Mulai el Hassen and his army enter Marakesh, for I had returned thither a few days before them. What was noticeable at Tafilet was doubly apparent now. The Sultan had become an old man. Travel-stained and weary, he rode his great white horse with its mockery of green-and-gold trappings, while over a head that was the picture of suffering waved the imperial umbrella of crimson velvet. Following him straggled into the city a horde of half-starved men and animals, trying to be happy that at last their terrible journey was at an end, but too ill and too hungry to succeed.

Mulai el Hassen found no peace at Marakesh. Affairs at Melilla had become strained, and no sooner had his Majesty reached the capital than a Spanish Embassy under General Martinez Campos proceeded thither. How it ended is well known. It added to the enormous expenses of the Sultan's summer expedition — which must have cost him nearly a

million sterling—a debt to the Spanish Government
of twenty million pesetas, at the same time necessitating the Sultan to abandon his idea of remaining in
his southern capital, and forcing upon him a long
march to Rabat and Fez, and an intended expedition
to the Riff to punish the tribes who had caused the
disturbance there.    Fez was never reached, the expedition never took place, and Mulai el Hassen's
entry into Rabat was in a coffin at the dead of
night.

Having thus briefly recapitulated the events preceding the Sultan's death, reference must now be
made to those who played important parts, for
better or for worse, in the days that followed.

With regard to the succession to the throne of
Morocco, no regular custom or law exists.    While
the new Sultan must be a relation of the late one, he
need not necessarily be a son, but is appointed by
his predecessor, and if approved of, acknowledged by
those in whose power the making of Sultans lies,—
that is to say, by the Viziers and powerful Shereefs.
Should the Sultan name no successor, it is these who
choose the man they may think suitable to fill the
post.

Of the great Shereefian families of Morocco that of
Mulai el Hassen is not the most important, for the
founder of his dynasty, rising in Tafilet, seized the

power from the more holy and reverend family of the
direct descendants of Mulai Idris, the founder of the
Moorish empire, who was the son of Abdullah el
Kamil, himself a grandson of Hassan, who with
Huseyn was the son of Fatima, Mohammed's
daughter. While the Fileli dynasty to-day holds
the throne, the reverence paid to the Fileli Shereefs
is not to be compared with that bestowed upon
Mulai Idris I. and II., one of whom lies buried in
the town bearing his name in Zarahun near Fez,
while the second is patron saint of the northern
capital itself, where he lies interred in a gorgeous
tomb.

Again, the family of the Shereefs of Wazan obtains far greater respect than that of the Sultan,
and the tombs of Mulai Abdullah Shereef and Sid
el Haj el Arbi are places of daily pilgrimages. In
order, therefore, to obtain the succession to the throne
of a new Sultan, the aid and influence of both the
Shereefs of Mulai Idris and Wazan have to be brought
to bear upon the question, as should either party
refuse to acknowledge the candidate, so powerful
are their followings that it is quite possible, more
than probable, that a civil war would be the result.
That a Shereef of Wazan could come to the throne is
practically impossible. The two heads of the family,
sons of the late Grand Shereef, are French protected

subjects; while what affects still more the native population is the existence of an ancient proverb which states that no Wazan Shereef can rule as Sultan, but that no Sultan can rule without the support of the Wazan Shereef. It is, in fact, a defensive alliance between the two great families.

Not so, however, with the Shereefs of Mulai Idris, who reside almost entirely in Fez, and whose influence there is very great. That a Drisite Shereef would have been ready to ascend the throne were it offered to him is only too probable, but fortunately it was not offered. In spite of their immense sanctity, the old adage that a prophet hath no honour in his own country holds good in Fez, where amongst the city-people they are considered as little above ordinary mortals. All their influence, and it is very extensive, lies amongst strangers and in the country districts, where being seldom seen or heard, all kinds of romance as to their marvellous powers are rife.

Therefore it will be seen that, powerful as are the families of Wazan and Mulai Idris, it was practically out of the question, unless civil war broke out, that a member of either should be put up as candidate for the throne. And had such an event happened, want of funds would have no doubt crushed the rebellion before any very serious results would have occurred. There remained, then, only the members of the late Sultan's family who could succeed. Of these, four had always been considered as likely candidates. First, Mulai Ismain, a brother of Mulai el Hassen, who for a long time was Viceroy in Fez. He is a man past middle age, of a quiet gentle manner, fanatical, and given to literary pursuits, and, while possessing very considerable influence, and still more popularity, is by no means a man to push himself forward—in fact, it was always said, on the best authority, that he had no desire whatever of succeeding to the throne. Certainly Mulai Ismain seemed the most probable successor to his brother, though every year lessened the likelihood of this by adding years to the age of the Sultan's favourite son, Mulai Abdul Aziz, the present Sultan. Although it was known that this boy was being trained by Mulai el Hassen, so that in the event of his own death he might come to the throne, his extreme youth for a time rendered it exceedingly improbable that he could succeed; and had Mulai el Hassen's death taken place only a year or two earlier, Mulai Abdul Aziz, instead of becoming Sultan, would have been merely an obstacle to whoever had succeeded—an obstacle that most likely would have been removed by assassination or secret murder. Fortunately, Mulai el Hassen lived sufficiently long

Y

to see his favourite son reach the age of sixteen—for
all reports as to his being then only twelve are false.
So great was his father's desire that he should succeed,
that during his lifetime he endowed his son with
very considerable wealth and property, and towards
the end of his life, since his return from Tafilet, made
it clearly apparent what was his desire in the event
of his death, by bestowing on him nearly all the
prerogatives of the Sultanate.

Mulai Abdul Aziz is the son of a Circassian wife
of Mulai el Hassen, a lady of great intelligence and
remarkable ability, who, though no longer in her
first youth, was able to maintain to the day of his
death a most singular and no doubt beneficial influence over Mulai el Hassen.  Her European extraction and her education abroad, her general knowledge
of the world, and her opportunities for watching the
Court intrigues, rendered her of more service to the
late Sultan than any of his Viziers.  She accompanied
him always upon his long and tedious marches, and
there can be no doubt that even in his dealings with
the European Powers her advice was always asked
and generally taken by the Sultan.  The affection
Mulai el Hassen bestowed upon her was also shared
by her son, Mulai Abdul Aziz, who, with the tender
anxiety of both an affectionate father and mother,
was brought up in a far more satisfactory manner

than is general with the sons of Moorish potentates.
While his elder brothers, of whom more anon, were
left to run wild and to lead lives of cruelty and
vice, Abdul Aziz was the constant companion of
his parents, who, both intent that he should one
day be Sultan of Morocco, lost no opportunity of
educating him, to the best of their abilities, to fill
the post.

The other candidates who may be said to have
had a chance of succeeding to the throne were Mulai
Mohammed, the late Sultan's eldest son, by a slave
wife, who has held the post of Viceroy in Morocco
City for a considerable time, and whose vicious life
has estranged him from the affections of the people.
This is the "one-eyed decapitator" of whom the
papers were so fond of speaking during the recent
crisis. Really the Englishman who invented the
name deserves popularity to the same extent as he
gave publicity to his brilliant imagination, for the
complimentary title is of purely English invention.
Unfortunately Mulai Mohammed never possessed the
power of decapitating any one, and had he ventured to
have done so, would have long ago been securely confined in prison. Vicious and immoral he was to an
extent that surpasses description, but beyond this his
sins were no greater than those of the ordinary Moorish
official. At times he was most lavish and generous

—often with other people's money; and although his open immorality estranged him from any affection on the part of the people, he still possessed a certain amount of popularity from his exceedingly unprincely condescension. On the whole, Mulai Mohammed is a very undesirable young man; but even his lax morality scarcely merits the outpourings of hatred and contempt that have been heaped upon him by the English press.

The remaining possible candidate to the throne was Mulai el Amin, another brother of the late Sultan, a pleasant, middle-aged man, who would scarcely have been capable of the amount of dignity necessitated by the position, as he possessed a temperament too affable and condescending.

It will be seen, therefore, that not only was Mulai Abdul Aziz his father's candidate, but that by his training and bringing up, in spite of his youth, he was by far the most likely to perform with any degree of success the arduous duties of the position. Again, his father and mother's care had kept him free from the immoral life usually led by boys of his age, and he came to the throne untainted by the vices of the country.

But one point more remains to be touched upon before referring to the events that have absolutely been taking place since the late Sultan's death early in June 1894—namely, a few words as to the Viziers and officials by which his Shereefian Majesty was surrounded.

The only members of the Moorish Government who enjoyed access to the person of their Sultan were some half-a-dozen Viziers, through whom the entire business of the country was carried on. These were respectively the Grand Vizier, the Minister of Foreign Affairs, the Lord Chamberlain, another Vizier answering to our Home Secretary, the Master of the Ceremonies, and the Minister of War. With these exceptions, no one was able to gain the confidential ear of the Sultan ; and should by any chance his Majesty listen to others, woe betide them, whoever they might be, did they attempt in any way to injure the position of these courtiers, who would be able, without the information ever reaching the Sultan, to revenge themselves as they might desire upon the man who informed his Majesty of their evil doings. Mention need be made only of those who have played important parts in the history of the last year. These are respectively Sid el Haj Amaati, the Grand Vizier, Sid Mohammed Soreir, the Minister of War, and Sid Ahmed ben Musa, the *Hajib* or Chamberlain. Between the two former—who are brothers, and members of the powerful Jamai family, which had already given another Grand Vizier before Haj Amaati was appointed, namely, Sid Mukhtar Jamai — and Sid Ahmed ben Musa, the *Hajib*, there had always existed a rivalry and hatred only to be found amongst oriental peoples. Sid Ahmed himself is the son of a Grand Vizier, the late Sid Musa, who for many years was the able and trusted adviser of the Sultans Sidi Mohammed and Mulai el Hassen.

While the Jamai brothers prided themselves on their great and powerful family, they scoffed at Sid Musa and his family as upstarts, for his father was a slave. But to such an extent did Mulai el Hassen bestow his confidence on both the Grand Vizier and the *Hajib*, that they were scarcely able to do one another harm in his Majesty's eyes. Haj Amaati had risen suddenly to his post, and his success with the Sultan no doubt caused much envy and hatred in the heart of Sid Ahmed. Two years ago Haj Amaati, on the resignation of the F'ki Sinhaji, became Grand Vizier, though at that time probably not more than thirty years of age. His elder brother had for a long time held the powerful and lucrative post of Minister of War, and with his support to back him, Haj Amaati commenced a career of amassing wealth by every possible means.

The power and influence possessed by a Grand Vizier

STREET LEADING TO THE SULTAN'S PALACE, MOROCCO CITY: A SECRETARY OF THE FOREIGN OFFICE GOING TO COURT.

in Morocco is almost incredible. Every official in the
whole country is under him; no one can communicate
with the Sultan except through him. In his hands
lie the disposal of the various governorships—one
should say the sale of the various governorships—and
the dismissal of all officials. In the hands of an
unscrupulous man there is every opportunity of
" black-mail," and of this Haj Amaati took an advantage unparalleled in Moorish history. He robbed
the Sultan and bought and sold appointments, and
in the two years that he was Grand Vizier he
amassed, in addition to his already considerable
fortune, a sum of nearly £150,000! That is to say,
he managed to ensure for himself, and entirely by
illicit means, an income of no less than about £70,000
a-year, and this in an open and unblushing manner.
So certain was he of his position and influence that,
soon after the Sultan's arrival at Morocco City on
his return from Tafilet, he attempted to oust from
favour Sid Ahmed, the Chamberlain, who, of all the
Court, was on the most intimate terms with, and the
most trusted servant of, the Sultan. For a time he
was successful: Sid Ahmed lost favour, and it
seemed that his dismissal was certain. Shortly
before Mulai el Hassen left Morocco City he was,
however, reinstated in his Majesty's regard; and
by the manner in which Mulai el Hassen appeared

to leave nearly everything in his hands, there is little
doubt that he repented of having distrusted him at
all.   This incident increased the hatred between Haj
Amaati and Sid Ahmed, and even had the late Sultan
lived, one or other would have been obliged to go,
as affairs at Court became too strained to continue
in that condition.

The late Sultan left Marakesh in May, accompanied by his whole Court, his army, and the
governors of southern Morocco and their troops, in
order to punish certain revolutionary tribes in the
district of Tedla, to the north - east of Marakesh :
thence it was his Majesty's intention to proceed to
Rabat, where the northern army was to join him,
and the entire forces were to pass on to Meknas
and Fez, punishing *en route* the tribes of Zimour
and Beni Hassen, whose depredations and fighting
had caused his Majesty very considerable anxiety
ever since his departure from Fez, a year previous.

Mulai el Hassen was ill when he left the southern
capital.   The anxiety, the heat of the desert, and
the intense cold on his journey to and from Tafilet,
had weakened a constitution already impaired by an
affection of the liver and kidneys.   Those who accompanied him on his departure from Morocco City
tell how the life and vigour had seemed to have
left him.   His parting with Mulai Abdul Aziz, who

had left the capital previous to his father, proceeding to Rabat, was said to have been a most touching one, and his favourite son rode out of the capital with all the pomp and paraphernalia of a Sultan. No doubt it was purposely done by Mulai el Hassen, who seems to have felt his end approaching, and considered this the most subtle means of exhibiting to his people his desire that Abdul Aziz should succeed him.

By slow marches, necessitated by the immense number of men and animals accompanying him, the Sultan reached the district of Tedla, and there fell ill.

At daybreak it was the custom of Mulai el Hassen, as already mentioned, to leave the enclosure of canvas in which his tents were pitched and proceed on foot to his office-tent, where he would transact business until generally about nine or ten o'clock, when he would retire within, not appearing again until the cool of the afternoon. For several days after the arrival of the camp in the region of Tedla, at a spot called Dar bu Zeedu, a halt was called; and although the Sultan from time to time visited his office-tent, it was generally known that he was unwell. After the 2d of June the Sultan did not leave his enclosure; and although the report was general that he was seriously indisposed, reassuring messages were given by the *Hajib*, Sid Ahmed, who had the *entrée* to the Sultan's tent, and his Majesty was pronounced to be getting on toward recovery. During the afternoon of Wednesday, June 6, Mulai el Hassen died, Sid Ahmed alone being present, the man who throughout his life had been his most confidential and trusted follower. Before his death he had spoken freely to Sid Ahmed, and had made him swear a solemn oath to support the succession of Mulai Abdul Aziz, and never to desert him as long as either of them lived. His Shereefian Majesty also left papers stating his desire that his favourite son should succeed him, and private letters to Abdul Aziz himself.

But besides the question of the succession, there were others as momentous, if not more so, to be considered. The camp was placed within the district of the Tedla regions, against whom the Sultan had intended to wage war; and the fact that he was dead, and that the camp would be left without any leader, would bring down an attack of the tribes and the sacking of the entire camp, if not the murder also of the Viziers and officials. Nor was the army to be trusted: Mulai Abdul Aziz was at Rabat, still some eight days' fast marching distant, and in those eight days who knew what course events might take? A hurried meeting of the Viziers was called; an oath of secrecy taken ; the drums were beaten for a start to be made ; and, to every one's astonishment and surprise, orders were given for a move, the reason affirmed being that the Sultan had sufficiently recovered to travel. The palanquin which always accompanied his Majesty was taken into the enclosure ; the Sultan's body was placed within, the doors closed, and, amidst the obeisances and acclamations of the camp, all that remained of Mulai el Hassen set out for Rabat.

Not a soul knew of the Sultan's death except the Viziers and a few of the slaves and tent-pitchers, whose mouths were sealed, knowing that death would ensue if they told.

The river Um er-Ribia was crossed, and a halt called on its right bank, near a spot known as the Brouj Beni Miskin. Meanwhile messengers had been secretly sent to Rabat to announce the Sultan's death and the accession of Mulai Abdul Aziz, to support whom the Viziers had all sworn.

The following day an early start was made, the dead Sultan still being carried in the usual position, with the flags and insignia of the Sultanate preceding him. As they passed along, the tribes-people are said to have kissed the palanquin, and one or two people of importance to have been allowed to see the Sultan within, whose ill-health was given as an excuse for his not speaking.

At the middle of the day a halt was called for his
Majesty to take breakfast, a tent pitched, the palanquin carried within, and food and green tea cooked,
taken into the tent, and brought out again as if it
had been tasted by the Sultan.

As yet no one knew besides the Viziers and the
handful of slaves that Mulai el Hassen was dead.
The military band played outside his tent, and all
the usual customs which were carried out when he
lived were continued.   But in a hot climate like that
of Morocco in June a secret of this sort cannot be
long kept, and on their arrival in camp, after a ten
hours' march, on Thursday, June 7, it was announced
that the Sultan was dead, and that messengers had
left the day before for the capitals, announcing the
accession of Mulai Abdul Aziz.   The proclamation
called upon the people and soldiers to follow the
desire of their deceased master, and to support the
Viziers in their intention of seeing Mulai Abdul Aziz
succeed.

The news fell like a thunderbolt upon the camp.
It was true that by the concealment of the Sultan's
death they had escaped from Tedla; but there still
remained dangers almost equally as great.   Would
not the tribes of Shauia, through which they had yet
to pass *en route* to Rabat, pillage the camp, for there
was plenty to loot there ?   And even if they refrained

from doing so, could the horde of ill-fed, ill-clothed, and ill-paid soldiers be trusted?

The camp split up into a hundred parties, each distrustful of the other, though all intent upon one object, a retreat to the coast. Each tribe represented in the camp collected its forces, and marched in a band together and camped together, not fearing so much any general outbreak as an attack on the part of members of some other tribe, between whom there may have been some long-standing feud, only prevented by fear of the Sultan from bursting into warfare.

By forced marches the camp and the army proceeded to Rabat, constantly hampered by the surrounding tribes, who, too timid to attack so large a force, contented themselves and satisfied their love of plunder by cutting off and robbing every straggler who happened to lag behind. The poor soldiers they killed for their rifles, and, if they possessed none, out of pure devilry. Many of the troops took advantage of the lack of order and government to run away and return to their homes—whence they had been taken by a systemless conscription to starve in the Sultan's service, or gain a precarious livelihood by theft.

Meanwhile Abdul Aziz had been proclaimed in Rabat, and letters were sent in all directions announcing his accession to the throne. In no period of modern Moorish history had there been a week of such suspense as then ensued. The Sultan was a boy, separated from his Ministers and Viziers by a long distance, in traversing which they ran a great danger of being plundered and murdered. Had such an event occurred, and Mulai Abdul Aziz's supporters been killed, his reign must have terminated at once, for the treasury would have fallen into other hands, and another Sultan been proclaimed.

With all possible speed the army marched towards the coast, bearing their now loathsome burden of the Sultan's body with them. There was a terrible mockery in the whole thing, — the decomposing corpse borne in royal state with the Shereefian banners waving before it, with the spear-bearers on either side, and the troop of mounted bodyguard and *askars* on foot.

On Thursday, June 14, Rabat was reached, and a halt called some little distance outside the city. The state of the Sultan's body was such as to render a public funeral impossible, so in the darkness of the night a little procession of foot-soldiers, with only a single Shereef attending, one and all bearing lanterns, set out. A hole was bored in the town walls,—for seldom, if ever, is a corpse carried into the gate of a Moorish city; and surrounded by this little band, Mulai el Hassen, Sultan of Morocco, was laid to his

last rest in the mosque covering the tomb of his
ancestor, Sidi Mohammed ben Abdullah.

At dawn, as the people bestirred themselves to
witness the funeral, it became known that all was
over; and amidst the acclamations of the populace
and the sounds of the Sultan's band, Mulai Abdul
Aziz was led forth, the great crimson - and - gold
umbrella waving over him, surrounded by his father's
Viziers, and mounted on his father's white horse, and
proclaimed Sultan.

Those who saw the spectacle described it to me.
The boy's eyes were filled with tears, for his love for
his father was intense, and report says that it was
only by force that he was persuaded to mount the
horse and be proclaimed. A touching story was
recounted to the writer by one who witnessed the
episode. On his return to the palace the mosque
where his father had been buried the previous night
was passed. Leaving the procession, Mulai Abdul
Aziz proceeded alone to the door, and, weeping
copiously, dismounted and entered to do his last
homage to his father and his Sultan.

The news of the Sultan's death had reached Casablanca on the coast on Saturday by a mounted express,
and thence two mounted men galloped to Rabat, a
distance of fifty-nine miles, in six and a half hours,
over an abominable road. A steamer was on the

point of leaving that port for Tangier, and her Britannic Majesty's Minister received the news shortly after 11 A.M. on Sunday morning,—a worthy record of fast travelling.   He was the first to obtain the information, and he immediately told his colleagues of what had taken place.   A special meeting of the European Ministers was called on Monday morning, after which the British Minister, Mr Satow, reported the information to Sid el Haj Mohammed Torres, the Sultan's Vizier resident at Tangier.   By mid-day on Monday the news was general in Tangier, and anxiety was depicted on every face as to what would be the results of so serious an occurrence. Not a few predicted a general massacre of the Europeans, which of everything that might occur was the least probable.   It is true that the tribes around Tangier disliked their governor, and might make some sort of attempt to assassinate him ; but their common-sense gained the better of them, and, on consideration, they realised that any such course would in the end but mean misery and imprisonment and even death to themselves, while by adopting an exemplary bearing they might so gain the favour of the new Sultan that their grievances would be heard and attended to.   At the same time they virtually threw off the jurisdiction of the Basha, each village electing a local sheikh, who would be responsible for the conduct of those under him.   So successful was this action that, so far from the country becoming in any way disturbed, things improved in every manner, cattle robberies ceased, and an unusual period of calm ensued, that spoke not a little for the credit of those to whom it was due.   The Moors have a proverb, and it is a very true one, that safety and security can only be found in the districts where there is no government—that is to say, where the government is a tribal one.

In talking over the crisis on that eventful Monday on which we received the news of the Sultan's death, one could not help feeling at what an exceedingly opportune moment it had occurred, as far as the general peace of the country was concerned.   For two or three years the harvests had been very bad ; but this summer had proved sufficient to repay the tribes and country - people for a period almost of starvation, and throughout the whole country the wheat and barley crops were magnificent.   Harvesting had already commenced, and every one was engaged in getting in the crops.   To the Moor wheat is life.   The country-people eat little or nothing else, every one grinding in his own house, or tent, as the case may be, his own flour.   To lose the crops would mean famine, and the Moor knows what famine means.   At all costs, at all hazards, the outstanding

z

crops must be got in—Sultan or no Sultan. So instead of taking up their arms to pay off old scores and to commence new ones, the peasant went forth on his errand of peace and gathered in his harvest. "The Sultan was dead," they said, "and his son had been proclaimed : everything was ordained by God— but the harvest must be got in." Had Mulai el Hassen's decease occurred at any other period than that at which it did, months of bloodshed and plundering would have been the result.

In spite of the opinion of most people, I was firmly convinced that, for the present at least, no serious incidents would occur. So strong was my conviction, that on Tuesday morning I left Tangier for Fez, accompanied by a Moorish youth, myself in Moorish clothes. We were both mounted on good horses, and hampered ourselves with absolutely no baggage of any sort. Alcazar was reached the following morning. The town was in a state of considerable alarm ; most of the Jews had already fled to Laraiche, and the officials were half expecting an attack on the part of the mountaineers. The following morning, that of the *Eid el Kebir*, the great feast of the Moorish year, I reached Wazan, where, at all events, I should learn from an authoritative source as to what was likely to occur. I found there that the news of the Sultan's death was already known, while

I was able to confirm that of Mulai Abdul Aziz's accession.

It must be remembered how important a part Wazan and its Shereefs play in Moorish politics. That the Great Shereef of Wazan should fail to acknowledge the accession of a Sultan would mean that 100,000 of their followers would do the same, and that all the mountaineers to the north-east of Morocco would rise in a body.

I was received as an old friend by the Shereef, in whose house I once lived for eight months, and was present at the afternoon court, at which, being the *Eid el Kebir*, or great feast, all the Shereefs were present, together with the principal men of the town. The scene was a most picturesque one: the gaily decorated room, leading by an arcade of Moorish arches into a garden, one mass of flowering-shrubs, amongst which a fountain played with soft gurgling sound—the large group of Shereefs in holiday attire of soft white wool and silk, the great silver trays and incense-burners, and long-necked scent-bottles,—all formed an ideal picture of oriental life. The one topic of conversation was what had taken place, the Sultan's death, and the accession of Mulai Abdul Aziz. It was, in fact, a sort of council of war or peace—happily the latter; and as we drank green tea, flavoured with mint and verbena, out of delicate

little cups, the Shereef made his public declaration
of adherence to Mulai Abdul Aziz, — a few words
uttered in the expressionless way that Moors of high
degree affect, words simple in themselves, but meaning perhaps his life and his throne to Mulai Abdul
Aziz.

Throughout the whole crisis the action of the
Shereefs of Wazan is highly to be commended. Their
every endeavour was to ensure peace and tranquillity,
and in this the Moorish Government owes a debt
that it will be difficult ever to pay to Mulai el Arbi
and his brother Mulai Mohammed.

This is not the place to talk of the charms of
Wazan, but as I left the little city, nestled in groves
of olives and oranges, early the next morning, it was
with a feeling of regret that I could not stay longer ;
but I wanted to be in Fez. If anything occurred, it
would be there. So I pushed on with my journey,
and after a thirteen hours' ride under a hot sun, put
up for the night at a village overlooking the river
Sebu. Here bad news met us : the neighbouring
tribes of Mjat, who are Berbers, Hejawa, and Sher-
arda, were up in arms, with the intention of taking
advantage of the opportunity to wipe out old scores.
Already a small skirmish had taken place, and the
morrow threatened to dawn with further fighting,
which would entirely block the road to Fez, and also

the road I had passed over the day before from Wazan.

At daybreak armed bands of horsemen could be seen scouring the country, and it was not until the afternoon that we learned that the three tribes in question had met and decided to postpone any hostilities until after the harvest had been gathered in. I set out at once, and the following day before noon reached Fez in safety. So insecure were the roads reported to be, that we met not a single caravan *en route*, with the exception of one, whose camel-drivers appeared to be very much more afraid of us three horsemen than we were of them. At eleven we entered Fez—myself, a Shereef who had accompanied me, and my native servant.

Meanwhile the new Sultan still remained at Rabat, and a time of immense activity was passing at the Court, couriers without number leaving daily with letters for every part of the kingdom, announcing the accession of Abdul Aziz to the throne ; and though it was exceedingly important that his Shereefian Majesty should proceed as quickly as possible to Fez, it was found impossible for him to make an immediate start, so great was the press of business.

By this time Europe was being flooded with so-called information as to what was taking place. The " one-eyed decapitator " was reported by three daily papers of the same date to have raised a rebellion in Morocco, to have organised an army of 20,000 men in Fez, and to have been imprisoned at Rabat; while a most pathetic and graphic account appeared in nearly all the London papers of the funeral of Mulai el Hassen, at which every pomp was observed, and at which all the members of the consular body at Rabat were officially present! It was witnessed, the informant said, by the entire population; whereas the funeral was secretly carried out in the dead of night, only a few soldiers accompanying the body to its grave.

The news of the late Sultan's death had been received in Fez on the evening of Tuesday, June 12, in a letter addressed to Mulai Omar, his son, by the Viziers. The Viceroy at once imparted the news secretly to the governor, and criers were sent throughout the town calling the people together to hear a Shereefian letter read in the mosque of Bu Jelud. Suspecting nothing of great importance—for this is the ordinary custom of making known a decree—the people sauntered in.

Meanwhile Mulai Omar had caused to be drawn up the paper acknowledging the new Sultan, and headed the list with his own signature, the second to sign being Mulai Ismain, who had been considered by many to be the most likely candidate to the throne.

As soon as the mosque was full, the doors were
closed, and the announcement of the Sultan's death
made known, together with the proclamation of the
accession of his son. As the letter was concluded,
the Basha of the town rose and said, "If any one
has anything to say, let him speak." Not a word
was uttered, and in perfect silence the lawyers
drew up a document to be forwarded to Mulai Abdul Aziz announcing the readiness of Fez to accept
him as their sovereign. Intense indignation reigned
amongst the audience in the mosque. They felt that
they had been tricked into giving their consent
without the opportunity of discussing the affair; but
escape was impossible, and a murmur of discontent
would have meant their going straight to prison, for
the doors were closed and a strong guard in readiness.

What was the real state of feeling in Fez it is very
difficult to say, but it is doubtful whether they would
have at once accepted Mulai Abdul Aziz had not
the authorities obtained their signatures in the manner they did. In all probability they would have
bargained with him, offering to receive him should
they be free from certain taxes — the *octroi*, for
instance—for a certain length of time, if not for ever.
Of all the inhabitants of Morocco there are none more
grasping, more cowardly, and more given to intrigue,
than the people of Fez. Their meanness is prover-

bial, and while they give themselves airs over every-
one else's head, they are despised and hated by the
remainder of the population.    Given up to every
vice, they go about the streets covering their hands
for fear of sunburn and muttering their prayers,
talking of their importance and bravery, yet frightened by a spider or a mouse.    The women of any of
the other cities of Morocco could defeat the men of
Fez.    However, whatever may have been the ideas
of the inhabitants of Fez as to the advisability of the
succession of Mulai Abdul Aziz, their allegiance had
been given, and there was now no drawing back.

By this time the news had spread throughout the
entire country, and Hiyaina, a neighbouring Arab
tribe to Fez, came in considerable force, some 400
horses, and commenced petty robberies just outside
the town walls.    The scare amongst the effeminate
Fezzis was amusing to witness.    Trade became at a
standstill, and they secured themselves within their
houses under lock and key, leaving the authorities
and the strangers in the city to settle with the wild
tribesmen.    However, the affair came to nought in
the end ; for the very Arabs who had come with a
possible idea of looting Fez were bribed into the
Government service to keep the roads open for caravans—a most important point, as scarcely any wheat
or barley existed in the capital, and any lengthened

delay in the arrival of the grain-bearing camels from the country would mean famine and revolution.

On Wednesday, June 20, a deputation left Fez for Rabat to bear an address of welcome to the Sultan, a document magnificently illuminated. On the 24th, the first letter written in the new Sultan's name, with all his titles and dignities, was received. It announced his accession to the throne, and called upon the people to be obedient. Its receipt was honoured by an almost endless salute from the artillery in the palace square.

On Monday, June 25, the Sultan left Rabat for Meknas and Fez, travelling through the tribe of Beni Hassen, which, together with their neighbours the Berbers of Zimour, had already sworn allegiance.

At Tangier things were proceeding quietly. The French Government sent a man-of-war and an armed despatch-boat, while the English were contented with the presence of the Bramble, a small gunboat from Gibraltar. The Portuguese and Spaniards both sent vessels of kinds. An act of gross stupidity on the part of the commander of one of the latter nearly caused an unpleasant disturbance in the country. The Isla de Luzon was sent by the Spanish Government to the coast. Now the first town down the Atlantic coast of Morocco is the almost deserted and entirely ruinous Arzeila, a place of absolutely no importance, and where there is no harbour of any sort. For some reason known only to the adventurous Spanish commander, he was pleased to come to anchor and to fire a salute of twenty-one guns in the roadstead, which Arzeila had no means of returning, for neither cannon nor powder are to be found ; and as never in the memory of man had any vessel of any sort ever approached the place, the few inhabitants were filled with consternation and terror, which was only increased when a boat was noticed coming ashore. There was no doubt about the question in the minds of the natives —a European invasion was taking place! A few stayed to see what was going to happen ; the greater part fled, spreading here, there, and everywhere the news of the invasion of Moorish territory by the Christians. · Meanwhile the water-kegs which had been sent on shore in the boats were filled, and the officer in charge, having taken coffee in the house of a certain Jew who calls himself Spanish Consular Agent, returned to his ship, and the man-of-war departed, steaming away just as volunteers began pouring in from every direction to prevent the infidels landing their troops. Before night some 2000 mountaineers and tribesmen had assembled in the neighbourhood. For a time the wild reports that were circulated in Tangier caused a little anxiety ; but soon it became known that the whole scare was due to either the ignorance or wilful stupidity of the commander of the Isla de Luzon in saluting and sending a boat ashore at Arzeila, which is a closed port, not to say a picturesque ruin.

On July 1, Mulai Abdul Aziz reached Meknas from Rabat, having *en route* prayed at the tomb of Mulai Idris I., in Zarahun, who lies interred on the steep slope of the mountain above the Roman ruins of Volubilis. Although his Majesty entered Meknas at an extremely early hour, long before he was expected, he was accorded an enthusiastic reception.

At Court affairs were fast proceeding to a stage which must end tragically. Mulai Abdul Aziz, it is true, was firmly on the throne, but the boy Sultan was only an item in the palace. The hatred and jealousy of the Viziers amongst themselves was a public secret, and all watched anxiously for the termination of the crisis which, in spite of every outward and visible show of accord, it was well known must soon arrive.

The fact that Sid Ahmed ben Musa had been chosen by Mulai Abdul Aziz as almost his sole adviser had stirred the hearts of the rival Jamai Viziers, the brothers Haj Amaati and Sid Mohammed Soreir, to their very depths. Those who do not know the Moors are ill acquainted with the strength of their passions ; and there is no saying to what extent their hatred and jealousy might not carry them. No one could have been better aware of this than Sid Ahmed himself, the most faithful and devoted follower the Sultan could possess, whose mixed blood of Arab and negro strain gave him all the force and cunning of the former and all the fidelity of a slave.

On Tuesday, July 10, at the sitting of the morning Court, Haj Amaati and Sid Mohammed Soreir, the Grand Vizier and Minister of War, were dismissed, the return of their seals being demanded. Both must have realised that their end was practically come ; and as they mounted their mules and rode away from the palace, they were ruined men.

The dismissal of Ministers in Morocco is a very different affair to what it is in Europe. It means disgrace, and more than that, the almost certain confiscation of all their property—if not imprisonment. The immense pride inherent in a Moorish official of high degree renders all the more degrading his fall ; while the intense jealousy and hatred felt for the unscrupulous officials, to whom all injustice and taxation is, often very rightly, accredited, prevent any sympathy on the part of the public. The man to whom every one had to bow and cringe had fallen ; no longer was his wrath to be feared ; and the feelings of the populace, pent up for so long, burst forth.

No name was too bad for the late Grand Vizier, no crime too fearful not to have been committed by him.

A sort of stupor fell over the Court. No one knew what would happen next. This dismissal of two of the most powerful men, if not the two most powerful, in the *entourage* of the Sultan, was so sudden and so far removed from the usual course adopted by a new Sultan, that all held their breath, awaiting a future the details of which they were not even able to guess at. Terror reigned amongst the officials; wild reports were heard on every side as to who was to be the next to fall; and expectation on the part of those who had nothing to fear, and terror on that of those whose position rendered them liable to a similar fate, was rife.

It was no secret whence the blow had been struck, for no sooner were the posts of Grand Vizier and Minister of War vacated than they were filled, the former by Sid Ahmed himself, the second by his brother Sid Saïd; while to the Chamberlainship, which Sid Ahmed had left to fill the still higher position, another brother was nominated. Sid Ahmed thus obtained an overwhelming majority in the surroundings of the Sultan, for the three most confidential positions were annexed by himself and his two brothers.

The following Friday, July 13,—unlucky combination of day and number, — Haj Amaati and Sid Mohammed Soreir were seized in their houses and thrown into prison. Although it had been thought possible that such a course might be pursued, the actual event caused an unparalleled excitement. The work of arrest was quickly but roughly done, but such are the ways of the Moors. The Basha of Meknas, with a small band of troops, proceeded to the Grand Vizier's house first, and, gaining admittance, announced his errand. The horror of the situation must have been fully appreciated by the Vizier, for, giving way to one of those violent fits of rage to which he was prone, he attempted to resist, and a soldier in his employ drew his sword upon the Basha. In a minute both were seized, but not before, in the struggle, Haj Amaati's rich clothes had been torn to shreds. Four ropes were fastened to his neck, each held by a soldier; and, dressed only in his shirt, he was dragged through the streets, amidst the derisive laughter and the curses of the people, to the prison. The very crowd that now rejoiced in his degradation had bowed low to him only a day or two before, as he passed through the streets to and from the palace. One incident is worthy of mention, as showing the feelings of the Moors. As he was paraded

along, a common *askari*, one of the riff-raff of Morocco, passed. "God!" he cried, "why, the infidel
has a better fez than mine!" and with these words
he lifted the turban and cap off the Vizier's head
roughly, placing his own filthy head-gear in its
place.

And the crowd laughed and jeered!

As soon as Haj Amaati was confined in jail, Sid
Mohammed Soreir was arrested; but, with far more
pluck and courage, he followed his captor without
resistance, and entered prison like a gentleman.

Wild rumours spread all over the town as to the
reasons of the imprisonment of the Viziers, and it
was generally stated that a plot had been discovered by which the Sultan and Sid Ahmed, the
new Vizier, were to have been assassinated that
very day, *en route* to mid-day prayers. But
whatever may have been the truth of this asser-
tion, the fact remains that no attempt was made,
and Mulai Abdul Aziz was driven in his green-
and-gold brougham to the mosque, surrounded by
his Court. Both his Majesty and Sid Ahmed
looked extremely nervous, and every possible pre-
caution was taken to prevent assassination. During the afternoon a lesser Vizier, who acted as
*amin el askar*, or paymaster of the troops, Sid
el Arbi Zebdi, was seized and imprisoned. This

but added to the terror of the remaining officials, who had escaped, but dreaded a like fate.

I had the opportunity the same evening of discussing the course events had taken with two men, who hold in different ways almost the highest positions in Morocco. One was himself a Vizier, the other far above all fear of arrest. They both told me the same tale; but, in spite of the high authority on which I heard it, I do not think it is to be credited, and in my opinion it was the officially agreed upon story, that was to give justice to the arrest of such important members of the Sultan's Court.

I was told that both the Viziers in question had addressed letters to Mulai Ismain in Fez, and to Mulai Mohammed in Morocco City, the young Sultan's uncle and brother respectively, inviting them to seize the opportunity of attempting the throne, and offering all their large fortune and influence in the event of their doing so. These letters, it was said, were intercepted and the plot discovered.

Although both the Viziers in question were quite capable of such a plot, I cannot believe that either pursued the course stated above. To a Moor a document of any sort is a far more important thing than to us, and any one who is acquainted with the Moors knows how extremely difficult it is to obtain any kind of matter in writing. Had such an idea as that stated above entered the minds of Haj Amaati and his brother, and had they formulated any conspiracy to that effect, they would never have been so foolish as to commit themselves to writing, and any communication with the two Shereefs in question would have been made with the aid of a trusted envoy. It was easy to see that one of my informants at least discredited the story he was telling me, which he only knew from official sources. My own opinion is this, that the whole affair was the result of Sid Ahmed's jealousy, and that he was actuated no doubt also by a feeling that the course he pursued was the safest in the Sultan's interests—for by removing his own two most dangerous enemies, he at the same time would find further scope for his influence and policy. That the Viziers deserved their fate none can deny. Haj Amaati had impoverished the whole country by his enormous and insatiable greed and black-mail, and his brother had deprived the soldiery of a very considerable portion of their pay.

Immediately the arrests were made the entire property of both — together with that of Sid el Arbi Zebdi — was confiscated, and their houses at Fez seized. Haj Amaati had just completed the building in the capital of a palace second to none

there in size and decoration, a block of buildings
rising high above the level of the other houses,
which will be an eternal landmark of the Vizier's
rise and fall. It had been completed only during
his absence in the south with the Sultan, and so
much pride did the Vizier take in this new palace
that he had ordered all the decorations in stucco
and mosaic, of which the Moors are perfect mas-
ters, to be draped with linen, so that none should
see the general effect before himself. A rope attached to these curtains would allow the entire
drapery to fall, when the every beauty of the
decoration would be exposed. Within a week of
realising this dream of oriental fancy, he was cast
into a dungeon, and his house and all his wealth
confiscated to the Sultan.

With the fall of the two Viziers it became more
apparent than ever that Sid Ahmed meant to be
master of the whole situation; but he was wise
enough not to attempt alone what could be done
equally well, and very probably better, with the
advice of trusted counsellors. There were two people
at the Court in whose hands might lie the power
of treating him as he had treated the others.
These two were respectively the Circassian mother
of the Sultan, and Sidi Mohammed el Marani, an
influential Shereef, who had married the sister of

Mulai el Hassen, and into whose hands a considerable part of the upbringing of Mulai Abdul Aziz had been intrusted. Both must be conciliated, for over the Sultan both held great influence—so great, in fact, that should Sid Ahmed's conduct in any way displease them, their united power might easily persuade the Sultan to dismiss him. Not for this reason alone, however, did Sid Ahmed, as it were, invite these two to join him in a sort of council of regency, for he knew fully well the ability of both and their devotion to his lord and master.

In the hands of these three persons the welfare of Morocco lies. But before entering upon any conjectures as to the future, the history of past events must be continued a little further.

On Thursday, July 19, a start was made from Meknas towards Fez, the army and the governor of the tribes and their escorts having camped the previous night a slight distance outside the town near the Fez road.

Two events worthy of mention had meanwhile taken place at Fez—first, the behaviour of Mulai Omar, the Sultan's brother and viceroy; and, secondly, the fact that the *enkas*, or local taxation upon all goods sold, had been removed, together with the *octroi* at the city gates.

With regard to the former a few words must be

said.  Mulai Omar, who had been left as viceroy by
Mulai el Hassen, whose son he was by a slave wife,
is a young man of extremely vicious and degenerate
habits, nearly black in colour, and with an expression as ugly as it is revolting.  While beyond his
immorality no actual charge of crime can be laid to
his door, he may be said to be incapable of filling
the position he held, and to want discretion and
common-sense.

It appears—and I knew of the event at the time
—that on his learning of the death of his father,
he sent to the Jewish silversmiths, by whom all
Government work is done, and ordered one of their
number to make him a seal.  Now in Morocco a
seal is an exceedingly important object, and no one
uses a seal of office unless it is actually presented
to him by the Sultan.  So far the story is generally
known, but here my version—the true version—
differs, for while the European press harped upon
the fact that Mulai Omar wished to make himself
a seal with the inscription of Sultan upon it, the
fact was that the seal was to bear Mulai Abdul Aziz's
name, and that the reason of Mulai Omar's ordering
it to be made was not in order to stamp documents
himself as Sultan, but probably to have in his possession a means of forging letters supposed to have
come from Court.  Whether his idea was by this

to make the best of the short period that remained to him as viceroy to amass money, or whether in case of any outbreak or disturbance on the part of the population to be able to forge conciliatory or other letters that would keep them quiet until his brother's arrival, it is impossible to say. But whatever may have been the desire, the result in the suspicious eyes of his brother was this—that he had attempted by some means to usurp the throne.

However, the seal was never made. The Jew artificer, knowing the penalty that would meet him at the hands of the Sultan were he even the innocent instrument in this, fled and sought the protection of an influential member of the Government, and the affair was knocked on the head at once.

A second charge was also laid at Mulai Omar's door—that of having ordered the music of the drums and pipes to cease on the occasion of the announcement of Mulai Abdul Aziz's succession to the throne. On the players refusing, his Highness sent a slave, who enforced silence by splitting up the drums with a dagger. For this act of treason he was afterwards punished by having the flesh of his hand sliced, the wound filled with salt, and the whole hand sewn up in leather. It is a common belief that this punishment causes mortification to set in, and that the hand decomposes; but such is not the case, for by the

time the leather wears off the wound is healed, the
result being that the hand is rendered useless, and
remains closed for ever. It is a punishment not
often in use, but is sometimes done in cases of
murder or constant theft, as, without in any way
injuring the health of the man, it prevents his com-
mitting the crime a second time, or for the hundredth
time, as the case may be. It is a punishment that
cannot be applied except by the Sultan's orders.

It was no doubt on account of these offences that
letters were received by Mulai Omar from the Sultan,
forbidding him to leave his house, and placing him
under surveillance—a course that was supplemented
on his brother's arrival by chains upon his legs.
Meanwhile his Majesty had been pleased to treat
his brother, Mulai Mohammed, in Morocco City, in
the same manner.

As to the remitting of the local taxes and *octroi*
in Fez, but little need be said. Certain unfriendly
remarks had been overheard regarding the new Sultan, and the general tone of the Fez people was
not satisfactory. Fearing that an outbreak might
occur, and knowing that the avaricious inhabitants
were open to no persuasion except money, the Amin
Haj Abdesalam Makri, the Chancellor of the Ex-
chequer of Fez, on his own authority, remitted this
most unpopular tax, which is contrary to Moorish

law. It turned the tide, and the Fez citizen, finding himself a few dollars, or a few pence, the richer, changed front, and was loud in his acclamations of the new Sultan. The charm of the situation was, however, that as soon as the Sultan had safely entered Fez, and was thus securely upon the throne, he instituted once again the tax, and the population rose on the morning of Tuesday, July 24, to find the tax-gatherers returned to their accustomed haunts.

On Saturday, July 21, Mulai Abdul Aziz made his State entry into Fez.

From an early hour all was stir and bustle in the capital, and before the sun had risen the streets were full of long strings of men, women, and children, mounted and on foot, pouring toward the upper part of the city, New Fez, where the entry was to take place. The crowd was large but orderly, and, like all Moorish crowds, silent, though now and again a shout burst forth when some native, gay in colour, galloped along on his richly trapped horse and fired his gun.

Without the city the crowd ranged itself on each side of the road, which was guarded by long lines of troops, the cavalry near the city, and beyond in the plain the infantry.

The Sultan had spent the night at a distance of

some six miles away, where the great camp had been pitched, and early as it was when I arrived upon the scene outside the gate of the city, stragglers and troops from the *mahalla* were already arriving,—wild tribesmen, mounted or on foot, Kaids of districts with their troops of irregular cavalry, mules and camels laden with baggage, black slaves and women. I was soon free of the crowd, and riding slowly along behind the line of soldiers toward the camp.

A murmur passed through the people, and turning to the west, I could see a great cloud of dust appearing above one of the low elevations in the plain.

The morning was lovely ; the sun, although scarcely risen, was hot, while a not unpicturesque, though by no means pleasant, addition to the scene was the fine cloud of dust that hung over everything. Soon one was able to distinguish the tops of the gold and coloured banners that preceded the Sultan's procession, and still nearer the white draped figures of the women, mounted upon mules. Some eighty of these there were, and as their mules were hurried along by the soldier guard, every one, soldier and sightseer, turned away their heads, as etiquette demands. Two women, covered, except for the eyes, in soft white draperies, preceded the rest, and it was easy to guess who they were,—the Circassian mother of the young Sultan and his newly married wife.

Then came the artillery on the back of mules, followed by a troop of bodyguards, handsomely dressed and mounted. After them the band, mounted and discoursing music as they rode. Then again a forest of banners, of every hue and colour, of cloth, velvet, and silk, of gold embroidery and gold brocade,—the sacred flags of the great saints and Shereefs of Morocco.

Behind these rode the Sultan Mulai Abdul Aziz, mounted upon a dark roan horse with cream mane and tail, seated upon a saddle of apple-green and gold embroidery, while over his head, borne by a mounted soldier, waved the umbrella of crimson and gold. He was dressed in white, a fine long *bernus* hanging lightly over his *haik* of soft silk and wool. A cord of white silk bound round his head held these two garments in place over his turban.

Mulai Abdul Aziz appeared nervous but dignified. Immovable as a statue, one could not help noticing that his eyes wandered here and there amongst the crowd, as though fearing some attempt upon his life; but even to a greater extent than this was his anxiety apparent in his mouth, for his lips wore a pout, with him a sure sign of excitement.

Close at the young Sultan's elbow rode Bu Ahmed, the Grand Vizier, while following him came a crowd of officials and soldiers.

All rode quickly, stopping every now and again to receive some deputation, or when the crowd caused a block, and the spear-bearers and foot-guard that surrounded the royal horse had often to run. At the gate of the city a long delay occurred, and the crowd pressed on every side, for the entrance is small, and the artillery-mules, in their hurry to push through, had completely blocked the road. I was mounted on an Arab horse and saddle, and dressed in native costume, so that my appearance attracted no attention on the part of the natives, and in the crowd I found myself within a very short distance of the Sultan, whence I was able to obtain an excellent view not only of his face, but of his every feature. Dust-strewn and sun-burnt with his summer journey, he looked darker than he really is, for his colour is little more than that of a southern European. The eyes, surrounded with heavy black lashes, are dark. No signs of beard or moustache are traceable on his lip or chin, and altogether he possesses the face of a nice-looking boy, wanting only in vivacity and expression.

Once in the city, the procession broke up, and

accompanied only by a trusty band of guards, his Majesty rode to the tomb of his ancestor, Mulai Idris II., the patron saint of Fez, where he took the oath of the Sultanate; and a few minutes later the great gates of the white palace closed upon Mulai Abdul Aziz, Sultan of Morocco.

# INDEX.

PRINTED BY WILLIAM BLACKWOOD AND SONS.

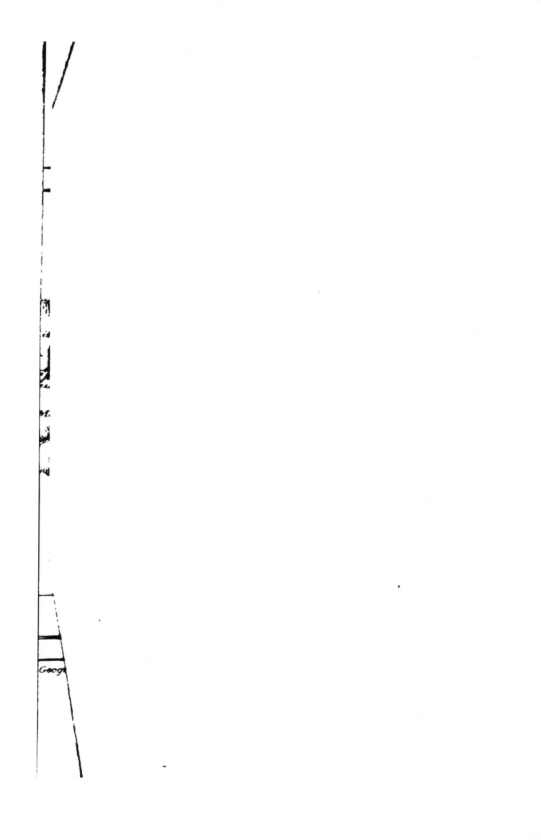

Check Out More Titles From HardPress Classics Series In this collection we are offering thousands of classic and hard to find books. This series spans a vast array of subjects – so you are bound to find something of interest to enjoy reading and learning about.

Subjects:
Architecture
Art
Biography & Autobiography
Body, Mind &Spirit
Children & Young Adult
Dramas
Education
Fiction
History
Language Arts & Disciplines
Law
Literary Collections
Music
Poetry
Psychology
Science
…and many more.

Visit us at www.hardpress.net

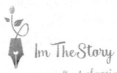